# DEAR REGINA

A publication of the
Stuart A. Rose Manuscript, Archives, and
Rare Book Library at Emory University

SERIES EDITOR
Clinton R. Fluker
Emory University

FOUNDING EDITOR
Pellom McDaniels
Emory University

*Dear Regina*

# Flannery O'Connor's Letters from Iowa

EDITED BY MONICA CAROL MILLER

The University of Georgia Press

*Athens*

Published by the University of Georgia Press
Athens, Georgia 30602
www.ugapress.org
© 2022 by the Mary Flannery O'Connor Charitable Trust
All rights reserved
Designed by Erin Kirk
Set in Garamond Premier Pro
Printed and bound by Sheridan Books

The paper in this book meets the guidelines for
permanence and durability of the Committee on
Production Guidelines for Book Longevity of the
Council on Library Resources.

Most University of Georgia Press titles are
available from popular e-book vendors.

Printed in the United States of America

22  23  24  25  26  C  5  4  3  2  1

Library of Congress Cataloging-in-Publication Data

Names: O'Connor, Flannery, author. | O'Connor, Regina Cline, addressee. |
Miller, Monica Carol, 1974– editor.
Title: Dear Regina : Flannery O'Connor's letters from Iowa /
edited by Monica Carol Miller.
Description: Athens : The University of Georgia Press, [2022] | Series:
A publication of the Stuart A. Rose Manuscript, Archives, and Rare Book
Library at Emory University | Includes bibliographical references and index.
Identifiers: LCCN 2021062321 (print) | LCCN 2021062322 (ebook) |
ISBN 9780820361857 (hardback) | ISBN 9780820361840 (ebook)
Subjects: LCSH: O'Connor, Flannery—Correspondence. | O'Connor, Regina
Cline. | Iowa Writers' Workshop. | Women authors, American—20th century—
Biography. | Creative writing (Higher education)—United States. |
Mothers and daughters—United States.
Classification: LCC PS3565.C57 Z48 2022 (print) | LCC PS3565.C57 (ebook) |
DDC 813/.54 [B]—dc23/eng/20220203
LC record available at https://lccn.loc.gov/2021062321
LC ebook record available at https://lccn.loc.gov/2021062322

# CONTENTS

# INTRODUCTION

In the fall of 1945, twenty-year-old Flannery O'Connor arrived at the University of Iowa in Iowa City, Iowa, to begin graduate school after earning a bachelor of arts degree in social sciences from Georgia State College for Women (GSCW) in Milledgeville, Georgia. Although she had been admitted to Iowa's Graduate School of Journalism, once there she sought out Paul Engle, the highly respected director of the Writers' Workshop. Their memorable first meeting has often been recounted:

> When she finally spoke, her Georgia dialect sounded so thick to his Midwestern ear that he asked her to repeat her question. Embarrassed by an inability a second time to understand, Engle handed her a pad to write what she had said. So in schoolgirl script, she put down three short lines: "My name is Flannery O'Connor. I am not a journalist. Can I come to the Writers' Workshop?" Engle suggested that she drop off writing samples, and they would consider her, late as it was. The next day a few stories arrived, and to his near disbelief, he found them to be "imaginative, tough, alive." She was instantly accepted to the Workshop, both the name of Engle's writing class and of his MFA graduate writing program, the first in the nation, to which she would switch her affiliation from the Graduate School of Journalism by the second semester. (Gooch 117–18)

O'Connor's education at Iowa was an important step in her evolution as a writer as well as an introduction to the writer's life and community in which she would spend the rest of her short life and career. It was at Iowa that she wrote the beginnings of *Wise Blood*. There she met Allen Tate, Robert Penn Warren, Andrew Lytle, and others who would help her gain traction in publishing as well as provide the connections that would get her into Yaddo's artists' community. The work she accomplished at Iowa and the connections she made there formed the foundation for her future writing success.

While scholars have written about how her time at Iowa shaped her writing, there has been less focus (and few resources freely available to scholars and others) on how her time at Iowa shaped her personally. The correspondence in *Dear Regina* has only been freely available to scholars in the manuscript collections at

Emory University since 2014; even since then, access required travel to Atlanta and appropriate credentials. Up until she left for graduate school, O'Connor had grown up in Savannah and then Milledgeville, Georgia: both smallish, southern towns in which she was a member of well-respected, long-established families. Iowa was a revelation for many reasons: she was away from home, away from her known climate, region, family, and habits. Iowa gave her an opportunity to reinvent herself, as this was when she started going by Flannery O'Connor, rather than Mary Flannery, as well as creatively, as her work evolved from the cartoons she first came to Iowa to create to the incisive fiction that she produced as a student in the Writers' Workshop.

Yet while her graduate school experience allowed for such reinvention, much about her former life stayed constant: her daily mass attendance, her spiritual devotion, and—surprising to many—her strong relationship with her mother. When scholars and fans of O'Connor alike consider the mother-daughter relationships in her work, they tend to assume that the dynamics in the stories have their basis in O'Connor's relationship with her mother, Regina Cline O'Connor. To be sure, much of this interpretation is based on Flannery's own descriptions of their relationship. Often referring sardonically to Regina as "the parent" in letters to her friends,[1] Flannery seemed at times to chafe at living her adult life with her mother, who disapproved of anything remotely inappropriate. (Flannery's father, Edward O'Connor, died of lupus in 1941, when she was fifteen.) In a letter to Elizabeth Hester, O'Connor admitted to sharing a disposition with her character Joy-Hulga Hopewell in "Good Country People," even giving her character an unattractive sweatshirt, a source of real-life contention between O'Connor and her mother: "The only embossed [sweatshirt] I ever had had a fierce-looking bulldog on it with the word GEORGIA over him. I wore it all the time, it being my policy at that point in life to create an unfavorable impression. My urge for such has to be repressed as my mother does not approve of making a spectacle of oneself when over thirty" (Letter to A., 5 Aug. 1955). Biographical readings of O'Connor's work have been further encouraged by Louise Westling's foundational 1978 article on the "sour, deformed daughters and self-righteous mothers" who appear in her fiction (511). Scholars have continued to read O'Connor's stories through this lens of mother/daughter animosity, as Claire Kahane's identification illustrates: "[I]t is most often maternal figures, mothers and matriarchs," she argues, "who are the objects of assault by enraged and misfit children of all ages who haven't gotten what they need" (3). Many readers continue to assume that the relationship between Flannery and Regina was similar to that of Joy-Hulga and her mother in "Good

Country People," that of an overbearing mother preoccupied with appearances and her petulant, overintellectual daughter.

However, the 2014 acquisition of a significant collection of Flannery O'Connor's papers by the Stuart A. Rose Manuscript, Archives, and Rare Book Library at Emory University has provided access to a significant amount of material previously unavailable (see Justice, "Flannery O'Connor Archive"). Within the nineteen linear feet (forty boxes) of papers in this archive is a collection of letters that Flannery wrote to Regina nearly daily from 1945 to 1947, while she was a graduate student at Iowa. Collected here for the first time in print, the letters in *Dear Regina* reveal that their day-to-day relationship had much more depth and affection than the generally accepted narratives would allow. Indeed, I believe such characterizations have exaggerated and overemphasized the contentiousness between the two women. Flannery is clearly a willing participant in their correspondence, noting early on that "I am the only one here who hears from home every day and should like to continue to be" (5 Oct. 1945). I have argued that psychobiographical readings such as Westling's distract from what I see as several striking currents of critique in O'Connor's work, including those of southern pastoralism and gender stereotypes.[2] Indeed, I believe that exaggerations of the contention between Flannery and Regina have led to misreadings of the mother-daughter relationships in O'Connor's stories. A willingness to take such mother figures as Mrs. Hopewell in "Good Country People" or Mrs. Crater in "The Life You Save May Be Your Own" seriously, rather than reject them as flat, comical characters, offers enticing new readings of O'Connor's fiction.

The letters from Flannery to Regina during her time in Iowa collected here bolster such sympathetic readings. Written from September 1945, when she first arrived in Iowa City and began her graduate studies, through the fall of 1947, the letters provide insights not only into this mother-daughter relationship but into Flannery's own personal and professional development.[3] Some letters are brief reports of hard work and regular meals. Others include detailed accounts of the logistics of life away from home, the complexities of travel arrangements, dental appointments, getting typewriter ribbons, and food—so much food!

One notable aspect of these letters that has surprised and interested scholars is Flannery's preoccupation with food (see, e.g., Davis and McCoy). She reports on her window-ledge "delicatessen," where she keeps eggs and milk chilled in the cold Iowa winters, as well as her hot-plate dinners, the casseroles offered at the school cafeteria, and the comfort foods from home she misses and craves. For example, during the fall of 1946 Flannery writes to Regina what have become known among

O'Connor scholars as her "mayonnaise letters." In many letters, food plays an important role: she consistently comments on her acquisition of food, her meals, and the care packages she receives from home. She also makes references to food shortages, providing important insights into daily life in the 1940s. Despite the end of World War II, food shortages continued in the United States and worldwide in 1946, as Flannery's experiences reflect (see, e.g., Leuchtenberg). In one letter, she mentions that she has not been able to find mayonnaise anywhere, and she asks Regina to send her a jar of homemade mayonnaise. Over the course of twelve days, Flannery mentions mayonnaise in eight letters, asking Regina repeatedly to send her some, to see if one of their relatives will send her some, lamenting her lack of mayonnaise—and, when it finally arrives in the mail, rejoicing at her good fortune.

Scholars have already begun considering the meaning of Flannery's extended preoccupation with mayonnaise, particularly with regard to what these letters reveal about the mother-daughter relationship. Certainly, mayonnaise represents the comforts of home, especially the homemade version; it is easy to read her repeated requests as "evidence of homesickness, the kind of nostalgia favorite foods are intended to cure," as Caroline McCoy observes ("Flannery O'Connor's Two Deepest Loves"). Indeed, citing Brad Gooch's biography of the author, David A. Davis suggests that, "Although O'Connor insisted on several occasions that she was not homesick at all, she wrote to her mother every day and craved food from home, which suggests that food was a form of familial connection for her, so the mayonnaise represents attachment to her mother" (32). Davis extends this biographical reading to her fiction, arguing that "food acts as a language of connection in her mother-daughter stories, so we can read the stories' internal dynamics and character tension through food" (32). The myriad food references throughout *Dear Regina* not only provide a window into Flannery's day-to-day life for her readers and fans but also open up possibilities for new readings of her work through the framework of food studies.

Unlike Davis, however, Caroline McCoy dismisses the idea of Flannery's homesickness, noting how often Flannery writes to Regina of "thriving in Iowa and her intentions to develop her literary career outside of Georgia." Rather, McCoy believes that "O'Connor's penned testimonials to mayonnaise are, to me, small attempts at connection. A thousand miles from her mother's kitchen, the absence of the ingredient could become a shared curiosity and an acknowledgment of maternal influence. I imagine her wishing to affirm her love of home and family, even as she anticipated leaving both behind" ("Flannery O'Connor's Two Deepest

Loves"). Despite their differences in interpretation, both Davis and McCoy see Flannery's preoccupation with mayonnaise in these letters as proof of a strong connection between the daughter and mother, though the tenor of that bond is complicated.

The letters in *Dear Regina* depict a complex and dynamic relationship between mother and daughter during the time that Flannery was developing her writing craft in graduate school. They document her growth as both a writer and a young woman as she navigates a new chapter of her life in completely unfamiliar territory: in the Midwest, in graduate school, and—importantly—in Engle's challenging community of writers at the University of Iowa. Engle's strong vision existed within the wave of post–World War II creative writing programs whose long-lasting effect on American letters continues to be felt and understood. According to Eric Bennett in *Workshops of Empire: Stegner, Engle, and American Creative Writing During the Cold War*, Engle's creation of the workshop found itself at the cutting edge of a movement that "transformed the institutions of American literature" (88).

Flannery originally enrolled in the Graduate School of Journalism in 1945, submitting drawings and cartoons to the Art Department with the goal of being admitted to the advanced drawing course sequence. Her original goal was to continue creating the kinds of cartoons she had published in various publications in high school and during her undergraduate career at Georgia State College for Women (now Georgia College and State University), aiming for an eventual career publishing in venues such as the *New Yorker* (Gooch 121–22; see also O'Connor, *The Cartoons*). From her first days at Iowa, Flannery exhibits a focused, confident attitude toward her work. Writing to Regina about her submissions to the Art Department, she reports: "Saw the Art people today and they looked at my stuff and seemed much interested, helpful, appreciative, etc. Am signed up for an advanced drawing course with a man who has done cartooning and says he can help me" (21 Sept. 1945). In this same letter, she describes that first meeting with Engle, which became nearly mythic in Engle's retelling. For Flannery, however—at least in her letter to Regina—it was a much less dramatic experience: "Also got into the Writer's Workshop that was supposed to be so difficult—without any trouble." The differences between Flannery's succinct account of her admission to the workshop and that of Engle provide important insights into Flannery's inner confidence in her work, regardless of how she might have appeared to Engle upon their first meeting.

At Iowa, Flannery's craft developed in an environment where her work was taken seriously. After the first meeting with Engle, Flannery reports, "The more I

stay around here, the more I think I will be able to make money after this training. These people know how to do things" (21 Sept. 1945). Flannery saw her time
in the workshop as an important apprenticeship; she approached the development of her writing as the honing of a craft. In her letter about Paul Horgan, an
American writer who taught at the workshop while she was there, she describes
him admiringly as "very thorough and seems to be above all a craftsman which is
what I need" (21 Feb. 1946). Flannery's understanding of writing as a craft reflects
the larger movement in MFA programs at this time, of which the Iowa Writers'
Workshop was an exemplar. Christopher Kempf describes the "craft" sensibility
of this era's workshop approach as a "synthesis of expressive labor and guild-like
programmatic discipline" (4), a succinct description of Flannery's experience.
After Horgan leads a critique of one of her stories, for example, Flannery writes:
"He is a colonel, by the way, just got out of the army—big discipline man—insists
the writer should write a certain number of hours a day at a given time regularly
and without interruption. Which is what I will have to do this summer, as I have
to have 20 or 30 thousand words done before September on the novel I will have
to do for my thesis" (1 Mar. 1946). These letters in particular chronicle the birth
of Flannery's work ethic as a writer. The resulting discipline would last the rest
of her life.

The letters in *Dear Regina* show Flannery's introduction to a community of
writers and publishers that would play an important role in her professional life
and success. Engle brought in writers such as Robert Penn Warren, Allen Tate,
Andrew Lytle, John Crowe Ransom, and Robert Lowell, all of whom quickly became admirers of her writing. Certainly, their critiques and celebrations of her
work were both enlightening and pragmatically useful to her revision process.
However, these established authors also showed a remarkable willingness to provide resources for her practical success. In these letters we find stories of Flannery's
mentors offering to help her find fellowships, jobs, and publishing opportunities.

In addition, their recognition of Flannery as an emerging writer also contributed to a palpable increase in her sense that a writing career was a very real possibility for her. During her first semester in the workshop, for example, she expresses
feeling encouraged by a classmate's suggestion of "a possible market" for her story
(22 Oct. 1945), though that same month she says that there is only "a vague possibility that I may be able to sell a story somewhere, but that is slight" (28 Oct.
1945). One year later, however, after a summer at home in Milledgeville spent dil-
igently writing and revising, Flannery's letters are full of inquiries after the mail at
home, expecting to hear back from such literary journals as the *Sewanee Review*

and *Accent*, journals whose publication of her work would be a benchmark of her success as a serious writer. By the time she graduated in 1947 with her MFA, she had won the prestigious Rinehart-Iowa Award, which would support the completion and possible publication of her first novel, *Wise Blood* (1952), and she had also secured a teaching fellowship for the following year. Her letters during the fall of 1947 reveal in Flannery a clear understanding of what it will take to complete and publish her work.

However, the letters in *Dear Regina* reveal more than the evolution of Flannery's writing career. They also tell the story of a young woman on her own for the first time, whose views on life are developing and changing in response to new experiences and encounters. Over the course of these two and a half years, Flannery grows from a young woman who seeks her mother's advice about travel arrangements and what she should write in letters to family members to a confident woman who explains the finer details of her publishing contracts and even expresses concern over her mother's own career. It is true that there are numerous moments of recognizable, sardonic complaint from daughter to mother, such as Flannery's requests that Regina "Please restrain yourself from sending me any more aprons. I know it will be hard but please restrain yourself" (13 Oct. 1945). However, the letters also contain ample evidence showing their relationship to be one of mutual respect.

In one notable example, O'Connor expresses concern as her mother begins to take over the running of Andalusia, the family farm she inherited from her uncle. These letters not only demonstrate that Flannery understood the difficulties that her mother faced in running the farm but also provide a different picture of the relationship between the two women than is generally recognized. Upon learning that her mother is taking over running Andalusia,[4] Flannery expresses concern for the difficulties she expects her mother to face in taking on this arduous responsibility. Over the course of several letters, O'Connor offers suggestions for renting out the house; frets that the farm will increase her mother's worries; and, finally, reassures her mother that her reservations about the situation are more regarding the realities of farm life than they are doubts about her mother's abilities. These letters highlight the fact that Flannery understands the expenses and troubles of running a farm are real and significant and offer a new perspective for reading the many characters in her stories created in Regina's likeness: tough negotiators and driven businesswomen who also find the responsibilities of running a farm to be seriously demanding. Reading stories such as "The Displaced Person," "A Circle in the Fire," or even "Good Country People" in the context of these letters allows for a more complex reading of O'Connor's work, especially as characters such as Mrs. McIntyre, Mrs. Cope, and Mrs. Hopewell acquire more depth than is typically attributed to them.

Indeed, *Dear Regina* revises somewhat the image of Regina Cline O'Connor as an overbearing mother and businesswoman. It is frustrating as a reader that we only have Flannery's side of their correspondence, but much can still be gleaned from the context of Flannery's letters. In addition to details about the farm, Flannery's letters are filled with chatty questions and news about close family members and members of the Milledgeville community. For example, Flannery makes several references to her friend Mary Virginia Harrison, her closest friend in high school who was "the daughter of the postmaster Ben Harrison and her mother's friend Gussie Harrison." Although "[t]heir match was made by their mothers," their friendship thrived throughout high school and college (Gooch 58). Despite grumbling about the details, Flannery even ultimately admits enjoying her friend's visit to Iowa in the fall of 1947. The letters also contain regular references to Regina's sisters Katie Cline, nicknamed "Duchess" by the family, and Mary Cline, whom Gooch characterizes as the "impresario of the Cline Mansion" in Milledgeville (54). Flannery's letters also frequently reference "Cousin Katie" in Savannah, Regina's cousin Kate Flannery Semmes, who lived next door to the O'Connors during Flannery's childhood in Savannah. Regina named her daughter "Mary Flannery" after Cousin Katie's mother, Mary Norton Flannery. As biographer Jean Cash notes, Regina "had dual motives in naming her daughter 'Mary Flannery': she gave her the name both to honor Mrs. Semmes's mother and to influence Katie Semmes herself to assist the family financially" (11). Indeed, throughout the letters in *Dear Regina*, Flannery refers to the financial assistance from Cousin Katie, which helped her afford graduate school.

While the importance of Flannery's family remains a constant in these letters, her sense of self undergoes remarkable changes. Certainly, her adoption of "Flannery" rather than "Mary Flannery" is the most visible marker of these changes. Several scholars have quoted from Flannery's 1946 letter to Regina about her adopted pen name, in which she explains: "As far as writing is concerned, the Mary is so much impedimenta. All my writing will be done under Flannery O'Connor. That is what I am called here and that is the way I want it" (13 March 1946). However, less well known are her later letters to her mother in which she directly asks Regina herself to call her Flannery, rather than Mary Flannery: "That is who I am, that is who I am always going to be, and the people whom I will associate with and do associate with know nothing else" (4 Nov. 1947). Flannery's assertion of her adopted identity in not only her professional life but also her personal life provides important insights into her evolution as a writer. Indeed, her insistence upon her preferred name offers intriguing opportunities to analyze Flannery's conception of identity in her work and in her personal life.

Among the most significant aspects of Flannery's psychosocial development revealed in *Dear Regina* is her changing understanding of race and racial dynamics. As the question of O'Connor's own views on race, racism, and civil rights continues to be a focus of both scholarly and readerly inquiry, these letters are of particular interest because in them we see a definite evolution of O'Connor's understanding of race. In her early letters, she complains about having to lock her door because of other boarders she describes as "Cubans." She also admits that having a black classmate made her feel uncomfortable enough about a story she wrote (which included a black character) that she passed on reading the story out loud in class (19 Oct. 1945). Later in the correspondence, however, she defends having lunch with her black classmate to her mother (27 Oct. 1945) and rejects what she characterizes as Regina's "moral lecture on the race problem" in a previous letter (2 Nov. 1945). This ambivalence stands in stark contrast to the previously published correspondence from later in Flannery's life, after her lupus diagnosis and her move back to Milledgeville, where she lived with Regina until her death in 1964. Paul Elie characterized these later letters as possessing "a habit of bigotry that grows more pronounced as O'Connor's fiction, in matters of race, grows more complex and profound—a habit that seems to defy the pattern of her art" (327). Putting the letters in *Dear Regina* in conversation with the letters previously published in *The Habit of Being* and *The Collected Works of Flannery O'Connor*, along with scholarship about issues of race in O'Connor's work, allows for a fuller understanding of how racism inflected her worldview.

Indeed, in the first book-length study of racism in O'Connor's fiction and correspondence, scholar Angela Alaimo O'Donnell notes the contrast between how "O'Connor's fiction often enabled her to escape the limitations of her white perspective" yet how "the limitations in her own attitudes and behaviors [were] a more challenging enterprise" (8). Hilton Als concurs with this assessment in his 2002 *New Yorker* article on O'Connor's depiction of race, as he compares her inability to understand the Civil Rights Movement to that of William Faulkner, noting that "O'Connor herself had difficulty assimilating the push toward integration which took the region so suddenly and violently in the fifties and sixties. She clung to the provincialism she satirized, and she was sometimes clumsy at conveying real life among blacks beyond her own circles—their class distinctions, their communication with one another apart from whites." Despite Als's criticism of the limitations that O'Connor's racialist thinking placed on her writing, he does praise her depiction of black characters in comparison to other white writers such as Faulkner, whose character Dilsey, for example, he criticizes as a "fulcrum of integrity and compassion" rather than a human being. In contrast, Als says that O'Connor's black characters "are not symbols defined in opposition to whiteness; they are the living people who were, physically at least, on the periphery of O'Connor's own world." O'Connor's upbringing in the overtly racist, pre–Civil Rights era South contributed to what Als characterizes as her "most profound gift": "her ability to describe impartially the [white] bourgeoisie she was born into, to depict with humor and without judgment her rapidly crumbling social order." As O'Donnell explains, "O'Connor knows the thoughts of her white racist characters because she herself has entertained them. Such toxic animosities [of racism] are in the air O'Connor breathes and, inevitably, become part of her way of seeing the world" (19).

To be fair, the letters in *Dear Regina* do not contain any specific epiphanies of racist reckoning on O'Connor's part; rather, they are Flannery's reports on the various experiences of a young woman—whose horizons are expanding—confronted with racially integrated environments and people from backgrounds very different than her own. In these new situations, Flannery's worldview expands and changes from that of a sheltered, southern white girl from the Jim Crow South. O'Donnell points to her return south, forced to live with her mother in Milledgeville after her lupus diagnosis, as "a return that meant, to some extent, readaptation to the culture that had produced her and was part and parcel of who she was" (21). In *Dear Regina*, we see Flannery's growth before this return and readaptation. In no way do these letters exculpate Flannery from the charges of racism that haunt her work—quite the contrary, in fact. Flannery's potential for evolving a less racialist worldview apparent in these letters makes the casual racism in her later letters even less acceptable.

Not all of the insights into Flannery's character are this serious, however. As readers of her previously published letters understand, Flannery's epistolary writing reveals a strong, insightful, entertaining personality. One particularly amusing thread running through these letters is Flannery's apparent enjoyment of what might now be referred to as "hate-watching" movies. Throughout *Dear Regina*, she reports going to a variety of movies, from *The Lost Weekend* to *The Bells of St. Mary's*, few of which she enjoyed. Most of them she dismissed with a disdainful

"It was punk" or "It was gruesome"—descriptions I particularly enjoy. She gives herself a home permanent; she complains about her neighbors' enjoyment of football; she describes her changing preferences in fashion, from white blouses under pullover sweaters to smart suits. And she provides numerous recipes for hot-plate cooking with canned pineapples.

### NOTES

1. See, for example, O'Connor's letter to Sally and Robert Fitzgerald, Thursday, (undated), 1952.

2. See my article "Country People" in *Reconsidering Flannery O'Connor*, edited by Alison Arant and Jordan Cofer.

3. Unfortunately, letters from the spring of 1948 are not included in this collection; the collection picks up after Flannery's graduation from Iowa, when she is in residence at Yaddo. However, they do cover the two years she spent earning her master of fine arts degree, including her graduation, and then her first semester as a postdoctoral fellow.

4. See the letters from February 1947 as well as the introduction to the academic year 1946–1947.

# EDITOR'S NOTE

In the fall of 2014, I had just moved to Atlanta to begin a three-year postdoctoral fellowship at Georgia Tech, after spending a month in Milledgeville, Georgia, for the National Endowment for the Humanities' summer seminar on "Reconsidering Flannery O'Connor." That fall, Emory University's Stuart A. Rose Manuscript, Archives, and Rare Book Library announced their acquisition of a significant collection of O'Connor's correspondence, manuscripts, personal writing, and other ephemera. This acquisition was an important addition to their already important O'Connor collections, which included other O'Connor-related materials: namely, letters to her friend Betty Hester (which had been unsealed in 2007) as well as papers belonging to another friend, scholar Sally Fitzgerald. Living not far from Emory, I was fortunate to be among the first scholars to work with this collection after it was made available to the public, and I have returned to the Rose Library several times in the years since: to read through not only these letters but also much of the rest of this collection, such as cards she made for her parents, her high school notebooks, and even the lino stencils she used to print cartoons for her college newspaper.

Nearly all of the 486 letters in this book were handwritten by O'Connor, usually on yellowed 8½ x 11 inch newsprint. Some of the shorter notes are on penny postcards, and more formal stationery (e.g., hotel stationery) also makes an occasional appearance. The handwriting at times appears rushed, but it is generally legible. While she generally wrote to Regina every day, there's an occasional gap in their correspondence—including one unusual ten-day break in late March and early April 1947. At times, Flannery explains the reason for the lapse, though not always.[1] Overall, the two and a half years represented by these letters reveal the growth of a young artist as she hones her craft and takes her place in the world of American letters. I am grateful to Emory and the Rose Library for the opportunity to see a new side of such an important American writer.

I found Brad Gooch's *Flannery: A Life of Flannery O'Connor* an invaluable resource for clarifying the occasionally unclear references in these letters, such as "Miss Bancroft" and "Mary Virginia." Salutations and closings have been included, so that readers can see the evolution of Flannery's relationship with her mother. Dates have been added, though O'Connor generally only wrote the day of the week on her letters. Most of the letters included the postmarked envelopes, so any missing dates could be determined by comparing the letter to its postmarked date. Most typographical or spelling errors have been corrected, with the exception of some of O'Connor's idiosyncratic spellings (such as her various attempts at spelling "mayonnaise"). Some names have been spelled out for clarity, and a few perfunctory notes (e.g., regarding flight times) on postcards or outside envelopes have not been included. Otherwise, these letters are unabridged and transcribed from original documents. Brackets indicate editorial insertions beyond those noted above.

### NOTE

1. It may be, of course, that some letters have been lost in the seventy-five years that have elapsed since they were first written. Overall, however, this collection is remarkably intact.

# CAST OF CHARACTERS

## *Correspondents*

(Mary) Flannery O'Connor
> American writer of critically acclaimed novels, short stories, and essays. A native of Savannah and Milledgeville, Georgia, she earned her MFA from the University of Iowa in 1947, where she was a student in the prestigious Writers' Workshop. Though known as "Mary Flannery" by her family and friends growing up, over the course of her time at Iowa, she drops the "Mary" from her name professionally and socially.

Regina Cline O'Connor
> Mother of Flannery O'Connor. As Mary Flannery was an only child, she addressed both of her parents by their first names, as her letters reflect.

## *Family*

Bernard Cline ("Doctor")
> Older brother of Regina Cline O'Connor and owner of Andalusia, the Milledgeville farm where Flannery and Regina would live after Flannery's diagnosis of lupus.

Mary Cline ("Sister")
> Older sister of Regina Cline O'Connor, the "impresario of the Cline Mansion" in Milledgeville (Gooch 54).

Katie Cline ("Duchess")
> Older sister of Regina Cline O'Connor, who also lived in the Cline Mansion.

Louis Cline ("Uncle Louis")
> Older brother of Regina Cline O'Connor who inherited Andalusia along with Regina.

Louise Florencourt

> Cousin of Flannery's who visited Milledgeville with her three sisters each summer from her home in Boston, Massachusetts. Louise Florencourt was one of the first three women to graduate from Harvard Law School, and she is the trustee of the Mary Flannery O'Connor Charitable Trust.

Garners

> Large family of Flannery's cousins who visit Regina on several occasions.

Kate Flannery Semmes ("Cousin Katie")

> Cousin of Regina Cline O'Connor and daughter of Flannery's namesake (Mary Norton Flannery) who lived next door to the O'Connors in Savannah, Georgia.

Tarletons

> Family of Helen Cleo Cline Tarleton, older sister of Regina Cline O'Connor. They lived in Atlanta.

### *Georgians*

Miss Bancroft

> An unmarried teacher at Georgia State College for Women who boarded with Flannery's Aunt Mary in the Milledgeville Cline mansion.

George Beiswanger

> Taught Flannery in "Introduction to Modern Philosophy" course at Georgia State College for Women.

John Sullivan

> A friend of Flannery's whom many suggest was one of her great unrequited loves, they met when he was a Marine sergeant stationed at Georgia State College for Women. He left the military for the seminary and kept up an active correspondence with Flannery. He ultimately left the seminary, married, and went into business.

Mary Virginia Harrison

> Friend of Flannery's since seventh grade in Milledgeville.

*Iowans*

Gloria Bremerwell (aka Bremer)

Black classmate of Flannery's at Iowa whose race is both a point of contention between Flannery and Regina as well as a source of concern when Flannery read her work out loud to her classmates.

Sarah Dawson

Flannery's roommate her first semester in Currier House.

Ruth Sullivan

A white housemate in Currier House and fellow graduate student in the workshop.

Louise Trovato

Flannery's roommate in Currier House.

# Academic Year 1945–1946

This collection of letters begins the day that Flannery moves into Currier House, a dormitory for graduate women at the University of Iowa (Gooch 118–19; Cash 80). Her first letters are full of details about her moving in, her neighbor, and especially her concerns about the inhabitants she characterizes as "Cubans." Currier House consisted of double rooms and housed about twenty women (Gooch 118). Flannery expresses relief at being assigned Louise Trovato as her roommate, whom she and Regina apparently met on their trip to Iowa City; Gooch notes that Flannery and Louise formed a close friendship during their time at Iowa, as these letters demonstrate (399).

Reading about Flannery's friendship with Louise provides insight into Flannery's perspective on heterosexual romance. Although she does mention her correspondence with John Sullivan, a friend she met in Milledgeville when he was stationed there as a Marine, her letters to Regina reveal no sense of disappointment at any lack of romantic relationship with Sullivan. Rather, Flannery's sardonic and dismissive references to Trovato's love life imply her disdain for such dalliances. And while it is true that her sarcasm may be motivated to some degree by jealousy (or it may be an attempt to convince herself of her lack of desire for a love life), her commentary on Trovato's romantic life to Regina sheds light on her own lack of romantic entanglements, despite our inability as readers to fully ascertain her true feelings on the subject. Indeed, it is possible that Flannery herself was unaware of her own feelings in this area, and her letters to Regina are an attempt to forge her feelings as she wished them to be.

Among the notable developments in this group of letters are Flannery's references to Gloria Bremerwell (whom she originally identifies in a letter as "Gloria Breemer"), a black woman in the workshop with her. Flannery seems to taunt Regina with her account of having lunch with "Gloria Bremerwell, colored," whom she describes as being "in the workshop, writes poetry, and is very nice indeed. . . . Shall I bring her home for Christmas?" (27 Oct. 1945). In a later letter, she jokes that she might go to Miss Bremerwell's home for Christmas, if snow prevents her from getting to Georgia. It is particularly frustrating to lack Regina's side of the correspondence here, as she apparently did rise to Flannery's bait, what Flannery refers to as her "moral lecture on the race problem" (2 Nov. 1945). These references to Bremerwell have been the subject of substantial analysis by many O'Connor scholars in the continuing consideration of the role of race and racism in O'Connor's work.

In these letters we see Flannery's work being taken seriously in the workshop from the beginning. Her confidence in her abilities as a writer is clear as she is accepted into the workshop, even as she notes that there remains much for her to learn in the apprenticeship of graduate school. In November, Paul Engle is already encouraging her to consider sending out her stories for possible publication; over the course of these letters, her references to him evolve from Mr. Engle to the less formal Engle (and by the fall of 1947, she will refer to him even more informally as "Paul"). By the end of this academic year, she will have her first story accepted for publication ("The Geranium," published in the Summer 1946 issue of *Accent*) (Cash 102), will fully adopt the professional name "Flannery O'Connor," and will be preparing to spend her summer fully immersed in writing her creative thesis at home in Milledgeville.

Tuesday [18 Sept. 1945]

Dear R—

I moved myself in here this afternoon. There are 2 girls in next room, 2 in other downstairs room, 1 upstairs and no supervisor or roommate so far.

Louise Trovato passed by and I called her in and she stayed a while. Try sending me a couple of postcards at 32 Bloomington and see if I get them—my packages I suppose would have to go to the other address. Throat feels better. I could profitably use a dozen coat hangers.

The girl next door is interested in saving her money and we have discussed getting an electric heater and fixing our own breakfast. How much do those 1 eye electric burners cost? Could Louis get me one.

Those easy chairs you thought were so nice are anything but easy but the bed does very well. I have the cotton blanket on it.

Regards to all concerned.

    Love

    MF

* * *

Wednesday [19 Sept. 1945]

Dear Regina,

Am trying out typewriter to see if it will be too high and am afraid it will. Had supper with Louise Trovato last night as planned then she came back here and sat a while. We are going to the picture show tonight. She has changed and got a double room in the same house on Market Street and she doesn't think she will care for the roommate she has drawn. Mine still hasn't shown up but I am well ensconced in my corner and she will have a hard time dragging me out of it. I don't care for the bathroom arrangements here but I presume they are better than elsewhere. I like the girl next door from Minnesota fairly well but don't care for her roommate who is one of these Physical Education specimens from Colorado.

Louise Trovato is trying to get an Assistantship in her work here.

It has warmed up considerably but don't send me any lighter clothes.

The supervisor hasn't come but she will be a graduate student like the rest of us and no older.

Louise Trovato is on the scent of a boarding place where you get breakfast and supper (dinner). I may try it for a month—if anything comes of it—and see how I like it.

I am preparing a small delicatessen in the 2nd shifferobe drawer which is going to serve me for breakfast—bread and fruit. I can get the milk and eggs at other meals.

I keep my door into the hall locked to discourage the walking through and visiting business.

Regards to Duchess, Sister, and Miss B.

Love,

MF

[*Handwritten on back of letter*]

There are some Mexicans or Cubans or something that are here visiting the girl in that back west room most of the time. I am afraid there won't be any way to lock the closet in the hall and I check every hour practically to see if my coat etc. is still there. I can lock my door but if the people in the next room don't lock theirs—and they don't—somebody could walk off with everything.

Still can't find the right people to tell me about the work.

MF

[*Back of envelope*]

My cold much better.

\* \* \*

Thursday [20 Sept. 1945]

Dear Regina,

Still no roommate but the reckoning day will be here shortly I fear. I just learned today that the Supervisor of this house is from *Atlanta*. I trust she will not be one of Atlanta's lesser products, but from the looks of her last year's roommate who is reputedly her best friend and here in this house, she may not be much. The girl who was her roommate is from Cuba and has Cuban friends running all over this place—male and female—until all hours of the night. My door remains locked and I think I have created the general impression of not caring to be disturbed.

The girl next door that I didn't like moved out, so both the one that is still there and I are waiting on roommates.

Most of the people in this house are Assistants or Fellows (me).

Louise Trovato got her Assistantship which pays her $40.00 per month and furnishes valuable experience. I have had supper with her every night so far, and tonight we are going to the tearoom thing that is supposed to open. She said if she hadn't met us and known me, she would have been on the train and back in New York. She apparently gets decidedly despondent at times. She doesn't think she will like her roommate and she has an application in for a room in this house, but I don't think there is any chance of her getting it. She is going to take one course that I am taking. We went and talked to the man this afternoon, and he was very nice. Said the object was to sell and find markets. Brother Schramm still out of town.

My delicatessen is gradually being built up. I found the bottled prunes. They cost 32 cents. You might send me some cheaper, I don't know. I have some Dutch Rusk toast that comes in a box and probably won't mold like bread. I bought me a tin pan, a dish and a glass and my food looks like something you would put out for the cat, but it is plenty, nutritious, and tasty if not artistic. (breakfast, that is).

You may tell my relatives, if it wouldn't disappoint them too much, that I am not homesick. All I miss is you and free access to the bathroom. I have to go into the next room to turn the light on in this room. It bothers me more than the people in there though—although only one of them is here since the one I didn't like moved out. I also have to use their trash can unless I want to buy one which I don't.

Just got your letter and so glad Uncle Goolsby was thereabouts. Louise Trovato would like to go to Chicago some weekend, maybe Thanksgiving, with me, so I will contact him at the proper time.

    Love,

    MF

P.S. Ate dinner (middle of day) with Jo Stoneberg.

* * *

Friday [21 Sept. 1945]

Dear Regina,

Still no roommate. The girl next door's *new* roommate arrived last night. She is a Catholic but pretty looking. Brought a teddy bear with her. That sort.

Louise Trovato and I went to that tearoom last night, and it was hot and stuffy, and after so long a time they brought the food, which was all right but nothing extra and about 20¢ more than you'd pay at the Union.

Saw the Art people today and they looked at my stuff and seemed much interested, helpful, appreciative, etc. Am signed up for an advanced drawing course with a man who has done cartooning and says he can help me. Also got into the Writer's Workshop that was supposed to be so difficult—without any trouble.

The more I stay around here, the more I think I will be able to make money after this training. These people know how to do things.

I found a screen in the hall closet which they said we could use in this room. I have incorporated it around my section and hope the other party is not inclined to want to share it with me.

If you can send me some 6–16 film, I will take some pictures and send you.

No news.

Supervisor from Atlanta hasn't come yet.

Love,
MF

* * *

[Saturday 22 Sept. 1945]

Dear Regina,

There is a very bossy girl in this house who is a friend of the supervisor and who is the one always entertaining the Cuban Republic. Today, someone cancelled a room in the house here, and by accident I happened to be in the hall and hear this girl say that, since there had been a cancellation, she was going to have her two Cuban friends changed from their graduate house and come in here. One, she informed me, could go in the room upstairs that had been cancelled, and the other was to go in my room and be my roommate, because whoever was in this room had apparently cancelled their reservation, too. I just stared at her and walked off, because I didn't know what to say. When she left, I got my coat and went and got Louise Trovato and hotfooted it to the office of Student Affairs. Louise had said she was next on the list and was to get the first vacancy. The Office of Student Affairs sent us to Currier to another lady, where we found the bossy girl making arrangements for the Cuban to get into my room. We waited while she talked and heard that the vacancies were not as she had planned, but the lady told her she would see what she could do to get the Cubans in. Then, we talked to her when the girl left and after much red tape got Louise in my room.

So my roommate has arrived, and I am much relieved. If it had been the Cuban, I would have had to move myself to a crate in somebody's backyard. They are dirty-looking, always entertaining greasy boys, and always playing rhumba music. Louise is glad to be in here, because she didn't like her roommate. She isn't much of a Catholic—said she never went to church at home.

More later.

MF

\* \* \*

Saturday [22 Sept. 1945]

Dear Regina,

It promises to be very nice having Louise in here. Anything would be better than those Cubans. If she leaves in Feb. the problem will come up again so you might pray that the Lord will be with me. The Catholic in the next room (an ex-model) Gloria Breemer (the one with the teddy bear) found out about the Newman Club and we are going next Friday. Hope Louise will go with us. She is a Catholic in name only but I think she is going to church with me tomorrow. She said her mother was a very good Catholic and was always mad that she didn't go to church. I think from what she says of when she graduated etc. that she must be hitting the 36's or 7's.

I bought me the rain boots today—$3.00. It is raining.

If you have sent any cards to 32 Bloomington, don't send any more since I haven't got them.

Regards to the others.

Love,

MF

\* \* \*

Sunday [23 Sept. 1945]

Dear Regina,

All the upstairs sewerage has overflowed into the tubs etc. downstairs. Started last night and plumber came this A.M. Don't know whether it's fixed yet or not. This house is always going to be coming apart in some section. We go to the Union for bathroom purposes today. I haven't taken any baths yet and I don't know if I will until Christmas.

Louise, Gloria (teddy bear owner), and I went to St. Mary's today. No charge for admission. Liked it much better than St. Patrick's. They have the Novena to Our Lady of Perpetual Help which I shall attend if possible.

Louise says to tell you she is very glad to be in here.

I still haven't registered because Mr. Schramm is not back but so far as I know now I won't have a class before ten o'clock.

I have some grim [*sic*] crackers to go with my prunes and Dutch rusk. Louise has some orange juice and apples. Did you find anything out about the burner?

Supervisor is supposed to come today. Somebody told me she lived in Birmingham now so that lets Atlanta out.

I bought an egg at the drug store and put it in my hair today because I was afraid to wash it with the cold. It is rainy here.

Regards to Auntery and Unclery. Presume Miss Bancroft got off. Wrote her to North Carolina.

Got one box of kleenex which gave out yesterday. Please send me some if you can get it. Also some of that Evening in Paris talcum powder which I can't get here.

Start school tomorrow.

> Love,
> MF

* * *

Monday [24 Sept. 1945]

Dear Regina,

Our plumbing is fixed. The supervisor arrived last night. She looks like she couldn't supervise anything short of a flea circus. She is a great friend of the girl who tried to put the Cuban in my room so neither care for me since Louise is in here instead. The supervisor is 22.

Mr. Schramm is still not here and won't be here until the end of the week so I am going to the classes I want to not knowing if he will let me stay in them.

The girl next door (with the teddy bear) is not too nice about our going through their room to the bathroom but I don't know anything she can do about it.

Louise is very agreeable to have in here.

We have eaten a couple of other places than the Union but they are all dirty or not cheap.

I got me some professional kleenex that they use in hospitals which will do for the time.

When does uncle come back? Has anything happened about the blouse?

They have laundry service for sheets here for 50¢ a week. You have to use their sheets and they give you two clean ones a week. You don't have to use this service if you don't want to. I reckon I'll just send mine home.

I was asking the cashier on the Union sun porch thing how to use the telephone book the other day and she asked me if I would come in and talk to her some time—she liked to hear me talk. There aren't many Southerners up here that I can see.

Regards to Aunts Mary and Katie.

> Love,
> MF

[*on back of envelope*]

Just got letter and Recorder. Much obliged.

* * *

Tuesday [25 Sept. 1945]

Dear Regina,

The maid is in here with the vacuum cleaner. She cleans up twice a week which is all right because I would never do it. They have also washed the windows. I have just washed my night clothes and hung them in the basement. There is a very good place there where the furnace is and they get dry in a short time.

They have a high mass at St. Mary's every morning at 7:30—over by eight—with music which I attended this morning and will probably continue to do.

Got Lizzie's card also Union Recorder which I enjoyed. Why don't you try to sell that accordion to some of those people?

Sorry you are having to eat Estella's cooking again. I enjoy my meals. I spent $9.60 for food in 7 days, which will come to about $40.00 per month—as I suspected. This is a pretty cheap place to get an education.

Tell Sister I bought a bottle of mineral oil today.

> Love,
> MF

* * *

Wednesday [26 Sept. 1945]

Dear Regina,

My glasses came last night. They are thinking about letting us get mail at this house but it hasn't gone through yet so until it does, continue sending mine to Currier Hall.

I have been to two classes only so far. Am still waiting on Mr. Schramm. Liked the two classes I went to very much—one Art, the other magazine writing.

It is raining and cold here today. It rains a great deal. The fountain at Currier Hall is very nice. You can get an egg sandwich—very big—for ten cents there.

Thursday the people upstairs are giving a surprise birthday party for a girl up there and we are invited. You bring your own utensils and help pay for the cake. They also plan to have something for the convalescent children next door. They are orthopedic cases, I understand.

Hope you enjoyed meeting the faculty, etc.

Regards to Duchess and Sister.

> Love,
> MF

P.S. I wrote Mary Virginia and all those people.

\* \* \*

Thursday [27 Sept. 1945]

Dear Regina,

They turned the heat on in this house yesterday and got it up too high and we all roasted last night. They are going to turn it down sometime today. It is still wet outside. I found a grocery down the street only 2 blocks and am now stocked up on Gerber's custards and puddings, also 7 Ups. They have Coca Colas on Tuesday and I plan to get some of those if possible.

Louise went for a physical and they gave her 2 or 3 shots and those with the heat on have got her down. She is a very despondent soul anyhow but brother am I glad she's in here. She says she won't be back after Christmas but I don't know. It will depend on how she feels at Christmas I reckon.

Still no Mr. Schramm.

Regards to household—

> Love,
> MF

\* \* \*

[Friday 28 Sept. 1945]

Dear Regina,

The address is now:
Currier Graduate House
32 East Bloomington St.

Saw Mr. Schramm today. Said he could either fit me for a job I didn't want or make me a better writer and drawer. I took the latter. My work is very intensive writing. On Tuesday and Thursday I have 8 o'clock classes. On all other days, I don't have to go until after dinner. It has turned very cold here all of a sudden. We are supposed to go to the Newman Club tonight, but don't think I will as I am sick and don't want to risk this weather. We can get an electric plate for $4.80. If you can't get one any cheaper, I am going to buy this one, but please let me know so I can hurry up and do it before they are all sold here.

I am in class with a lady of color named Gloria Breemer—the same name as the Catholic with the teddy bear in the next room.

In case you care to see my schedule, it is as follows:

Mon.:  Advanced drawing from 2 until 5
Tues.:  Political Science from 8 until 9, Fiction Analysis from 2 until 3;
        Magazine Writing from 4 until 5
Wed.:  Nothing
Thurs:  Political Science from 8 until 9; Fiction Analysis 2–3;
        Writer's Workshop 4–6
Fri:    Advanced Drawing from 2–5
Sat.    Advertising from 10–12

The rest of the time I have to spend writing.

Don't dig up too many people for me to write to. I've got more than my hands full. Will write Dr. and Louis as soon as I can.

Regards to Sister and Duchess.

> Love,
> MF

* * *

Sunday [30 Sept. 1945]

Dear Regina,

Sell the book to Yvonne. Don't send the Who's Who. Save the New Yorkers.

Am enclosing clipping Cousin Katie sent me of "Uncle" Georges. Also ad from Daily Iowan. Competition! Will send one of the latter to Cousin Katie.

When do the Garners arrive and in what force? Whose idea was it their going to the farm? Why won't it be nice for Uncle to go live with them? Where is the dear boy?

We are going to high mass at St. Mary's in a little while.

My Saturday advertising class has been changed to Tuesday night.

We didn't go to Newman Club because it was too bad out but will go next Friday if same conditions do not prevail. The priests at St. Thomas Moore [*sic*] are the Revs. Leonard J. Brugman, J. Walter McEleney, J. Ryan Beiser—for his Reverence's information.

We bought an electric burner but took it back on account of there was no way to turn it off without taking it out of the socket and that didn't work. There is a girl here with an electric cup. Haven't seen any more however.

Will write Josie.

Regards to Aunts.

Love,

MF

FIGURE 1. Ad from the *Daily Iowan* that Flannery referred to as "competition" (30 Sept. 1945). Flannery O'Connor papers, Stuart A. Rose Manuscript, Archives, and Rare Book Library, Emory University.

FIGURE 2. Clipping sent by Cousin Katie about the hurricane in Savannah from the *Savannah Morning News* (30 Sept. 1945). Flannery O'Connor papers, Stuart A. Rose Manuscript, Archives, and Rare Book Library, Emory University.

\* \* \*

### Monday [1 Oct. 1945]

Dear Regina,

Got your Wednesday letter today but no package yet. Also no package from the Binions if they are going to send me one. I got a can of carrot juice this morning that I am going to try. I make frequent rounds of all the grocery stores. Have not seen that A&P yet.

Louise poorly on account of a TB test. It puffed her arm out pretty bad. Says she won't be back in February. Hope she changes her mind. We went to high mass yesterday and I think she enjoyed the music if nothing else. The sermon was sorry. All the sermons seem to be so that I have heard. Her trouble is she has had no Catholic education and doesn't know what it's all about.

I won't be able to go to the Newman Club on account of my Tuesday night class—that's when it meets apparently. Louise and Gloria will probably go.

Regards to the Duchess and her Sister.

Tell Miss Mary I am thinking about buying some agar agar for my grim crackers.

Love,

MF

\* \* \*

### Tuesday [2 Oct. 1945]

Dear Regina,

The box came last night and I was glad to get it. I immediately ate a box of the wafers—all but three, to be exact, which the girl next door had. Much obliged for the Kleenex powder etc. but please do not send me anymore earrings and that stuff. I have no place to put them and I do not wear them. And no accordion *please. Don't send me anything I don't ask for*—except food.

We can't get the Currier laundry service because we didn't sign up for it in time. Louise is going to take some of hers to the laundry today but my sheets aren't dirty and I have no intention of changing them for a good many weeks. They don't even look dirty.

My art class is very tiring—3 hours—and my work is vastly inferior to the others. I may pass the course but I doubt it. Anyway I am staying in it on the assumption that I may get help later on with the cartoons. The man is very busy but he said bring some in Friday and he would criticize them. The class period we devote to sketching from the model. We sit on these newfangled art easels that look like ironing boards and draw at arm's length. With no back support it gets very draggy.

I can't tell how I stand in the other classes because there is no way to compare work but mine should by all rights not be equal to the others.

You get to the basement in this place through our bathroom. It is hot as hades down there and things dry in a minute. The girl next door with the teddy bear has more or less got used to our coming through. She had the tooth ache yesterday and went to the Dental School to have it looked at. They said she had 15 cavities and needed an extraction. Her dentist in Cleveland told her they were all right before she came. She has gone to have it pulled today. I wouldn't let them pull any of mine without consulting elsewhere. Which reminds me, have you made the appointment with Dr. Rogers to get my front one fixed?

Must go eat another box of Nabiscos.

> Love,
> MFO'C

P.S. I enclose the letter from Mary, thinking Duchess might enjoy it.

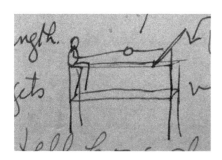

FIGURE 3. Flannery's illustration of her "ironing board" drawing desk (2 Oct. 1945). Flannery O'Connor papers, Stuart A. Rose Manuscript, Archives, and Rare Book Library, Emory University.

\* \* \*

### Wednesday [3 Oct. 1945]

Dear Regina,

About the cards—don't get any for me. I don't like them and am not going to send that kind if I send any.

Can you send me one of those 10¢ pencil sharpeners? I need one bad and can't get it up here. Also a can opener if you can get one.

The girl next door had her tooth pulled at the dental school. A student did it. It was his first extraction and she said he had to stick the novocaine needle in three times before he got it in the right place.

I went to my Tuesday night advertising class last night and enjoyed it. I think I will enjoy all of them but the art.

I bought a book of meal tickets for the Union cafeteria. You can't save any money but you don't have to take much money around with you and you can tell how long the five dollars will go for food.

I eat breakfast in my room. Louise has that kind of powdered coffee you mix with boiling water—also buns of some description or cereal. I have some kind of juice—pineapple this morning—prunes, Dutch Rusk, grim crackers, etc. I ain't starving.

Regards to aunts.

> Love,
> MF

P.S. Would you like me to send you a little jar of the powdered coffee? All you do is put it in the hot faucet water. She says it's not bad.

> MFO'C

Send letters to 32 E. Bloomington and don't put Currier anything on them as it takes longer for them to come.

*  *  *

Thursday [4 Oct. 1945]

Dear Regina,

Got your letter of Sunday and card of Monday both just now. Am glad we can get a burner because we can have eggs. The party for the girl upstairs was very nice, costing us 17¢ a piece. She and her husband were stationed in Savannah about a year ago. He is now in the Pacific and she is getting her MFA. Just had an extended conversation with the maid. The help around here is very efficient and a good deal more polite than some of the powers that be. The girl next door with the teddy bear and the ex-tooth joined me in a can of Gerber's this A.M. I like the Union cafeteria a great deal. Louise likes to eat out occasionally but it is greasy, dirty, and expensive. I eat dinner by myself and usually have supper with her. She is getting so she will go to the Union all the time, too.

I got to go there now.

> Love,
> MF

\* \* \*

Friday [5 Oct. 1945]

Dear Regina,

Will enclose the letter Dr. sent as proof of the fact that I have met obligations.

The laundry is coming for Louise's and my sheets today. They weren't very dirty, having been used only 3 weeks—but as long as she sent hers, I sent mine. I don't know how much it will cost.

My radio won't play.

She (Louise) didn't have to have a physical but she thought she did, so she got one. I was waiting to see if I couldn't get out of it some way so I didn't get one and then we found out they didn't make graduate students get them.

We aren't going to put up any curtains in this room. We haven't time for such and it looks all right like it is. Plenty of other people don't have them either.

Enjoyed Agnes's letter, what I could read of it.

Haven't got one from you today. I am the only one around here who hears from home every day and should like to continue to be.

I have to go to the art today and sit astride the ironing board affair for three hours. I am not looking forward to it.

They have been having very good muffins at the Union lately.

When does Catherine de Gerner arrive? Regards to Uncle.

    Love,
    MFO'C

\* \* \*

[Saturday 6 Oct. 1945]

Dear Regina,

We went to the Newman Club party last night and it was (lousy) but I paid my membership and although I can't go to the meeting on account of my Tuesday night class, I am a member and the Lord be with me.

Please get from Fr. Toomey the author and publisher and city where published of a book called "The Spirit of Catholicity" which he at one time lent me. I want to get it for Louise. She is interested in the subject and has requested a book, and I think this is the one for her.

This room and whole house is kept very hot. At night, regardless of the low temperature outside, we sleep under only a sheet. They say it will be this way all winter, but I doubt it.

I need a couple of white shirts with collars that can stick out of the top of a sweater. Nothing else. It is never necessary to dress up around here. I like it very much.

> Love,
> MF

\* \* \*

### Sunday [7 Oct. 1945]

Dear Regina,

We have just got through going to St. Mary's for high mass and are now going to the Union for boiled ham. This afternoon I plan to walk over to St. Wenceslaus since I have figured out where it is.

It is now Indian Summer, I am told. A bitter disappointment it is. The weather is much better but not anything to get hot about and I hear it doesn't last but 3 or four days.

There is no need for a fur coat yet. With a sweater underneath I do very well. Yesterday I ironed 2 shirts.

> Love,
> MF

\* \* \*

### Monday [8 Oct. 1945]

Dear Regina,

Your letters of Wednesday and Thursday, a card from Cousin Katie, Union Recorder, the letter from John, and a rejection slip arrived today.

The girl next door who rooms with Gloria is from Minnesota—is named Connie Quinelle. Lutheran, very nice indeed—aged 22. She has an assistantship in French and makes $60 a month.

Louise talks of leaving because she doesn't feel she is getting the courses she wants. I am satisfied with mine. However, I want to get the second year's training elsewhere if that will be possible, and if I want or need it. I will not be prepared for a job after this year here. Outside of teaching, of course.

Yesterday the supervisor had some tea bags and she invited us in to bring our glasses and put hot water in them and have her tea, which we did. I took the marshmellers and they finished them off in short order. Will be very glad to get the can opener.

John Sullivan says when he gets back, he is going to the University of Cincinnati. I must write him that I have a friend in Chicago who recommends it highly.

It is cold again today. I have to go sit on the ironing board three hours this afternoon.

We went to see "Conflict" last night. It was all right.

A box of church envelopes has been sent me. It doesn't say for which church. Louise and Gloria haven't got any.

They are having 40 hours at St. Mary's next week.

> Love,
> MF

* * *

Tuesday [9 Oct. 1945]

Dear Regina,

Your letters of Friday and Saturday all came today. The can opener last night. It is a very superior looking can opener. It won't open the Gerber's but it does very well on the fruit juice. I am highly obliged. I presume my thanks can be relayed to Mrs. Lewis.

Last night, two of the people upstairs had open house in their rooms to show off their decorating. We went. They had fruit juice, and in the cans they had a contraption that you stick on the can, it opens it, provides a spout that opens and closes, thus making it possible to leave the juice in the can indefinitely and to pour it without getting all over the top of the can. They said they got them at the hardware store, and I plan to get some if I can.

Tonight one of the people upstairs is having a birthday, so we are all supposed to eat at the Union together. They are having a cake and a tablecloth.

The girl in that west back room off the porch is a Jewess from N.Y. named Serena Weismann. Very flossy. She had to take a practice test for a ten year old's intelligence. She got me to be the guinea pig. She couldn't tell me how much I made but she looked worried. One of the questions was, what is similar in a cow, a snake, and a sparrow? I couldn't get it. The answer: they all grow.

Regards to aunts Mary and Katie.

> Love,
> MF

* * *

Wednesday [10 Oct. 1945]

Dear Regina,

We got our laundry back yesterday. I sent two sheets, a pillow case, and towel, and it cost me thirty cents. This was not bad, except that the sheets etc. were dirtier than when I sent them and practically rough dried.

I got my check for $15 today. Louise got one for $39. She has to teach, however.

It is rainy again here but so hot in the house we can't hardly stay in it without all the windows open. Our food keeps refrigerated in the window. Don't send the extra night clothes if you haven't made them. I wear one pair a couple of weeks and wash the other in the meantime.

Know you are glad Marie is coming back. Hope her health permits her to stay. What is Dorothy doing these days? Mable?

Regards to Aunt Mary.

Love,

MF

P.S. I still don't know when Catherine Carner is coming back. I forgot to tell you John Sullivan is on the Marshall Islands.

MF

* * *

Thursday [11 Oct. 1945]

Dear Regina,

Letter and pencil sharpener arrived this A.M. Also card from Miss Bancroft. Pencil sharpener does very well, and am glad to get it.

Tell Miss Mary that I opened the door this A.M. and there stood the reincarnation of Mrs. Griffin. She was trying to get in the door, of course, and then walked down the walk between my two feet. I might could get her in a bag some night and send her back if you all want her.

It is fairly decent here again in the weather line. Louise regulates the air in this room and appears to know what she is doing. I don't get contaminated with any more air than is necessary.

We have bugs but we didn't attract them. I understand they have always been here. Silverfish, they call them.

I have only had to buy 1 textbook ($1.75) but a lot of art supplies.

Will see about getting me a shirt or two. Don't send that one you spoke about.

Love,

MF

\* \* \*

Friday [12 Oct. 1945]

Dear Regina,

The stove came last night, and we were mighty glad to get it. However, I was afraid to use it because the plug sparked when you put it in the socket, so I took it to the electrical place and am going back for it tomorrow. Don't tell Louis, since I wrote him I had already had four boiled eggs, a dish of oatmeal, and a cup of boiling water off it. I don't know how much it will cost to get it fixed. The lady couldn't say. I know it's not the wall socket's fault since other things work in that all right.

Haven't had time to look at the radio yet.

If Brother McDonah designs any ironing boards, I hope he puts backs on them.

Had a letter from Miss Hallie today saying she had ordered me a Shakespeare. I will write her, but if you see her, tell her how much I appreciate it. Also that we tried to get to see her.

Louise has met an eligible male principal. I hope he pays her enough attention to keep her here next semester. She says she is in the market for a rich old man with money.

I am off to sit on the ironing board for three hours.

Love,
MF

\* \* \*

Saturday [13 Oct. 1945]

Dear Regina,

The box with the blouse came this morning and I am highly obliged. It is a nice one—fits fine—and I am glad to get it. Also the other edible portion. Please restrain yourself from sending me any more aprons. I know it will be hard but please restrain yourself. It just makes more for me to bring home. I haven't spilled anything on myself yet.

I shudder to think of what you have done to my room. There will not be left a paper upon a paper, I know.

Had a letter from Frances Lewis, which didn't say anything so I don't enclose it.

This morning, I walked around to St. Wenceslaus. It is on the same street as Currier Hall, down six blocks. They were apparently having school in there, so I didn't go in. On my way back I came down a block and ran into the Mercy Hospital.

Yesterday in the art, the man said my study of the pose was a very good drawing, and that is the first time he has had anything to say about my stuff. He usually just looks at it and walks away like he can't stand to look. Then in a little while, when we were working on another drawing, some visitors—professors in the art department—came in and one of them said my drawing showed that I was very sensitive to line movement. So maybe the class is not too advanced for me after all. I still dislike the ironing board, but I ought to get used to that before the year is up.

I take political science from an old boy named Briggs who came to my chair the other day and said he wanted to get my name straight—he thought I might be a tackle (football player).

It takes 3 days for your letters to get here.

Regards to the aunts.

Is the new cook still there?

> Love,
> MFO'C

\* \* \*

Sunday [14 Oct. 1945]

Dear Regina,

The heater is working and this A.M. I had two eggs on Rusk and a can of vienna sausages. I went to 7:30 mass at St. Mary's and went to Communion for the 40 hours and came home and fixed my breakfast. I went back to church with Louise because I was afraid she wouldn't go if I didn't, so I've been twice.

We went the 2nd time to the St. Thomas More's Chapel. It is over the river about four uphill blocks. It is very modernistic etc.

Next week, I plan to go to St. Wenceslaus if it kills me. I've been trying to get there, but Louise is usually late and we have to go to a later mass elsewhere.

We are now going to the Union for baked ham. I am very fond of the Union.

You wouldn't send me one of my silver spoons? I don't like to eat eggs off this thing—and I presume I could keep up with it.

Gloria's boyfriend came to see her this weekend and left her with a quart of liquor. So tell Miss Mary anytime she wants to drop a little in her aspirin bottle, I think I could get by with it.

> Love,
> MF

How's Uncle's trim?

* * *

Monday [15 Oct. 1945]

Dear Regina,

Got your two letters today. For breakfast I had three eggs on rusk. I am not starving. I have tomato soup and beef broth for anytime I feel faint, which ain't likely to be often. Regardless of the heat in the room, the window refrigerates things. They are so cold, in fact, you can hardly touch them. I am not overworked but my time is filled. I would rather be shot than have to room with Gloria—she is very fractious and addicted to loud noises. Furthermore, you don't choose your roommate. I can only complain if I don't like her and hope they will change her. I think, however, that Louise may stay. She likes it better now.

Will you please look in my room and send me the folder or as many of them as you can find that I made up of my work when I sent off for the fellowships. There ought to be two of them around the vicinity of the high desk. If you will remember, they were black and had articles from the Corinthian in them, also a few block prints, and typewritten poems. Mail them *flat* in one of those large envelopes or between cardboard. It is essential that I have these and I need them right away. If you cannot find them, please look in the old Corinthians that were lying around and send me copies of the following articles. (DO NOT SEND THE BOOKS— JUST CUT THE ARTICLES OUT).

"Fashion's Perfect Medium"
"Biologic Endeavor"
"Doctors of Delinquency"

I will be much obliged to get these. In fact, I gotta have them. Don't forget the continuations, please.

Last night we went to see "Anchors Aweigh," which was pretty good for a musical. This afternoon, I have to go sit on the ironing board.

John Sullivan said, according to his points, he should be home sometime before 1961. He had seen a Japanese Lt. Cmdr. who had on some fancy shoes and he asked the Cmdr. where he could get some like them. He said the Jap grinned and ran off and came back 4 days later with a pair of the shoes. He had had his steward make them for John.

Regards to aunts.

[*No closing signature*]

\* \* \*

Tuesday [16 Oct. 1945]

[*With a note asking "What kind of bug is this?" where she smashed a bug at the top of the page.*]

Dear Regina,

The letter from Newman was from some girl asking for information to put in the Alumna Journal. Just something else to take up my time which I haven't got.

Did you find the papers I asked for?

They call you when you have a package at Currier and they haven't called me about that one from the Binions. They probably haven't sent anything.

Miss Hallie's book came yesterday.

The bug at the top of the page just walked there and I flattened him. Is it a bed-bug? If it has dropped from up there, it is probably in the letter and you can shake it out. There are many bugs around here.

The address for Duchess is

TSgt. J. J. Sullivan, USMCR
Marine HqSq-4, c/o FPO
San Francisco, Calif.

You can put it on the separate piece of paper.

Eggs up here are 38¢ a dozen—I eat a couple a day—eggs not dozens.

Regards to Aunts, Uncle, and Trawicks.

Love,
MF

\* \* \*

Wednesday [17 Oct. 1945]

Dear Regina,

Much obliged for the name of the book. I will see if I can get it now.

I had a conference with the man under whom I do most of my writing, and, from his remarks, the fiction I handed in for criticism stands up very well. The poetry he found devoid of imagery, music, and everything else (with the exception of one or two he liked) but the fiction he liked. I presume my thesis will be a book of short stories. The next story he may not like, so it really doesn't mean anything.

A girl just came in and told me that one of the girls upstairs had left her brief-case on that coat rack at the Union and had gone to get it and found it not there.

She lost her notes and $9, and in coming up the Union stairs she fell and sprained her ankle and is now at the hospital.

If you know anything to kill the silverfish, send it.

Hope you have found those papers I want.

Regards to aunts etc.

> Love,
> MFOC

P.S. If you've got another pair of the pajamas made, you'd better send them. I thought I had two pair, but I only have one.

* * *

Friday [19 Oct. 1945]

Dear Regina,

Didn't get to write yesterday as I was rushing to get a manuscript typed for criticism. I read one of my short stories in the workshop next week. Somebody reads a manuscript every time and the others criticize it—otherwise, you do all the work out of class. I had a story dealing with Negroes that the man thought was good, but I couldn't read it on account of the colored girl in there. I was afraid it might make her self-conscious. Now I am going to read one that's not so good.

The girl upstairs who is the Assistant in Art and who lived in Savannah a year is going to take over the art class I am in because the man who has been teaching it has too much to do. I don't know but what this will lessen the value of the course for me, but it may not. I will have to wait and see.

We bought some hives for the silverfish.

They had a picnic at the city park last night (the people in this house), and we went. It was tolerable.

Somebody put the girl's stuff back who lost it at the Union.

I use the stove on the floor like an Indian and push it around. It hasn't made the floor swell.

I sent the Bulletin to Mr. Curtis.

What about my ducks?

> Love,
> MF

P.S. Louise had a cyst cut on her ear but her spirits are unusually high, nevertheless. I believe she will stay.

* * *

Saturday [20 Oct. 1945]

Dear Regina,

Got your letter and Cousin Katie's enclosed. Enjoyed. My face is OK—no trouble. Will you be able to see her? Wouldn't you love having Auntie Tarleton come stay with you while Sister went to Savannah? My cold is gone. Louise is the one that ails around here. I go to mass every morning while the weather is decent but won't be able to do it much longer.

Tonight we are going to the A&P.

Tomorrow I hope to get to St. Wenceslaus.

    Love,

    MFOC

* * *

Sunday [21 Oct. 1945]

Dear Regina,

We finally got to St. Wenceslaus. It was about the size of St. Patrick's. The walls were in grey and grey-blue and the altars in white. They have a small statue of the Infant Jesus of Prague that is dressed up in a silk smock with ruffles. When they have Communion, they pull a white tablecloth over the rail. They also do that at St. Thomas More's. The sermon was about the best we've heard. At St. Mary's, the priest stutters, but the music is very fine.

*Don't mark the silver*, please.

The papers came last night, and I was powerful glad to get them, as I have to take them to my magazine writing class Tuesday. *Much highly obliged.* They are having another picnic for a girl upstairs birthday. These are an awful nuisance, and they make you pay for them.

Last night, we went to the A&P. I see where I will be spending many pleasant hours there. It was lovely. Prunes for 27¢.

Today we went to the Union for baked ham. I am very fond of the Union.

Regards to my relatives.

    Love,

    MFO'C

My cold is not here. Louise has one.

* * *

Monday [22 Oct. 1945]

Dear Regina,

Have just come from the A&P, where I spent a pleasant half hour. Eggs 49¢ a dozen. Got your two letters, also one from Miss Bancroft (enclosed) and one from Mary Virginia and the Colonnade. Very nice of her. Please give her a dollar and ask her to give it to the Alumna Journal people so I can get an Alumna Journal.

The girl upstairs is teaching my art now, and I think I will get even less out of it, but now I don't get as tired sitting on the ironing board. She is a nice girl.

Louise is upset these days because her mother and father have sold their house in Jamestown (NY) and are talking of moving to California. She also has a terrific cough. She sure is nice, and I am very fortunate to have her for a roommate. I couldn't stand the two in the next room—Gloria and Connie. They are too noisy, etc. We have no trouble about the bathroom, except they can't understand why I lock the door when I go in it. I do just the same. So does Louise.

Regards to Aunts Mary and Katie, Willie and the new cook.

Wrote Cousin Katie yesterday.

> Love,
> MF

* * *

Tuesday [23 Oct. 1945]

Dear Regina,

Got your Friday letter tonight but no package. Am much obliged for the things when they come. Will give the chocolate bars to Louise if she wants them, but don't send any more. Will attend to the sugar wafers myself.

Did Frank Jr. get out on a medical discharge? Where does he think he will go next? What about Peter? Did he get to go to Northwestern? Frankly, I hope he doesn't come up here. I wouldn't know what to do with him, and I am working most of the time.

There is a preflight school at Ames—also one here. Iowa State is Ames, so I presume Mr. Butts' boy is going there.

Do you ever see Mary Thomas Maxwell?

Regards to Aunts, Uncles, and help.

Louise says thank you for the chocolate bars. She also appreciated your card a great deal. She is certainly very nice.

> Love,
> MFO'C

\* \* \*

Wednesday [24 Oct. 1945]

Dear Regina,

Today I went to see Miss Updegraph, one of the ladies Dr. Scurry knew. I wanted some information for an article dealing with child psychology that I am trying to write for my magazine writing class. So since she is an expert in that field, I went and asked her for a reading list and told her that we have a mutual friend etc. etc. She was very nice—fat, sort of reddish hair. She asked for my telephone number and said there was a girl interested in writing she knew that I might enjoy knowing, so she may have me come to see her. The Miss Cockeran is the one under whom the girl next door has her assistantship, and she asked Miss Cockeran about Dr. Scurry at my request, so they both know I'm around.

Louise and the girl upstairs who is a Catholic went to the Newman Club last night. She seemed to enjoy it.

There are only four of us who use the bathroom, so it doesn't get dirty with the maid cleaning it out twice a week. I spend as little time in it as is consistent with community living, however.

Tonight, Louise and I are going to a play.

I appreciate their sending me the paper free. I hope they remember to send it at that rate.

The package with the night clothes hasn't come.

My regards to Aunts Mary and Katie, etc.

> Love,
> MF

\* \* \*

Thursday [25 Oct. 1945]

Dear Regina,

Today I got a card from Annie Bruce with the enclosed slip in it, return receipt. I appreciated the card. She made up a verse and wrote it in it, so I wrote her back one. Also got a card from Dr. Tigner, who said he was in BM Hospital. Is he still there?

Louise's family are moving away from Jamestown and plan to come by here on their way out to California and see her.

There are a lot of people here who want to go to their respective homes for Christmas a la airplane. There is nobody going my way, but most of them will have to go to Chicago.

The underskirt Mrs. Bell gave me, upon being washed, shrunk to almost un-wearability. I washed the blouse you sent me today but don't know if it did the same.

You should go in for the croqueting; it might develop your muscles.

The package came after I had written you it hadn't. Immediately ate crackers and gave bars to Louise, who said she had wanted to write you for some time to thank you for inviting her to the picture show with us. She is very busy most of the time. Much obliged for the pajamas. Regards to Duchess, who owes me 4 cards, and Miss Mary.

> Love,
> MF

\* \* \*

Friday [26 Oct. 1945]

Enjoyed clippings—the advertising is nothing breathtaking.

Dear Regina,

I was supposed to read my short story in the workshop yesterday, but when I got there, Mr. Engle, the man who runs it, announced that he would read it himself, since nobody would understand it if I did. He thereupon proceeded to read it with great gusto and expression and did it great justice. The people in the workshop thought it had its points, and their criticism wasn't as violent as I have heard on other people's work that has been read. One woman in there mentioned a possible market for it, so I am somewhat encouraged. I have handed him in three short stories since I have been here—one of which I wrote this summer and two here. He hasn't criticized the last one for me yet, but the other two he gave the impression of thinking were more good than bad.

Give the Geographics to whomever you please.

They call me Flannery here—Miss O'Connor in class.

What is the name of the school Regina Sullivan goes to and where is it located? My friend upstairs who is a Catholic and also in the workshop (Ruth Sullivan, her name is) has a younger sister who is a freshman at that Ursuline Convent at New Rochelle just out of New York. I wondered if that was the place Regina went to. This one's name is Nancy Sullivan.

There's no place around here to get asbestos, and we don't leave the stove on but about 10 minutes once a day to do the eggs. There is no visible swelling in the floor.

Hope Cousin Katie will enjoy the devil in my room. Regards to aunts.

> Love,
> MFO'C

\* \* \*

Saturday [27 Oct. 1945]

Dear Regina,

Got your Tuesday and Wednesday letters both today. As far as I know, the silver is in the third drawer to the left in the high desk. Either kill Miss Fannie or leave a drake with her—preferably, leave a drake. I wanted the pure-blooded bantam rooster. He is the smallest. The others, I said you could give to Willie and Annie Bruce, but do not give away that good rooster.

Do not mention that man I told you was in Louise's class in your letters or any communication you might have with her. I merely said he was in her class, and I can't keep up with the conclusions you jump to. I wished to imply no such as you have asked about.

Today for dinner I ate with Ruth Sullivan, white, Miriam Johnson, white, and Gloria Bremerwell, colored. She is in the workshop, writes poetry, and is very nice indeed. She was the one whose name we understood was Breemer but it is Bremerwell. I like her better than Gloria Breemer, white. Shall I bring her home with me Christmas?

Tonight, Louise and I and all the Hook and Eye-Dutch are going shopping. Louise wants a coat and I want some fig newtons.

It is hot again today.

Regards to aunties.

> Love,
> MF

P.S. Delighted you don't need the operation, but don't get too proud of yourself—you ain't got no muscles.

* * *

Sunday [28 Oct. 1945]

Dear Regina,

Please look in the 1st drawer to the right in the table I draw on in my room and send me, if you can find them, the returns on my Graduate Record Examination. I showed them to you at the time I got them, so you should know what they are. If I can show I have had that examination once, they won't make me take it again. Otherwise, I will have to.

We went to St. Mary's 10:15 today. I have to go when Louise wants to or she will decide not to go at all. She says when it gets cold, she's not going. So then, I'll start going to an early one. She thinks her people will be through here in about a month.

The enclosed is for Aunt Mary, to keep her up to the minute on the latest medical literature.

Louise didn't find a coat to suit her. The prices here are high and the stuff is cheezy looking.

Tonight we are going to see "Junior Miss." Usually, we go to the picture show on Sunday.

I am enjoying the work here very much but have no hope of getting any job or any other stipend for next year here. There is a vague possibility that I may be able to sell a story somewhere, but that is slight.

We are off to eat boiled ham. (The food here is just as good as at home when you stick to the Union.)

    Love,
    MF

* * *

Monday [29 Oct. 1945]

Dear Regina,

Got your Thursday letter and enclosure today. Chewing gum reminded me of my Aunt Mary—it tasted like calomel.

I wash the dishes after I eat out of them—when else?

It is drizzly today, and I am told that this will be the last of Indian Summer and that it will now get cold. I have been told that three times before.

Do I understand you are also doing my room over in orchid? If so, it must be rare.

The Union Recorder is coming to Currier Hall. Could you have them send it here? Is it Grandpa Goodrich who has bought E. E. Bell out?

On Mondays at the Union, they have the ham scraps left over from Sunday, mixed up in an egg casserole-like arrangement, and it is powerful tasty. They do the same with salmon—also tasty. They have salmon loaf and tartar sauce—delicious. Yesterday, they had muffins with blueberries in them. They have very fine pineapple and carrot salad. I eat the lettuce under it, since I am paying 10¢ for it. Last night we had to eat at the Huddle because the Union isn't open on Sunday night. It was punk. We saw "Junior Miss," and it was very good indeed.

Do silverfish bite?

> Love,
> MF

* * *

Tuesday [30 Oct. 1945]

Dear Regina,

Got your Friday letter today, also one from Cousin Katie, replete with intelligence of the Doyles, etc.

The Writer's Workshop is not the same as the magazine writing class. Have you found the silver? When are Betty Ann and Cousin John arriving?

I never have had time to get my radio looked at, so it just sits there. We don't have time to do anything but work, but most of it I enjoy. Louise is now talking about going to California after this semester. She doesn't know what she is going to do or wants to do.

The people next door had a mouse last night, sitting in their crackers eating. Currier is going to put out some traps, I understand.

I saw Jo Stoneberg the other day. She looked overworked, but otherwise agreeable.

We are going to hear William Primrose tomorrow night on their concert association. We do not have to dress up. That's one thing I like about this place—also the food. I had baked hash at the Union today for 15¢—delightful.

Regards to relatives.

> Love,
> MF

\* \* \*

Wednesday [31 Oct. 1945]

Dear Regina,

Just returned from A&P where I spent a pleasant half hour selecting a bottle of sauerkraut juice. Figure it will vitaminize my breakfasts more than pineapple juice.

I had egg custard at the Union today like Cousin Katie had in Savannah. This is certainly a nice place.

The man who teaches magazine writing gave me a paper back with "clever as hell" on it, so I presume I am doing all right in his class.

Tonight they are having the party—Halloween party—for the convalescent children next door.

Wrote American Airlines yesterday. If you still have those railroad schedules, send them to me so I can tell where to write to in Chicago to see about the train. I understand people have been snowed in up here and couldn't get out for Christmas. Maybe Miss Bremerwell will invite me home with her for Christmas if that happens.

Like the girl upstairs as an art teacher very much. I get more help.

Louise wrote you yesterday.

Regards to aunties.

Love,
MF

\* \* \*

Thursday [1 Nov. 1945]

Dear Regina,

Just returned from an "inquisitorial summary," which is what they call a test. It was fairly easy, but I don't know what I'll get on it.

There being no help for it, we cleaned up the room this morning. It was very uninteresting and debilitating. I don't think I will do it again.

There are only about 12 children next door. They are very lively not to be able to walk.

I have seen people in fur coats a couple of times, mostly those mouton things. They look cheap. Ruth Sullivan and I are going to Cedar Rapids a coming Saturday. I don't want anything there, but it only costs 50¢, so I will go to see Cedar Rapids.

Saw Dr. Updegraph again last night at a concert, and she asked me to call that girl up, so I reckon I will have to. Dr. Updegraph looks like Mrs. Toomey, only she has reddish hair.

Give the books and magazines to whomever you please, I thought I said.

Did you take the nails off your fingers?

Is Duchess so much better that she can go automobile riding, or are they just taking her because they know how to handle her better? Does she ride in front or in back? Is Mrs. Digby ever coming back?

Regards to Aunts Mary and Katie and Uncle.

> Love,
> MF

\* \* \*

Friday [2 Nov. 1945]

Dear Regina,

Got your Monday and Tuesday letters today with Graduate Record stuff and am much obliged, also moral lecture on race problem. My sitting with Miss Bremerwell was unavoidable, but I would not hesitate to sit with her again under like conditions. Let me remind you that I am able to take care of myself in this regard. Also that conditions you can't see, you can't judge.

Louise doesn't have to go to her Saturday classes tomorrow, so we may go to Cedar Rapids. She is still after a coat. I don't need mine yet.

I had a conference with Mr. Engle of the Workshop yesterday in regard to the story that was read there. He said he had been delighted with it. He does not pass out such remarks too liberally, so I am encouraged. I do not think he considers it marketable, however.

Give Annie the *young* rooster. The old one, I want. The old one is small and fat and middle-aged looking.

Louise's sister sent her a picture of her mother. She looks sort of like Duchess.

Regards to relatives.

> Love,
> MF

\* \* \*

Saturday [3 Nov. 1945]

Dear Regina,

I am on the trolley going to Cedar Rapids—also Louise and Fern, the girl upstairs. It costs 88¢ round trip—trolley looks like a caboose—sign at one end of it saying "toilet" but not denoting sex. Will not visit. Country so far is very like at home. I am hoping it will hurry up and get flat. They have a lot of all-white cows, but they are dirty. Have passed some lovely chicken houses that look like beach cottages.

Today is a big day, it seems, for football people. They aren't having classes so everybody can go to the football game, so we are going to Cedar Rapids. I may come back with a pair of low-heel Sunday shoes like I tried to get in Atlanta. I may just come home.

I reckon I will write Margaret for my fur coat, as it is now cold and I see a lot of people wearing them.

Regards to relatives.

Love,
MF

* * *

Sunday [4 Nov. 1945]

Dear Regina,

I got me a winter head rag in Cedar Rapids and some heavier drawers. As soon as you finish the knitted gloves, I would be obliged to get them. It is fairly cold, and the ones you made me bring are in several ineffectual strips. We came back at 7:45 on the trolley—a very nice trip—like going to Macon. We had supper at the hotel and had to pay $1.25 for it, which distressed me no little.

Today we are going to the 11:30 mass and thence to the Union. Louise isn't going to the Union or eat dinner at all as she wants to study. My stomach means more than my studies to me, so I will be there.

How is the new nurse working out?

Regards to Aunts M and K and Uncle.

Love,
MF

* * *

Monday [5 Nov. 1945]

Dear Regina,

Got your two letters today. Cannot believe Dr. Murphy looked like anything but Dr. Murphy. Did Mata Hari have the goat with her?

I can get a plane out of Chicago at 2:50 P.M. and get to Atlanta at 8:55 P.M., or at 7:05 A.M. and get to Atlanta at 1:20 P.M., or 5:15 P.M. and get to Atlanta at 12:33 P.M. However, I plan to write several airlines for their schedules before I get my reservation. If possible, I want to get one to Macon, but I don't know if there is a company that runs one from Chicago straight there.

It is warm again today after being cold for a few days.

Can't send you the stories, as I have to give the carbons to Mr. [Wilbur] Schramm and Mr. [William E.] Porter for criticism and the original to Mr. Engle for criticism. The magazine writing class has nothing to do with the workshop. I read the story in the workshop—Engle read it, rather. If I ever get one published will be time enough to read it.

We don't have any classes Monday the 12th, as Sunday is Armistice Day.

Louise and Fern are talking about going to Des Moines, then I reckon I will if they do.

Regards to relatives.

 Love,

 MF

* * *

Tuesday [6 Nov. 1945]

Dear Regina,

There is a girl in my art class whom I have talked to sometimes when we have a resting spell. Yesterday, she asked me where I was from. It turned out she was an ex-WAVE who had been to Stonekeepers School during Commander Stubbs's reign. She hadn't liked it because it was so strict. She had been through our house and remembered it. Said someone told her that some of the scenes from *Gone with the Wind* had been taken in it. I assured her to the contrary, lest it get out that I was the niece of Scarlot [*sic*] O'Hara. She was there from November to January of '43–4 when the last of the Marines were leaving. Apparently, she was glad when she left.

I got a paper I wrote for political science back with an A–, which was all right with me. He probably gave everybody the same thing, however. I have a test in my advertising tonight. I find the course very dull. Have not heard from the other inquisitorial summary.

Just got your letter with railroad schedule. I am not coming on the train, except as a last resort. I don't get out until the 22nd, which is a Saturday, which will involve the weekend and all that. Is it all right not to go to mass when you are travelling? Since I have no Saturday classes, I hope to leave Friday on the rocket and spend the night in Chicago. Leave Chicago at 7:05 A.M. Saturday, get to Atlanta at 1:30 P.M. and come home with Doctor that afternoon or on the 4 o'clock bus.

That is the only way to do it—otherwise I would be two days about it and get there on Christmas day. I think that rather than spend the night in Chicago, I will leave Friday night on the slow rocket ~~and leave Chicago~~ Nope—couldn't do that, so will probably come first way as stated above on 7:05 plane. All this if I can get the plane reservation.

Regards to aunties.

Love,

MF

* * *

Thursday [8 Nov. 1945]

Dear Regina,

The gloves came this A.M., and I am much obliged as they are needed; however, the fingers are all too long, so I reckon I will have to send them back, which I will as soon as I can.

I sent a pair of the flannel pajamas to the laundry last week because I was sending the sheets and didn't have any time to wash them. They came back today rough dried and shrunk. The sleeves are almost up to the elbow. I had washed that pair before and didn't shrink, so I presume it was the laundry's fault.

We wasted our money on the picture show last night, as it wasn't any good.

It is raining with a high wind here. I have just come back from the Union, and my umbrella blew inside out twice. I turned backward, and it blew back right. It is warm with the rain, however. They say you can't use an umbrella in the snow. I got my $15.00 today.

Regards to household.

Love,

MF

* * *

Friday [9 Nov. 1945]

Dear Regina,

Just received an Eastern Airlines timetable. They have a plane that leaves Chicago at 10:00 A.M. and gets to Macon at 5:15 P.M., and I plan to be on it. I am sure you would like to meet me in Macon Saturday, December 22nd.

It is too cold to send the gloves back. I will carry my loose change in the extra space, and you may use the rest of the yarn making me a pair of earmuffs.

Fern from upstairs (age 43) is going to take some pictures tonight of the room and Louise and me, which I will send you. She is an expert picture-taker, it seems. Regards to relatives.

  Love,

  MF

* * *

Saturday [10 Nov. 1945]

Dear Regina,

 Got your letter and Georgia Power stuff today. I don't exactly have what you might call time to enlighten the Georgia Power about the tourist potentialities of Milledgeville, but if I get an idea, I might jot down a 1000 words and send it to you to send in. Why don't you enter it—all they want are statistical facts.

 Don't send me any money for Thanksgiving—all I could do with it would be put it in the bank, and there is already enough in there to satisfy my needs. And don't send me anything, as I don't need anything, food or otherwise.

 I think I will buy me a pint of sherbet and eat it all on Thanksgiving—then go on with my typing. Louise has an invitation out to a fellow teacher's house for dinner then.

 I am going to try to take the radio to be fixed this afternoon. It is in the 30°s here, but I don't feel it. The house is hot as Hades. The head rag I got is plain grey-blue wool—very heavy—very large. It cost $2.02.

 Louise is probably going to Abakerky (sp?), New Mexico to see her sister for Christmas, she thinks.

  Regards to aunties.

  Love,

  MF

* * *

Sunday [11 Nov. 1945]

Dear Regina,

 We now go to 11:30 church and thence to the Union, which opens at 12 on Sundays. I haven't gotten any leaflet missals for some time. Have they been coming? Isn't it time that I should get some?

 Met the girl Dr. Updegraph wanted me to meet, and Louise and I are going to have supper with her in the near future at the Union.

Since the Union isn't open on Sunday nights, my Sunday supper consists of a pint of sherbet eaten out of the container. I follow it up with various assorted tidbits before I go to bed.

That I can tell, I have neither lost nor gained.

Coat hasn't come yet, but I am ready for it. Louise went to a teacher's party last night, and the ladies next door went out to hoot, so I had the apartment to myself and had a dandy time.

Fern took the pictures Friday night. I don't think they will be much.

Regards to others.

> Love,
>
> MF

\* \* \*

### Monday [12 Nov. 1945]

Dear Regina,

The fur coat came today. It is warm and wet outside (the weather, not the coat). They have my initials in it on the lining at the side. Will have to keep it either in the closet outside or in my room. Louise says the closet outside is better for the coat because it is cooler, but it doesn't lock. Will have to wait and see how it works out.

No mail today, on account of it being a holiday.

Saw a picture called "Guest Wife" yesterday. It was punk.

We bought some crackers from the A&P called "Triskets"—very fine. If they have them at the A&P there you ought to get yourself some.

When is Cousin Katie coming? Did Bessie ever see Billie?

Regards to Aunts Mary, Katie, Uncle.

> Love,
>
> MF

P.S. Plan to make my Christmas cards on postal cards. Will do a few each night, so don't go buying me any to send.

\* \* \*

### Tuesday [13 Nov. 1945]

Dear Regina,

Got your three letters, one from Mary Boyd and Dr. Taylor, and the Union Recorder today. Obliged for clippings, etc.

My regards to Cousin Katie and Bessie, since they are in Milledgeville. Tell them they should come back for Christmas.

Louise heard from her sister, and she is going to Albuquerque then.

It is fairly warm right now.

Am in a hurry, as I have to get a paper in and study for a test.

Regards to Aunt Mary, Katie, and Mary of kitchen.

> Love,
> MF

* * *

Wednesday [14 Nov. 1945]

Dear Regina,

Made my maiden voyage in fur coat this A.M. at 7:30 to church. Felt like a small size float, but very warm.

Yesterday, had the good fortune to get a carton of Coca Colas from the grocery down the street, and can get one every Tuesday.

Took radio to get it fixed today. Can get it back Saturday—don't know how much it will cost.

For dinner, I had—among other things—chop suey and egg custard, like they used to have at Cousin Katie's. Both very fine.

I am enjoying the work I am doing here very much indeed, with the possible exception of the advertising, which is dull.

Regards to Cousin Katie, Aunts Katie and Mary, Bessie, Uncles, etc.

> Love,
> MF

* * *

Thursday [15 Nov. 1945]

Dear Regina,

Got your letter and one from Dr. Tigner today, also a card from Miss Bancroft, saying she was sending a small package for Thanksgiving, which I will enjoy. I think it is edible.

Have to spend a great deal of my time typing, but am thankful I know how.

Dr. Tigner said he had seen Katie out on the porch, sniffing the breeze.

Some of the people upstairs have reserved a table at the Mad Hatter for Thanksgiving, so I presume I will eat with them, as I have been invited.

Louise soft boiled an egg yesterday morning, which she found not wholesome when she went into it. Otherwise, breakfasts compare favorably with those at home.

Regards to Cousin Katie, Bessie, Sister, Duchess, Uncle, etc.

Love,

MF

\* \* \*

Friday [16 Nov. 1945]

Dear Regina,

Had a conference with Mr. Engle yesterday about the last story. He liked it, and the criticism was constructive. Asked him if he thought it would be presumptuous on my part if I sent some to some small literary magazines after revision. He said he hoped that would be what I would do and that he would give me a list of places that might be interested—small, literary, non-paying markets. It will be very fine if I can get some of them in places like that. I find my writing compares favorably with first year graduate students. And I am very much encouraged.

Tonight we are going to see "The Affairs of Uncle Harry," which Louise wants to see. She is nice to me so I am going, but am not anxious to see it particularly. I think I spend about $10.00 a week for food, incidentals, and what have you. This is without a doubt a cheap place to get an education.

Regards to household.

Love,

MF

\* \* \*

Saturday [17 Nov. 1945]

Dear Regina,

Yesterday, a three-pound box of cookies arrived from Miss Bancroft, which was certainly mighty nice of her. Unfortunately, all the white ones have chocolate between them, so there are only a few I can eat. However, Louise and the ladies next door will enjoy them. The ladies next door sleep all Saturday morning and attend a football game in the afternoon; in the evening, they go out to hoot. Louise has classes all Saturday morning and sleeps Saturday afternoon. I type all morning—all afternoon—all evening. I eat dinner at 11:30 every day and supper at 5:30, which suits me fine. Today I had mincemeat pie, which was the first I ever had, but it was too sweet to suit my taste. They have pumpkin pie frequently at the Union, and I always get it. Rarely do they have sherbet now.

I have not heard from Eastern Airlines about my reservation, so if they don't hurry, I will have to make it with another company through Atlanta or take the Flagler. Am going to write them again tomorrow, however.

Got Cousin Katie's letter of the 13th and enjoyed it. Presume she and Bessie left yesterday.

Regards to Aunties.

> Love,
>
> MF

Ain't it a shame the Garners won't be with you?

\* \* \*

Sunday [18 Nov. 1945]

Dear Regina,

Last night we went to the Union and they had T-Bone steak. It cost 50¢ but it was very big—covered the plate—and was tender. Got the radio to the tune of $4.83, tube $1.10, transformer $2.65, tax 8¢, labor $1.00. Then we went to Strubes to get Louise a piece of ribbon she wanted for something and found they were having a hat sale. I bought a hat for $3, formerly $7, to use with the fur coat. It is the color of those $1.00 gloves you bought at some sale and you gave them to me because they were too small for you. Peach colored. You might send them if you see them around as I don't have any brown ones. My hands get stiff in this weather. Louise bought her a black hat and a coat—*white coat* for the winter—very classy but a little cracked but that ain't my business.

I am attending services alone this A.M. as she has to study. Thence to the Union for boiled ham. Tonight, a pint of sherbet.

Regards to household.

> Love,
>
> MF

\* \* \*

Monday [19 Nov. 1945]

Dear Regina,

Got your two letters and clipping. Do you all get the Macon News now? How long is Uncle staying in Louisiana?

We are going to a play Wednesday night and to hear the Don Cossacks Thursday night.

Had a pint of orange sherbet last night—very fine—hash at Union today, not so hot. Yesterday, had a combination of cabbage, grape, and marshmallow salad— an experience.

Am preparing to send some cartoons to some trade journals. Don't pay much, but less competition. Hope I get them off.

Regards to relatives.

Love,

MF

\*  \*  \*

Tuesday [20 Nov. 1945]

Dear Regina,

The package came this A.M., and I have eaten my way down two layers of the cookies already. It is very nice of you to want to send them every week, and I will be looking forward to getting them. Gave the nuts to Edna, the maid who was delighted to get them. She's not such a hot cleaner, but she's very nice, and the nuts should improve her ability to see the dirt on top of the floor.

I am enjoying diarrhea today. I suspect the hash at the Union, but I feel all right withall [*sic*].

Typewriter broke down last night, so carried to place this morning and got it back just now (noon). Man put a new ribbon on it and oiled it up. Said I needed a new roll, which I will get some time, but can't spare it now. It works all right.

Have just applied for my social security number which I have to have to get my $15.00 per month.

Listen to the Falstaff Brewing Company's hour at 10:30 now and enjoy it. It irks the ladies next door that I don't play the radio all the time, but I am not going to have it interfere with my work, so I turn it on only when it suits me.

Got my inquisitorial summary back with a C—which goes to prove I am no better than average in that line. Got 90 in the advertising but most people made higher.

Regards to relatives.

Love,

MF

P.S. Anytime you want to send any more cookies, don't hesitate a second.

* * *

Wednesday [21 Nov. 1945]

Dear Regina,

It is at present snowing. In fact, there is about a foot of it on the ground. Them what likes it can have it. It is now that the fur coat comes in, as it sheds it and the other one absorbs it.

I go to get the pictures Fern took today, but I don't think they will come out so hot, as she made time exposures, and I don't think she had the thing turned right.

Am still eating the cookies and enjoying immensely. They sho are good. I prefer the ones without the raisins. If you care to send anymore and want the box back, I will send it.

Found a hole in the coat to the grey suit Sister gave me. Presume I will leave it for you to handle, as I have neither the time nor the skill, etc.

Regards to Aunts Mary and Katie.

    Love,
    MF

* * *

Thursday [22 Nov. 1945]

Dear Regina,

Cousin Katie sent me a box which arrived this A.M.—a fruit cake, a box of macaroons, and a little box of maple syrup candy. Much appreciated. I know she would have a fit if she knew I found a weevil in the box of macaroons. Anyway, Gloria kept right on eating them despite that, and Louise said they tasted good—tasted stale to me. Gloria will probably finish them up in spite of the fact that she has a dry socket after having a tooth pulled the other day.

It is still snowing, etc. We went to a play last night and I didn't fall down but once. Today I got a crick in my neck.

Went to the 9:00 mass today which was announced as a "high mass." Got there and found myself in the midst of a nuptial high double-ring ceremony—couple about 50 and 56, respectively—she the house mother at Currier Hall. It wasn't private, however, so me and some other ragamuffins sat to the side and enjoyed the proceedings.

Will enclose pictures which came out. Aren't so hot, but will give you an idea of the orderly way I keep my room. The one of Gloria and Connie was taken in their room.

Our eggs, fruit juice, Coca Cola, and prunes froze in the window last night. But I didn't even use the wool blanket on my bed. All you have to do is turn the register the night before.

Boy in the Union came up and asked me if my coat was mink. Said he raised mink. Informed him correctly.

Regards to Aunties.

> Love,
> MF

\* \* \*

Friday [23 Nov. 1945]

Dear Regina,

Just had word from Eastern Airlines that all their space is taken for the days I would want it, so that cuts my going to Macon out.

If I can't get a reservation on a Delta plane to Atlanta, I will arrive a la Flagler on the night of the 21st, so there will have to be a hotel reservation made in Atlanta. I will also have to make one in Chicago at the Stevens. Should I write Mr. Goolsby or just the regular channels?

It will take Louise three days on the train to get to Albuquerque if she can't get a plane.

I may just walk.

We are still eating the cookies. Louise discovered they had dates in them. The ones with the dates are very tasty. We only have a few left.

The weather is not to my taste but the education is, so I am sliding alone on the slippery pavements. I only fell once yesterday.

Regards to Aunties.

> Love,
> MF

\* \* \*

Saturday [24 Nov. 1945]

Dear R—

Got your two letters and gloves today. Found gloves didn't match, so if you want them back, I'll send them. If not, just leave them until I come home.

Am hoping I can get a reservation on the Delta plane, but haven't got their time table yet. Plan to come back on the Flagler anyway and to go on to Iowa City on that train that leaves that same night.

It has warmed up considerably and the snow is melting. Also the ice, which is the cause of my falling down so much. So I am glad of the rest.

Figure I will have to get some kind of long pants before this is over. I mean outside pants.

We are going to have steak again at the Union tonight. I reckon they will have it every Saturday.

I can't send Margaret any of that stuff and for heaven's sake *don't* send her *anything* you find around there. If I ever publish anything, that will be time enough to send it to the relatives.

We have eaten all the cookies, and the room looks very bare.

Regards to Aunties.

> Love,
> MF

* * *

Sunday [25 Nov. 1945]

Dear Regina,

Enclosed letter I sent to Mr. Goolsby about the room. It was all I knew to do. Still haven't heard about plane reservation. You can make a railroad reservation only fourteen days in advance.

Weather here is much more agreeable.

Louise is studying today. I go to church with Ruth Sullivan, thence to the Union for baked ham. Had the steak last night. Also what turned out to be turkey salad. I thought the Thanksgiving dinner at the Mad Hatter was putrid. It cost $1.22, which was also bad.

Regards to Aunts Mary and Katie.

> Love,
> MF

* * *

Monday [26 Nov. 1945]

Dear Regina,

Didn't get your letter today, but got the Union Recorder. Wonder if Margaret Oakey will come with her family visiting Milledgeville.

Enclose copy of Christmas cards I'm gonna do on postcards. Ought to get enough done by Christmas to send out.

They sent me a sheet of Christmas seals in return for which I was supposed to send them a dollar, which I (you) did, so will enclose them for you to put on your cards.

Very warm out and can use the other coat.

Have to be off for the ironing board session. Enjoy it much more with this girl from upstairs. Don't know whether I'm learning anything, though.

Who is with Duchess now?

I had cranberry sherbet today at the Union. It was very tasty and very pink.

Regards to Aunties.

> Love,
> MF

P.S. Just got your letter, which was delivered to Currier Hall for some reason. My health is all right now. Trust yours is the same.

FIGURE 4. Christmas card drawn by Flannery (26 Dec. 1945). Flannery O'Connor papers, Stuart A. Rose Manuscript, Archives, and Rare Book Library, Emory University.

\* \* \*

Tuesday [27 Nov. 1945]

Dear Regina,

Glad you got the Triscuits—I think they are very fine.

The flu is going around here. Last night, Connie came in with the back ache and dizzy. Gloria, who is nervous about catching things, moved out of the room for the night and slept on a cot in the study in the back. Today, Constance is up and about and Gloria looks sick. If I got to get it, I hope I get it before the 21st, or either have it while I am home—which should be nice for you. However, I eat an abundance of grapefruit juice, water, etc. I think I will start taking entoral. I feel very healthy. Do not mind the cold—only the ice. Fern says half the population up here have broken tail bones from falling. Fern and Louise are the oldest around here. All the others are 22 and 3 and 4, with that one that is nineteen.

I found a *worm* in the box of macaroons Cousin Katie sent, so I threw the whole box out. I enjoyed the fruit cake.

The cranberry sherbet at the Union is very fine.

Regards to relatives.

    Love,

    MF

\* \* \*

Wednesday [28 Nov. 1945]

Dear R,

I feel I am doing right well. John Crowe Ransom, the poet, is here for a couple of days and is going to criticize a manuscript at the workshop tomorrow. Yesterday, Mr. Engle told me he wanted to use one of my manuscripts. So, that's what will happen tomorrow—I have 3, two of which deal with negroes. The two which are the best, so Engle is going to ask Miss Bremwell if she would object or be embarrassed at having them read. If so, he will read the other one. But I am greatly encouraged to think that he picked mine to be read before John Crowe Ransom— who is, by the way, also editor of the Kenyon Review, a literary quarterly of high quality and little pay, such as I am trying to get my work into. There is a good chance that if Mr. Ransom likes my work, he will publish a story of mine. Of course, he may not like it, but his criticism will be very valuable to me anyway.

Nobody here has the flu yet.

Is it all right to eat eggs after they have been frozen in the window?

Regards to Aunties.

Does the cook affix her gum to the under or upper side of the sink?

    Love,

    MF

Have just heard that I can get a plane from Chicago to Atlanta (7:30 A.M. to 1:20 P.M.) on Delta. Have wired them to hold reservation for December 19 (Wednesday). Ruth Sullivan is also going then on a plane leaving half an hour earlier, so we will spend the night in Chicago together. Will have to write Mr. Goolsby and ask if I can get a reservation for the 18th at Stevens. If not, will enjoy railroad ladies lounge, according to Ruth. Send me Peter's address or telephone number and I will call him. Hope they can hold this reservation.

It will be $68.66 round trip.

* * *

Friday [30 Nov. 1945]

Dear Regina,

Didn't get to write yesterday, as was taken up with having a test and the workshop business. Mr. Engle said he thought the kindest thing to do was ignore the fact that Miss Bremwell was a negro and to go ahead and read the story with the colored character. So when we got there he announced that John Crowe Ransom would read the story as it was about the South and his voice would be more in keeping. So John Crowe read my story. His criticism was very valuable. He gave suggestions for the revision etc. He is a very nice old man. I am sure he won't want to use that story in the Kenyon Review but he liked my prose style and I will send him some other stories sometime probably.

Tonight about twelve of us in the workshop are having supper with him and Engle at the D&L—Pay-for-your-own-style.

Have not yet had the reservation I wired for confirmed so will probably be on the Flagler that I will come. Would certainly prefer going with Ruth Wednesday. She is very efficient and would see that I didn't get run over.

The Triscuits are hard to get, but if I see any more I'll send some to Mrs. R. D. and Duchess.

    Regards to Aunties,

      Love,

      MF

* * *

Saturday [1 Dec. 1945]

Dear R—

I am still trying to get a plane reservation. They haven't confirmed the one I wired for, but I think there is a possibility that I can get one that leaves Chicago at 7:30 P.M. and gets to Atlanta 1:15 A.M. Now, I know this is disagreeable to those who have to meet me. But, in this way I will not have to spend the night in Chicago in the ladies restroom. I have not heard from the Stevens, and other people are having trouble getting reservations, so I rather doubt I will get one. Anyway, I have requested a daytime flight for the 19th, 20th, 21st, or 22nd, or a night time flight for the 19th, 20th, or 21st. Now, if they write me, I can have one of those night flights, I want to know, can Louise or Doctor meet me at 1:15 A.M.—an imposition, but perhaps a necessary one. You might send me an airmail letter to that effect one way or the other.

We had a nice time eating with John Crowe Ransom last night. Asked Mr. Engle about the girl you sent the clipping about. He remembered her. She was in the workshop at one time.

Have to hurry to get this in. Will read about B.B.McC.

Love,

MF

* * *

Sunday [2 Dec. 1945]

Dear R—

Would you ask Dr. whether you shoot quail with a rifle or a shotgun or what. In the story I wrote that JC Ransom read I had a man shoot birds with a rifle, and he said that was wrong—that the man would use something else. I don't know anything about it, but a boy told me after workshop that he thought that a rifle was right. I got to have it right before I can send the story on anyway, so kindly find out, if you will.

We had steak last night and will have baked ham today. We are going to see "Over 21" this afternoon.

How long will Louise Florencourt stay in Milledgeville? Maybe I will see her in June, if I don't have to go to summer school to finish this degree.

Does Dr. Tigner want the picture back? I am not dying to keep it if he wants it.

Will probably hear from the Delta Airlines Tuesday one way or the other. The more I think about it, the better I think the night flight would be, since I have not got any hotel room.

Regards to relatives.

Love,

MF

\* \* \*

Monday [3 Dec. 1945]

Dear Regina,

Still haven't heard from the airline but expect to tomorrow.

It is fairly warm and dampish here. Don't feel the cold with the fur coat. Nobody here has the flu yet. I take the vitamin A. The shrunken pajamas don't worry me.

Am on my way to the ironing board.

We saw "Over 21." It wasn't so hot. I am going to quit going to the picture show. I have seen five since I've been up here and none any good.

Regards to relatives.

Love,

MF

\* \* \*

Tuesday [4 Dec. 1945]

Dear Regina,

Heard from the Delta. They can't give me anything now, but they expect cancellations by the middle of December and will write me as soon as I can get one. However, I will go on and get the Flagler reservation just in case. You can't do it but fourteen days ahead of time, however. If I get a plane reservation, I will cancel the other. If I come on the Flagler, will come the 21st Friday.

Today is Connie's birthday, and Gloria came in here this morning and asked Louise and me if we didn't want to chip in and buy her something, which I for one did not, but we said yes, so Gloria had already picked out something she (Gloria) couldn't afford, so we had to give her a dollar. It cost 3-something—some fool piece of statuary. I hated to part with the dollar that way, but I didn't know how to get out of it.

Still haven't heard from Mr. Goolsby, but there is no use getting a room, as I don't know when I want it.

It is fairly cold here, but no snow and ice, which is all right with me.

Fern gave us a recipe for stuff to kill the silverfish, so Louise had it filled, and we have arsenic paste about the room.

Louise has written a children's book which I am going to illustrate. I doubt if anything will come of it, but it is a try anyway.

Regards to Aunties.

Love,

MF

P.S. Just got your letter. Miss Bremwell had no visible reactions—she is still very pleasant. She is a very high minded person and I like her immensely.

\* \* \*

Wednesday [5 Dec. 1945]

Dear Regina,

Have just come from the railroad station where I ordered myself a Pullman reservation on the Dixie Limited instead of the Flagler. I decided this would eliminate hotels at both ends as I will leave Chicago at 3:00 P.M. and get to Atlanta the next morning at 9:40 A.M. I have ordered these for December 19th and will know the 1st of next week if I can get them. The price will be a couple of dollars less than the plane. If the plane reservation comes in and it looks any better at the time then I'll take it. If all this is confusing to you, it ain't any the less to me.

They are having caramel sherbet at the Union these days and it is very fine. The flu is very bad around here, but nobody in this house has it.

Regards to the aunties.

Does Mary Virginia *have* to have that thing for me? I don't plan to bring much, and I plan to pack myself a full meal and a half and put it in my suitcase, as I am not giving the railroad dining service any of my money.

Love,

MF

\* \* \*

Thursday [6 Dec. 1945]

Dear R—

Just got your letter and just make Mary Virginia understand that I *won't* have any evening dress with me. That will eliminate the whole problem. I am not coming with a lot of clothes. I will be doing good to get there myself and for *Pete's sake do not have any party for me.* Mary Virginia knows I don't like to wear long dresses and you can very easily tell her I haven't room to bring such, as I haven't. I am not going to have anything heavy in my suitcase as I will have to tote it myself. It is very fine weather here and I don't feel the cold with the fur coat.

I thought I'd better get Louise something for Christmas because she is so nice to me etc. and I didn't know what to get her. But there was a book she wanted, so I am going to give her that. It costs three dollars, but I want to give it to her.

Am glad the dress turned out well.

I can leave when I want to for the holidays—officially, the place gets out on the 22nd, but being a graduate student, I can go when I please. I don't mind cutting a few classes for convenience, so I will come a few days early. I would like to leave Sunday the 6th. The train leaves Atlanta at 7 P.M.

Regards to relatives.

> Love,
> MF

* * *

Friday [7 Dec. 1945]

Dear R—

Will enclose a letter I had from Frances for Duchess and Dr. Will write her, returning B. B. McC's article.

Had a test in my Analysis of Fiction last week and was sure I made a C in it. Yesterday, he gave the papers back and said he would read one that was adequate to the situation, and it turned out to be mine he was reading. I got an A+ on it, and he put "admirable" on the outside. There are about 60 in that class, so I thought that was doing all right. However, I got another C in my political science.

Had a conference with Engle yesterday about my stories. He said they were the best that had come out of the workshop this year—one in particular which he advised me sending to the "Sewanee Review" for a try. He didn't think they'd take it, but it at least meets their quality criterion, which is very high. A story published there means something—no pay—but a good literary start.

Regards to Aunties.

> Love,
> MF

* * *

Saturday [8 Dec. 1945]

Dear Regina,

Nothing going on around here right now. The weather is like spring, and I am enjoying the change. Am at present trying to type some stories to send out. It takes a great deal of time to type all this stuff.

Got your letter with Sherlock Holmes clipping—glad I am in good company. Please find out how many birds it is logically possible to shoot out of one covey. I got to know that, too.

Plan to have steak tonight.

Regards to relatives.

    Love,

    MF

* * *

Sunday [9 Dec. 1945]

Dear R—

Will have to eat by myself this day, as Louise is studying, and nobody else eats at the Union, which is all right with me.

Am preparing for test in Political Science, in which will probably get another C.

Supposedly, I will get my MA in June if I pass this work and get the thesis done. I think Engle may be inclined to give me a fellowship next year, but I have not broached the subject.

Still haven't heard from railroad reservation, but should tomorrow.

Regards to aunties.

    Love,

    MF

* * *

Monday [10 Dec. 1945]

Dear Regina,

I have an upper berth for December 19th final. Will get to Atlanta December 20th (Thursday) about 9:30 A.M., and thence a la bus. Will have a 7 hour wait in Chicago from 8:o'clock in the morning to 3 in the afternoon. If you send me Mrs. Curtis's telephone number, I will call her up.

Now, I want to come back Sunday the 6th. The train leaves Atlanta at 7 P.M., and what I want to know is—will there be an early mass in Milledgeville, so that I can take the bus to Atlanta if Dr. and Louis aren't going up? Kindly find out now and write me, as when I am in Chicago I will have to see can I can leave an order for a Rocket seat for that day.

Obliged for the fish. Will be a great aid to my studies.

> Love,
> MF

* * *

Tuesday [11 Dec. 1945]

Dear R.

Went to the RR station this morning and forked over $64 for my round trip ticket. When I get to Atlanta, I will have to make a Pullman reservation coming back and Rocket seat going out of Chicago. The man said I could do that from Atlanta, but it will have to be done Sunday the 23rd.

Am not going to mail any clothes—shoes—etc. I got no time for such. I repeat—I will be doing good to get there myself.

Louise didn't get her reservations to Albuquerque, so she will have to take her chances on the coach. It will take her three days, and she is mightily upset about it.

It is zero here, but I got no objection as long as it doesn't get icy.

Had a test today from the man who gave the "inquisitorial summary." He called this one an "adventure in theory."

Regards to Aunties.

> Love,
> MF

* * *

Wednesday [12 Dec. 1945]

Dear R—

Received no correspondence from you this A.M., but presume it may come this afternoon.

It has warmed up a trifle. All our eggs froze and popped and are now thawing out.

Josephine and Frank sent me an angel food cake yesterday, and it sho is tasty. I am having a fine time eating it.

Louise still has no reservations.

One of the hooks came off my coat, and the other is in the process, so you will be able to fix it when I come home.

Regards to Aunties.

Love,

MF

* * *

Thursday [13 Dec. 1945]

Dear Regina,

Got your two letters today. Why do you have to do so much for Joe Andrew's friends? Are they Catholics or something?

You may tell Dr. Keller I will be delighted to go to New England, Mexico, Cuba, and wherever he suggests, and he may leave the money on the kitchen table and I will pick it up.

Louise met a man in the Jefferson who suggested a way to get a reservation out of Kansas City, Missouri by wiring direct to the station, so last night she got a wire from the station with a reservation out of Kansas City. So now she goes to Des Moines on the milk train. From there to Kansas City; she has a plane reservation. Two days wait in Kansas City, and then a reservation on to Albuquerque. She is mightily satisfied.

It is snowing again here and altogether disagreeable, except that it's not so cold.

Regards to relatives.

Love,

MF

* * *

Friday [14 Dec. 1945]

Dear R—

Just had scalloped tuna fish at the Union. Tuna fish with eggs and green peas, cut up in it in a sauce. Very fine.

Icy out, but I haven't fallen down yet. Gloria fell down yesterday and knocked herself unconscious. She had the doctor last night and is down at the hospital being x-rayed. The doctor didn't think she hurt herself, but they do that as a precaution. I have been looking for a pair of "creepers." Old ladies use them on the ice so they won't fall, but I haven't found any yet. I walk in the snow, in the road, and off the sidewalks so I won't have to go on the ice. I don't aim to maim myself before I get a degree.

I washed some shirts to bring home. I only wash when I run out of clothes.

Regards to aunties.

> Love,
> MF

* * *

Saturday [15 Dec. 1945]

Dear R.

Got your letter with directions as to how to order my affairs on the railroad. I am thinking about keeping my extra money in my mouth and about wearing my pajama coat instead of a blouse. If Mary Virginia ain't having the tea (thanks to my special prayers) I am not going to bring that dress as I can wear the good suit on Sundays and Christmas and it looks just as decent as the other. Besides it is too cold to be changing from wool clothes to thin ones. It is 10 below here today. I got to get me some slacks or something. I wear the same clothes most every day here—one of the heavy sweaters, a skirt and shirt and am not going to bring more than that home.

Gloria is all right—no trouble about her fall.

Tell Miss Mary I will be obliged for a little nip to take back with me for the frost bite.

Have you got anybody anything for Christmas? I would like to bring something but I got no room for it, also no time to buy it, also nothing to buy. My monthly sickness is scheduled to overtake me Tuesday before I depart and I am not burdening myself with a heavy bag.

Regards to Aunties.

> Love,
> MF

* * *

Sunday [16 Dec. 1945]

Dear R—

Got your special last night etc. I got my reservation when I got my ticket. I will be glad when this little trip is over, as far as the railroads go.

On my way to St. Mary's and thence to the Union.

Bought a pair of slacks last night but will take them back because I don't think they are big enough. They are all wool and cost $10.00.

Will call Mrs. Curtis if it's not too cold. I will probably stay in the station 8 hours—with a book.

Regards until Thursday to the relatives.

Love,

MF

* * *

Tuesday [8 Jan. 1946]

Dear Regina,

Had a successful trip, at least. The train got into Chicago at 4:20. I got a taxi right away and got over to the other station just as the sign was going up for the rocket. So I made that and got in here about 9:30. Louise got in Sunday morning. I feel all right but tired, so I will stay in most of today and tomorrow.

Everything seems to be here which is a miracle, since they say our door and the front door were open most of the time.

I enjoyed my lunch in the small room on the train. I am very glad I won't have to go on another train until June.

What about Hicks? He had pneumonia when I left, and Dr. was on the warpath because they hadn't got him into the hospital.

I had a letter from J. Sullivan, who said he was studying Japanese.

It is very mild here and somewhat damp, but my face feels all right.

Tell Duchess I enjoyed the beaten biscuits, and any time she cares to send any more I'll be glad to get them.

Fern says the doctors told her to use cold packs on her sinus so the infection wouldn't localize. Ask Dr. about this.

Love,

MF

* * *

Wednesday [9 Jan. 1946]

Dear R—

My health is doing very well. I feel rested now, my nose is draining, and my hands don't itch. Fern says the doctors told her to inhale steam when she has sinus trouble—so she runs the hot water in the stationary stand and puts a towel over her head and inhales. Ask Doctor about this? I haven't done it, but she claims it's very good.

Today is Louise's birthday, so *she* is taking *me* out to dinner (supper) and the picture show (Weekend at the Waldorf).

Try to squelch that business of Doctor's having Peter come up here. I haven't got time to fool with him, and he wouldn't have a good time. It would be awful.

We are going to start getting a quart of milk every other day.

Regards to relatives.

    Love,

    MF

* * *

Thursday [10 Jan. 1946]

Dear R—

My health is doing nicely. We went to the picture show last night, and it was very funny—also had a dinner of tough steak at Smith's. Louise did the paying, so I didn't mind eating the steak.

Get me the name of a good dentist out here from Dr. Rogers as soon as you can. I don't want to wait. See what he knows about a Dr. Boreland—Gloria goes to him now.

The weather is very nice and dry and not too cold right now. This river is overflowing.

Put some egg in my head last night, and it didn't hurt me.

Regards to friends and relations.

    Love,

    MF

* * *

Friday [11 Jan. 1946]

Dear Regina,

My health is doing nicely and I trust yours is the same. Three Unicaps for my digestive system daily. The clothes came yesterday, and I was glad to get the sweater.

Had lovely salmon loaf at the Union, and the lady gave me a large helping of sherbet. She thinks it very amusing that I just get sherbet.

I am spending most of my time typing again.

Don't think I will wash my head until next Tuesday, as I have got used to its itching.

I think Louise is going to stay next semester. It looks that way now. It will certainly mean a lot to me if she does.

Regards to relatives.

> Love,
> MF

* * *

### Saturday [12 Jan. 1946]

Dear R.

Health still doing well. The house here is invited around to Miss Cutler's—the girl who teaches me art—to meet her husband, who has come back. So we'll have to go there this afternoon. I ain't looking forward to it.

The supervisor won't be here after February, as she finishes. The blond girl I don't like will probably get the job. One of the objectionable ones upstairs is moving out, also.

Wrote Dr., Louis, Julia, and Cousin Katie.

The plumbers are here fixing something. Something is always falling apart in the plumbing line around here.

Regards to Aunts M&K.

> Love,
> MF

* * *

### Sunday [13 Jan. 1946]

Dear R.

I went to the 9 o'clock this morning. Will eat soup in the room for lunch, and dinner downtown tonight, as that is what Louise wants to do.

I will be glad to see the write-up of the house. Gloria should be impressed.

I am wearing my union drawers today, as it is cold. They do very nicely.

My health is excellent. My hands have about quit peeling. Nose back to normal.

What about Hicks?

Regards to aunties.

> Love,
> MF

* * *

Monday [14 Jan. 1946]

Dear R.

Got your two letters and clippings etc. Thought the picture of the house nice.

Got my stories back from the Sewanee Review. The man wrote that he liked "many things about these stories," but could publish only four stories a year and was so far ahead of his fiction schedule that he would have to send them back. So I will try elsewhere. It was a very nice note.

I am in a hurry to go get my registration materials for next semester, as you have to stand in line a long time.

Regards to relatives.

> Love,
> MF

* * *

Tuesday [15 Jan. 1946]

Dear R.

I have finally washed mine head and feel considerably lighter thereabouts. I wish you would send those two white shirts soon. I could do with them.

It was so warm yesterday, the fur coat was uncomfortable, so I got out my blue one. I must have grown or something. The sleeves were two inches above my wrists, and I had to put the coat back up.

Louise says to tell you I look much better than when I came as regards my health. She says I look back to normal. She thought I looked punk when I got here—which was natural after that train trip.

Had a letter from Frances Lewis, replete with details of her various male acquaintances. Very funny.

Please hurry with the name of the dentist.

Saw in the Recorder about your book review—my literary parent—titch.

Perhaps that spray prescription is not necessary—I don't have a cough.

Regards to household.

> Love,
> MF

* * *

Wednesday [16 Jan. 1946]

Dear R.

The two packages came yesterday, and I was glad to see them. The blanket sho is nicer than these blue things, and I enjoyed sleeping under it. They have put a new iron in this house—very fancy it is, and those who have used it don't like it. I haven't tried it.

Gloria has applied for the supervisor's job here and for one at another dormitory. So if she gets either, we will have another person in the next room. I hope she gets one of them.

Just got your letter, and you may tell Duchess I will be waiting on the doorstep for the beaten biscuits.

Also, thank Miss Mary for the comb. Tell her it made my hair smell like Conyack (sp?)

It looks like Louise will stay.

> Love,
> MF

* * *

Thursday [17 Jan. 1946]

Dear R—

Got your Sunday letter and one from Dr. Glad Hicks's health is improved. Mine is also.

I think Miss Maxwell went away with the idea of keeping those stories, so I'd rather you wouldn't say anything to her. I would also be obliged if you wouldn't show them to anybody. As I have said—if I ever get any published will be time enough to show them abroad. I will try to write Mrs. Hines when I get a minute, but I have to study, so I will pass a few of these courses.

Right now, I am doing an advertising project that I dislike with great enthusiasm. At the beginning of the next semester (February 4th), I should have a little time.

We don't know yet if Gloria got her supervisory job.

Regards to aunties.

> Love,
> MF

The river don't get up to the bridge. It tore the man's boardwalk who has the canoe place, though.

* * *

Friday [18 Jan. 1946]

Dear Regina,

It is so warm here you don't need a coat out, hardly. Louise says she thinks it's around 70°, which is all right with me. There may be a blizzard next week the way it changes, though.

Mrs. Cutler has a very nice apartment a block from here. Her husband is getting his Ph.D. in Economics. He is very nice and very talkative. He looks like Peter Cline with a mustache—a jumpy little man. I will continue taking art from Mrs. Cutler next semester.

I haven't gotten my schedule worked out yet. We will have Friday, Saturday, and Sunday off between the two semesters, which will provide a bit of a rest.

Regards to aunts and kitchen force.

> Love,
> MF

* * *

Saturday [19 Jan. 1946]

Dear Regina,

It has gone down to 22 today, and I am powerful sorry. I enjoyed the Milledgeville section of the paper. How often does it come out?

They are having mid-winter sales at all the stores here, and I am hoping maybe I can get a pair of slacks cheap, if Louise will go downtown with me after supper tonight.

Bought me a box of Instant Postum to see if I would like that, but it tastes like old shoes smell. Nobody around here wants it. We can't get the same kind of coffee mix we used to, and the other mixes are messes. I bought me a box of tea balls and will probably start going in for tea.

We don't know yet if Gloria will get the supervisor's job, but I hope she does, because she is something of a nuisance in the next room. Of course, something worse could be put in there. There are four people leaving from this house—among them, Fern. She can finish quicker at Drake in Des Moines, so that is where she is going.

Regards to aunties.

> Love,
> MF

* * *

Monday [21 Jan. 1946]

Dear R—

Didn't write yesterday, as the weather was terrific and, after coming in from the 10:15 mass, I didn't show my face out again. Ate all my meals in—soup and prunes and triscuits for dinner. Eggs and sausages and toast and sherbet and milk for supper. We got our ice cream and sherbet Saturday night and kept it in the window. It is 8 below now and windy.

Louise has been studying late and it has been hard for me to sleep these last few nights so I have been having a tablespoon of spirits in some water which sends me off in a shorter time. However, that bottle you put it in makes it taste like vitamins which is disconcerting. Also I have used about half of it and would like some more when this gives out.

I didn't see any slacks downtown I wanted. Louise ordered herself a raincoat.

I plan to mail you a package Wednesday, as that is the day I don't have any classes—will probably be late, but it is a birthday present.

Your letters just came for the 17th and 18th. At present coats (in-between coats) are around $35–39, reduced. The enclosed is the measurement from the underarm seam down to where it should be. My fur coat is just right now without being turned up. Louise says I have grown.

I enjoyed the clippings. Regards to relatives.

    Love,

    MF

P.S. I saw some coats the other day reduced to $10. They were too little. Maybe there's an old coat at home you could cut down? *Don't* want green or beige or brown or rust.

* * *

Tuesday [22 Jan. 1946]

Dear R

Got your letter and Mary's. Who is she staying with? What does Jane O'Connor do? I wouldn't have known that was her picture. Is the neuritis Sister has like what Duchess thinks she has?

I will probably go to Gloria's dentist sometime at the first of the next semester.

I have a conference with Engle this afternoon about what I will take next semester. No more advertising for me.

These silverfish are walking all over everything. If you could find something that will stop them, I would be obliged.

Louise is feeling somewhat poorly.

Regards to aunties.

> Love,
> MF

\* \* \*

Wednesday [23 Jan. 1946]

Dear R.

Gloria got the supervisor's job, so we are waiting in some agitation to see what is in the next room next term. In the two places upstairs, there are going to be two very objectionable ones, from what I hear tell—people you wouldn't want using the same bathroom. Sho hope nothing like that gets in down here.

I had a conference with Engle yesterday, and he was delighted with my last story. Got my schedule made out. Next term, I won't have any classes in the morning at all. Only four afternoons a week will I actually be in class. He is letting me do an independent program of reading under his direction, which is a very fine thing. I also will have to write a great deal.

Saw a nice coat for $23 reduced, but didn't have a chance to try it on. I may go back and do it.

I will send your package tomorrow.

Regards to relatives.

> Love,
> MF

\* \* \*

Thursday [24 Jan. 1946]

Dear R.

I have wrapped your package up but may not get it mailed today, as the streets are icy. We didn't go out to supper last night, but had spinach soup in the room. Very fine. Instead of having the milk delivered, I go get it every day. It just costs 12¢ a quart, and I am saving money, because it is 6¢ a half pint at the Union.

Yesterday, Louise was fooling with her teeth with a toothpick and got a piece of it stuck in her gum. It stayed there all afternoon while she had to work, but last night she got it out. She said it was very painful having it in there.

We think we know who is going to be in Connie's room—Charlotte Some-bodyorother, but anyway Connie knows her and says she is a nice girl. She couldn't be much worse than Gloria, I reckon, although there are plenty around here who are.

You should try some of that spinach soup. It is the best soup I've ever tasted. Duchess would be powerful fond of it.

Regards to aunties.

> Love,
> MF

* * *

Friday [25 Jan. 1946]

Dear R.

Took your package to the post office yesterday and the man wouldn't let me send it because it was in a bottle and I didn't have cotton around it. I had excelsior but he said that wouldn't do. So not having any cotton I am going to stick a Kotex around the top of the bottle. That's cotton if he asks me. I will probably send it tomorrow, as I have to sit on the ironing board all afternoon.

I had a bottle of milk going down the street yesterday and fell on the ice but didn't break the bottle—me either.

Engle has asked me to do two or three illustrations for my last story. If he likes them, he is going to see if I can't be allowed to illustrate them as part of my thesis for the MFA degree next year. Ordinarily, you have to write a long paper on some phase of art (graphic art) in addition to the literary work you do. He thinks I may be able to illustrate my stories instead, which would be a great help, as I do not like to do papers of that sort.

Louise is going to write six children's stories for her thesis this semester, and she wants me to illustrate those, which I shall try to do. No money in it I am sure, as I doubt if she will be able to sell them, but it will be good practice for me.

I presume the executive vice president and his spouse twice blessed are in the city. Would relish some details.

Regards to same and aunties.

> Love,
> MF

\* \* \*

Saturday [26 Jan. 1946]

Dear R.

The shirt came and I am delighted with it and any more you might want to make, don't feel bad about doing it.

I am enclosing a piece about Porter, the man who wrote "Clever as hell" and "God, I like it."

I am going downtown now to meet Louise for dinner, and afterwards we are going to look at coats and buy our edibles for the week. She is much discouraged these days, on account of her work is so hard and is talking about not going on with it, but I think she will. She just gets that way.

Regards to relatives.

> Love,
> MF

\* \* \*

Sunday [27 Jan. 1946]

Dear R.

Well, I got the coat. It was a $45.00 coat and I got it for $27.00, including tax. It is all wool and plenty big, a sort of rust-gold thing. The woman called it "harvest," which isn't saying much. It was one of their fall coats, and I reckon they wanted to get rid of it. It is a plain box coat with a nice, brown lining. So that is that. We looked at all the other stores, and there wasn't anything under $39. So I am satisfied. Now I will send you the blue one as soon as I can. I am going to mail your other package Monday, Lord willin', and will try to send it then. It is 10 below here now and not wholly enjoyable out.

Gloria and Connie went beer drinking and got too much (eight glasses apiece only) and came in shot. Gloria was hysterical and Connie was sick, and they are profusely apologetic now—also sort of green-looking. I don't think it will happen again.

The girl Connie thought was going to be in the next room with her is not going to be so we don't know who will. It is some source of worry since so many slutty creatures roam these fields.

I saw in the paper where the Rev. Johnboy was going to be the priest in The Song of Bernadette. I bet that will be rich. I will send the clipping to John Sullivan.

We are mighty sorry Fern is going. She is a very nice person. I like her particularly well.

Regards to relatives.

> Love,
>
> MF

We will be much obliged for the coffee, but it is coming back in up here. We get the cheap kind—Barrington Hall—for 27¢. The Nescafe has always been too expensive. I've never tried it, but understand it's the best.

* * *

Monday [28 Jan. 1946]

Dear R.

The hot water is off in this house, has been since yesterday afternoon, so I am getting pretty dirty.

I have got your package rewrapped and will mail it tomorrow.

Louise is enjoying one of her periods of depression and threatens to leave every other hour. Boy, I sure hope she doesn't. The new people they are putting in this house are all objectionable that I know about.

The mail has just arrived with the coffee, two letters, and Recorder. Much obliged for the coffee—it should last until Spring. Also for the clippings. I sent the Colonnade no cartoon. Maybe they found an old one and are going to reuse it. I don't know.

It is warmer here today. The ice is off the streets, so I am navigating more freely.

Regards to aunties.

> Love,
>
> MF

* * *

Tuesday [29 Jan. 1946]

Dear R.

Edna the maid just came through and announced that one Veronica Rapp would occupy the next room. She is coming in tonight but won't be able to get in the room till Gloria gets out, and Gloria won't be able to get out until D. J. (the supervisor) gets out, and D. J. says she is not going until Monday. Legally, she should be out sooner. All very complicated. We don't know anything about Veronica Rapp, but that the name doesn't sound Latin American.

It looks like Louise may go to California. Her people have bought a house there, and she is delighted and strongly tempted to quit all this business here and go join them now. Lord, I hope she stays. Kindly pray that she will.

There is no telling what I would get in here. Louise's mind is much unsettled at present, and she is discouraged, and I wouldn't be surprised if she didn't go. I hope whatever is best for her will turn out, but I sure hope she stays.

I had some of the Nescafe this morning. It tastes much more like coffee than the Barrington Hall.

I am finally mailing your package today. I will not get to send the coat until this weekend. It is pleasantly warm here now, but snow is expected tonight.

I return the clipping herewith.

Regards to aunties and little cousins who should now be brightening your lives.

Love,

MF

\* \* \*

Wednesday [30 Jan. 1946]

Dear R.

Veronica Rapp is a medical doctor from Brazil. She is not greasy looking like the rest of these Latin Americans but is a thin blond and, from the glance I got of her, around 26 or 7. She is staying upstairs until Gloria gets moved, so I haven't met her, just seen her going in. I understand her English is not too adequate. Connie seems satisfied, but of course won't be able to tell until she sees what the girl's habits are. I shall feel at liberty to get sick on the slightest notice now. She is up here studying nutritional diseases.

Louise is getting herself registered today, which is encouraging from my point of view, but she is unpredictable and may take off notwithstanding that.

Tonight we are having supper downtown, and Louise is taking Fern, as it will be her last night here. As the weather is wet and slippery, we are eating the midday meal in the house—spinach soup, etc. I am supposed to go fetch my coat today, but I don't know will I or not, with this weather. It is not so cold, but damp. It is a size 16 and very roomy.

I got a political science paper back with a B on it, which is a slight improvement, but my final grade will still be a C.

I thought I would have no morning classes this term, but decided to take another course, so will have one 3 times a week—nine o'clock—Aesthetics.

Got your letter just now and one from Frank Jr. saying he would be going in the army soon—"right after the women and children."

Regards to combined forces of relatives.

> Love,
>
> MF

\* \* \*

Thursday [31 Jan. 1946]

Dear R.

Got my coat today, but of course will not be able to use it until it gets much warmer. It is now something below and snowy but not damp, I am thankful.

Talked to Dr. Rapp last night. She seems to be very refined and orderly and not like these others. She went to high school in Switzerland. I think we will enjoy having her. Apparently Louise is staying. That is today.

I have taken to eating hard-boiled eggs. That way, I don't have to wash any dishes. Louise says hard-boiled eggs aren't as good for you as soft eggs. Is this true?

I haven't washed any shirts since I came back. I like the seersucker shirt because I can just rinse it out and wear it rough dry, as all that shows is the bow.

Regards to aunties.

> Love,
>
> MF

| SCHEDULE: | Monday | 9–10 Aesthetics |
|---|---|---|
| | | 2–5 Art |
| | Tuesday | 3–4 Magazine Writing |
| | | 4–6 Literary Criticism |
| | Wednesday | 9–10 Aesthetics |
| | Thursday | 4–5 Workshop |
| | Friday | 9–10 Aesthetics |
| | | 2–5 Art |

* * *

Friday [1 Feb. 1946]

Dear R—

I put the coat you wanted sent and a jacket that has a hole in it that I'd be obliged if you'd fix and send back in the mail, but found I didn't have paper big enough to cover it, so I will have to try to buy some, after which I will send it.

It is very nice to have three days off. Everybody is moving today. I helped Gloria move her bed. She had to take it in the other room with her, as it is a special bed because she is so long.

Just came back from buying some paper and have wrapped the package up and will mail it tonight at the Union. I would be obliged if you would mend the jacket and send it back soon, as I wear it a good deal of the time. If you can let the sleeves down any, they need it. I stuck a safety pin where the hole is.

Got two manuscripts off today.

Weather improving.

Regards to aunties.

Love,

MF

* * *

Saturday [2 Feb. 1946]

Dear R—

Dr. Rapp has moved in and Gloria out. When Gloria was there, it smelled like cologne—now it smells like formaldehyde. I don't object, but I don't think Louise and Connie care too particularly about it. This doctor is a nice girl. She locks the door when she goes in the bathroom. Her people are Swiss.

Louise got the urge to clean up yesterday and has rearranged her part of the room around so that she has more room, she thinks. She is registered now, so I am hoping she will be here all semester.

Our milk froze stiff in the window and turned a yellow-green color. Louise said it was all right, that the butter fat made it do that way. It is terrible cold today.

I don't get whether Uncle is in Milledgeville or not. I thought you said he was going to stay with Julia until Mrs. Myer got back?

Louise is poorly today.

No news.

Regards to relatives.

    Love,

    MF

They have just called up here and said they are going to put new mattresses on all the beds, so we have to undo them all. I am satisfied with the one I've got. Nuts.

* * *

Sunday [3 Feb. 1946]

Dear R—

Do you think you could send me my animation board? All I would want would be the board and glass part with the felt around it. I wouldn't want the bulb, as I could use my own lamp. This would cut a lot of my work in half, and I would like to get it, if possible.

Well, we all have new beds! They are studio beds—no head, no foot. Just a steel frame on which is a box spring (covered) on which is a mattress. They are very narrow. I don't mind them so much. There was nothing wrong with the old ones. They just wanted to use them somewhere else.

Yesterday, I fell down twice. I cut myself on the second fall. I am having difficulty navigating freely today, as I am sore.

We went to see "What Next, Private Hargrove?" and it was very funny. It was the first time I had been since Christmas. I had my throat blessed this A.M. In this section, there should be something similar applied to the feet.

Louise is better.

Regards to relatives.

    Love,

    MF

* * *

Monday [4 Feb. 1946]

Dear R—

I went to my nine o'clock class, and the man decided to separate his graduate students from the others, so he is having them come to his house every Friday night for a two-hour seminar instead of at 9 o'clock Monday, Wednesday, and Friday, which means that now I have no morning classes at all, and so can do my reading and writing then.

Bought me a pair of woolen socks, as my feet perspire and get cold and damp. They seem to work better. They are only 50% wool.

The new beds are comfortable to sleep in but hard to sit in and work, as they have no backs and keep sliding away from the wall.

When I was at home, I got a book out of one of the cases called "Making of the Modern Mind" by Randall—a blue book. Will you see can you find it and send it to me? I will be much obliged.

Love,
MF

* * *

Tuesday [5 Feb. 1946]

Dear R—

Our beds roll around so that I have had to put coffee bottle tops under the rollers. They work pretty well.

It is as warm today as it was in Milledgeville Christmas.

Things are about straight here now. I like Dr. Rapp very much, including her formaldehyde.

Duchess must be doing pretty well to stand the trip downtown, if it didn't make her sick.

Louise just got a letter from Fern saying she was settled and getting along with her work.

No news. I am in a hurry.

Regards to aunties.

Love,
MF

* * *

Wednesday [6 Feb. 1946]

Dear R—

Yesterday was so hot, I could wear my new coat without a sweater under it. Today I need the big one, plus the two pair of Union products I brought back with me.

I am going to buy me another pair of woolen socks, so I can wear them every day.

I sent that package with the coat and jacket last Monday. I lugged it down to the Union to mail at supper. I told her I wanted to insure it, and she said they didn't insure things after five o'clock. It was just too icy and bad out to lug the thing home again, then bring it back the next day, so I sent it on like it was. I see no reason why it shouldn't get there all right.

I think that now that Louise has started, she will stay.

Regards to all relatives.

> Love,
> MF

* * *

Thursday [7 Feb. 1946]

Dear R—

Enclosed clipping about the new man who is going to be in the workshop. I don't know if I will have to work with him in conferences or not, but I presume I will.

We—Ruth Sullivan and I—are going to take the bus out to Mr. Zerby's house today so we will see where he lives, so we'll be sure to get there for his class tomorrow night. It is a long way out, and I don't relish going every Friday night—particularly when I have to sit on the ironing board all afternoon.

It is cold here but not icy. It snowed yesterday, and the wind blew it all away.

Gloria is proving herself very efficient, and the place is much pleasanter now with D. J. gone. Two new people upstairs are very nice. The other one isn't.

Regards to aunties.

> Love,
> MF

Figure 5. Newspaper clipping about Paul Horgan (7 Feb. 1946). Flannery O'Connor papers, Stuart A. Rose Manuscript, Archives, and Rare Book Library, Emory University.

**Novelist Will Join SUI English Staff**

Lt. Col. Paul Horgan, novelist from Roswell, N. Mex., will arrive at the university Feb. 15 to join the staff of the English department as a visiting writer.

Working with Prof. Paul Engle of the English department, he will assist students in the writer's workshop by individual consultations about fiction writing.

Horgan won the Harper prize novel competition in 1933 for his novel, "The Fault of Angels." His other novels include "Men of Arms" (1931), "No Quarter Given" (1935), "Main Line West" (1936), "The Return of the Weed" (1936), "A Lamp on the Plains" (1937), "Far from Cibola" (1938), "Figures in a Landscape" (1940), "The Habit of Empire" (1941) and "The Common Heart" (1942).

Among his other works are an American opera, "A Tree on the Plains," written in 1942, and a drama, "Yours, A. Lincoln," also written in 1942. Articles and fiction contributed to magazines have appeared in annual collections of best short stories for the year.

An alumnus of the New Mexican Military institute, he has been in the army since August, 1942.

* * *

Friday [8 Feb. 1946]

Dear R—

Engle read another of my stories in workshop yesterday and showed the illustrations. There are about 20 new people in there, most of them veterans. Seven of them thought there was no good in the story at all. A few liked it. Engle still thought it had its points. I am doing it over now according to the criticism, and I think it is much better. I think he was pleased with the illustrations, but I haven't talked to him about them yet. I didn't know he was going to read the story.

Ruth has a bad cold, and I am afraid I will have to go to Brother Zerby's by myself, which I don't relish. We rode out on the bus yesterday to see where it was and walked back. It is a far piece out.

I hope your dog committee prospers.

Regards to relatives.

    Love,
    MF

* * *

Saturday [9 Feb. 1946]

Dear R—

Ruth was all right to go to the Zerby's last night, so I had my moral support. You would have relished the evening. When we entered, this creature, half dog and half enthusiasm, sprang on me. Mrs. Zerby picked it off and gave it to Mr. Zerby, who kissed it and put it down. The house smelled like dog and baby— they have both—and immediately I sat down, I began to itch. After we had had the class, they had tea and cake. There were four of us sitting on this sofa-daybed arrangement. The dog was two laps down from me, and suddenly I heard a crash and felt some liquid spraying down upon me. The animal had turned a girl's teacup and an ash tray into the air. I didn't get much of it, fortunately. Every week for two hours, I got to go through this.

Last night, we had milk in the window and it froze and the bottle broke and the milk seeped all over the floor. Edna cleaned it up, for which I was thankful.

I had my good suit cleaned. It cost .75, and it doesn't smell like they do in Milledgeville.

I will try to write Cousin Katie today. I just haven't had time to write Sister.

Regards to relatives.

    Love,

    MF

P.S. I cut my leg on that fall, and it is all right.

* * *

Sunday [10 Feb. 1946]

Dear R—

On this day of our Lord, I plan to wash my dirty shirts, which includes all the shirts I own. If it gets this bad again, I may send them home to be washed. I just don't have time to do it. This course I am taking in philosophy from Zerby is much too difficult for me, and I will have to put much more time than I would like to on it.

If you see Dr. Beiswanger, tell him I am taking aesthetics and making a study of Croce (pronounced CROW-CHI) and don't like or understand it. We haven't got our grades yet, but I am expecting 3 Bs and 3 Cs. At least, that is what I hope I get.

The weather is fairly decent today. People talk about spring and such. I don't think there will be any blizzards now, since there haven't been any so far.

Regards to aunties and little second cousins.

    Love,

    MF

* * *

Monday [11 Feb. 1946]

Dear R.

Yesterday we took some pictures, so if they come out at all I will send them to you.

Last night was a party for one of the upstairs people's birthdays—milk and very bad cake are usually served at these affairs. Thursday, we are all eating supper together at the Union, on account of it is Valentine's Day. How sweet.

Last night it snowed, and in a few hours it will be slippery. You can't get anything to put on your shoes—I have investigated.

Louise seems satisfied with her work for a change, so I think she is safe the quarter out.

Trust relatives are well.

We are going to have the milk delivered.

>Love,
>
>MF

If at any time you would like to send any more of those cookies like you sent the time before (that you made), please feel free to do so.

* * *

Tuesday [12 Feb. 1946]

Dear R—

Enjoyed seeing your picture in the paper. Very fancy. Also will be delighted to see the cookies when they come. Also the animator. The book came yesterday, and I was mighty glad to get it. Much obliged. It was not slacks I bought. It was socks. Wool socks. My writing must be sorry. I am not going to get any slacks. The worst of the winter is over, I hear, and I am doing very well without them.

I wrote Cousin Katie yesterday. I haven't got time to send any Valentine business. Trust Gussie is better. My regards to her and her daughter.

What do you hear from Miss Bancroft? I haven't heard from her in a long time. Blessings to aunties.

>Love,
>
>MF

* * *

Wednesday [13 Feb. 1946]

Dear R—

The animator came yesterday afternoon in good shape. It works fine, and I am mighty glad to get it. Sorry you had to dig up the attic for it, though.

I have an appointment with the new workshop man—Mr. Horgan—for next Wednesday. I think he is going to take over all the fiction people. I hope he will be pleasant to work with. He hasn't come yet.

I will be happy to see the cookies. They sound very fine. I hanker for something tasty.

We are undergoing a snow storm today, but it hasn't got icy yet.

I will be glad to get the coat back. Also the extra contents of the package.

Regards to relatives.

>Love,
>
>MF

* * *

Thursday [14 Feb. 1946]

Dear R.

The cookies and the coat and the candy all came yesterday. I found them powerful tasty. I will send the tin box back for a refill as soon as I drain it—which should be in the very near future. We like the candy. I am not eating much of it, however, as I do not want to precipitate another session of sinus. Glad you let the coat sleeves down.

We got the pictures we took back, but Louise paid for them, and she wants to send them to her people, so I am getting some reprints of the negatives, which I will send you. Also a few to Cousin Katie. I am supposed to get them Friday.

It is still snowing and getting very cold. I don't like it.

Regards to aunties.

　　Love,
　　MF

* * *

Friday [15 Feb. 1946]

Dear R.

Cousin Katie sent me one of those heart-shaped boxes of candy. I opened it and extracted two caramels that weren't chocolate and am sending the rest to Duchess. Everybody around here has them, so there was no use to keep it. I am enjoying the candy and the cookies you sent me.

Tonight we have to repeat the Zerby performance. I hope the dog (Ingrid by name) will be in bed with the flu.

Last night I finished the bottle of tonic you sent me up here with. I use it when I can't go to sleep. You can send me some more if you put it in a prescription bottle. There have been no indications of my turning into a drunkard off what I have imbibed—one tablespoon in two tablespoons of $H_2O$.

I had a veal chop at the Union yesterday—never had tasted a veal chop, that I recall—very tasty. We had supper all together at the Union last night and invited Howard and Enid Cutler—Gloria's social instincts.

Regards to relatives.

　　Love,
　　MF

* * *

Saturday [16 Feb. 1946]

Dear R.

I am enclosing the pictures. I also sent the one of Connie and me to Cousin Katie. I had wanted to send one of me in the fur coat to Margaret, but didn't get one taken in it. Do you suppose it would be good to send her one in the other coat? Since she seems to be interested in what I am doing, I thought it might be a nice thing to do. Advise.

At the Zerby's last night, Ingrid was in the basement and Mrs. Zerby out, so it wasn't so bad. We ride out on the bus and walk back. It is about a 25 minute walk and I don't mind it. The buses do not run after nine o'clock out that way, so we have either to walk or call a taxi, and I prefer walking. I have no intention of dropping the course.

This afternoon I am going to take off and go to see the "Bells of St. Mary's."

Regards to relatives.

> Love,
> MF

* * *

Sunday [17 Feb. 1946]

Dear R.

Went to see the "Bells of St. Mary's" yesterday and thought it was punk. It certainly glamourized the good nuns. You ought to see it for curiosity's sake, however.

Connie has gone home this weekend to see her brother, who is just home from the war, so the bathroom is less crowded. We are now going to the Union for what sustenance we can get. I had a very fine steak last night.

I know you are enjoying your status of chief of operations. How long is Auntie staying in Savannah?

I am most through with the cookies.

Regards to household.

> Love,
> MF

\* \* \*

Monday [18 Feb. 1946]

Dear R.

Got your two letters and attendant clippings, also one from Miss Bancroft. I will be happy to see the two shirts. Anything to put off washing.

The new organ at the church looks very classy. I trust it sounds as well.

How long is Sister going to stay in Savannah? Is Duchess enjoying her temporary departure?

I know she is glad Louise is there.

Miss Bancroft seemed to be enjoying herself. She said she was a member of a Craftsman's Guild.

Nothing doing hereabouts.

Regards to aunties.

> Love,
> MF

\* \* \*

Tuesday [19 Feb. 1946]

Dear R.

Got two of your letters today. So I reckon I won't get one tomorrow. That is too bad about John Tarleton—I thought once you got high blood pressure, you had it for good. She sounded like he was looking forward to improving. How did she happen to communicate this intelligence to you? Why not Sister?

Catherine's little ones sound repulsive to the extreme. Is she aware of their obnoxiousness, or does she think they're perfect? I hope they will go off for a vacation this summer. I saw where their old man is now a Lt. Col. as well as an Ex-Vice President. That must add quite a flavor to the Exchange Bank. How does it look between Miss Fleeta and Catherine Martin?

I am getting more interested in my aesthetics as I go along. So, it's not bad, except having to go to his house and wonder at what moment his animal is going to burst from the basement and spring into my teacup.

Regards to relatives and cousin from Boston.

> Love,
> MF

* * *

Tuesday night [19 Feb. 1946]

Dear R.

I have just found out that I have to reapply for the fellowship next year this week. Engle said it didn't have to be done until April, but he was mistaken, I found on investigation. Since I want the fellowship in a different department, I have to reapply with three new letters, picture, etc. What I want is one of the pictures I had taken for the application last year. There were four or five left over. Either I gave them to you, or they were in the middle drawer of the high desk in my room. If you will send one to me right away or write me right away that you can't find them, I will be much obliged. I am glad I checked up on what Engle said—he is going out of town, and if he doesn't see about this before he goes, I won't get the fellowship, but I am doing all I can. I have an appointment with Mr. Schramm tomorrow and am going to get him to write one of the letters for me. Porter says he will write one, and then I'll get Engle to do the other if I can before he goes.

Send the picture airmail special. Sorry to have to bother you with this, but I want to be back here next year, a la fellowship.

[*No closing signature*]

* * *

Wednesday [20 Feb. 1946]

Dear R.

I have just had my conference with Mr. Horgan. He looks very much like John Tarleton but talks very nice, and I think it will be pleasant working with him.

I hope you can find those pictures.

Tonight we are going to a play. No news.

Regards to relatives.

Love,<br>
MF

* * *

Thursday [21 Feb. 1946]

Dear R.

Engle has gone east for 10 days. If the English board meets before he comes back, I won't get the fellowship. If it doesn't, maybe I will. I am making a novena to the effect of the latter and waiting on you to send the pictures.

More about Mr. Horgan—he is very thorough and seems to be above all a craftsman, which is what I need. He goes into things in a great deal more detail than Engle and I think he will be very helpful to me.

Louise has a cold and a sore throat, which I hope will stay on her side of the room. I am not likely to get it, as I have been around Ruth with one all week.

The play we went to see was putrid.

I enjoyed Miss Bancroft's letter. She said the same things in mine, practically.

Regards to relatives.

> Love,
> MF

P.S. Pray that I will get this fellowship—there's not much chance if Engle isn't here when they meet, because none of the others have had me, and he is the only one who thinks I ought to have it. It will mean a great deal to me to get it.

* * *

Friday [22 Feb. 1946]

Dear R—

I am on my way over to see Dr. Maxwell, the head of the English department, to see how long I can have to get my application in. I may be able to find out when the board will meet, etc.

Ruth has gone to Indiana for the weekend, so I will have to go to Zerby's by myself—will ride both ways, however. Nonetheless, I don't relish it.

Had very fine salmon at the Union today. They put egg and green peas in with it, cream it up, and sprinkle potato chips over the top. They have it every Friday and I always look forward to it.

This being a legal holiday, we get no mail.

Louise now has a cough and has gone downtown for cough syrup. My health is ripping. Trust yours is the same.

Regards to kin.

> Love,
> MF

* * *

Saturday [23 Feb. 1946]

Dear R.

The picture just came, and I am immensely obliged. That was quick service. I didn't expect it until Monday. I saw Maxwell yesterday and found out I don't have to have all the stuff in until March 1st. Engle will be back March 3rd. All I can do now is hand the stuff in and wait until April, when the business is announced. I think that if Engle can get me one, he will. Schramm said it would just depend on how many they had to give, whether Engle could get it for me or not.

Horgan is going to take the workshop over completely. He says he is going to insist on attention to details and treat all manuscripts as an editor would—with a view to helping us write publishable material. I don't like the man as well as Engle, but I think his system of teaching is going to be more valuable. I am glad that I have my reading under Engle, as that will still give me contact with him.

I went to Zerby's last night and enjoyed it—for the first time. They had the dog chained to Brother Zerby's chair, so I felt fairly secure. I walked home with some girl whose name I don't know, Ruth being in Indiana.

Louise's cough is improved.

Weather very spring-like.

Regards to kin.

> Love,
> MF

* * *

Sunday [24 Feb. 1946]

Dear R.

We are at the Union waiting for the line to slacken up before we start standing in it. There was some sort of game last night, and there are a lot of people eating that don't usually.

Got your two letters yesterday. I was going to send the picture to Margaret myself, but since you are, don't send the one of me by myself, as I don't like it. If you haven't sent it already, send the one of me and Connie. Gloria was not in that picture at all. Ruth Sullivan is the one on the end. The other girl with the glasses is somebody named Miriam Johnson.

We will now go get in line.

Regards to relatives.

> Love,
>
> MF

\* \* \*

Monday [25 Feb. 1946]

Dear R.

Got your two letters of 21st and 22nd. Will be glad to receive the peanuts—Louise likes them. It was very nice of the lady—I don't know her, by the way—to send them.

Last night we had a party for Gloria and Veronica, who had birthdays during the week—milk, cake, and stale doughnuts. These parties are always rare.

Had a letter from Margaret Florencourt, which I will enclose for Duchess.

I can't imagine his reverence being good.

Have just gotten my ticket to hear Robert St. John, who will be here Thursday. Louise is poorly.

I know you all are enjoying Louise. Will she be there when I get back—June 8th?

Regards to Aunt Mary, who should have returned by now.

> Love,
>
> MF

P.S. Isn't this rather sudden about Betty Cline? I rather imagine she doesn't know what she's doing.

\* \* \*

Tuesday [26 Feb. 1946]

Dear R.

By the tone of your Friday letter, I gather that Uncle is in his usual trim—glad you didn't let him get away with it. How is his daughter enjoying him?

Yesterday was decent enough for me to wear my light coat. Today it is snowing and I am back in the other one.

The peanuts haven't come, so I won't write the lady yet. Won't she think it silly hearing from me, when I've never seen her before?

Louise's health is better.

I am now eating some kind of cereal called "Bran and Fig." It looks like bird gravel and is pre-chewed, but it is quick to eat.

I had to wash two shirts last night. It was very painful. It would be as much trouble to send them home, though.

Regards to kin.

Love,

MF

* * *

Wednesday [27 Feb. 1946]

Dear Regina,

The peanuts came. Whew! Never seen so many peanuts. I wrote the lady and thanked her profusely etc. etc. I reckon I will start eating them for breakfast with the Bran and Fig.

Our bathroom door has been off one hinge for a week, but we have finally got it fixed. This house is continually coming off its hinge somewhere.

Weather disgusting right now. I have so far today managed not to fall down, but I still have to go to supper.

Had the blue suit cleaned. They did a fine job for 75¢. It doesn't smell like the odorless work in Milledgeville. The laundry here is rotten, though.

Regards to relatives.

Love,

MF

* * *

Thursday [28 Feb. 1946]

Dear R.

Presume you have returned from your culture tour of the city and hope you absorbed enough bookkeeping to sustain your position. Trust Uncle enjoyed your absence, you his.

How is Aunt Mary after her trip?

Engle has gone on a lecture tour. I don't know how soon he will be back now. I hand my stuff for the application in this afternoon.

Tonight, we go hear Robert St. John.

I regret to inform you that eating at the Union is not increasing the domesticity in me. I now see that it is possible to be well-nourished off other people's cooking, and I intend to keep the relationship between me and what I eat that way—i.e., let it start at the table, not the kitchen.

We have six days for Easter, and we thought we might like to go look at St. Louis. If I don't get this fellowship, though, I will have to start saving money hard, and I won't be going to any St. Louis.

Regards to kin.

> Love,
>
> MF

\* \* \*

Friday [1 Mar. 1946]

Dear R—

Had quite a surprise yesterday. Went to workshop as usual, Horgan presiding. He said he had two stories he wanted to read. One was mine. He didn't know, of course, that I had never read my own stories in there. Well, anyway, the other story was read first and critiqued, and then he turned mine over to me to read. I read about three sentences, which nobody understood. They all started hollering they couldn't understand, and somebody said, that's the one from Georgia, so I told him I had never read my own before because nobody could understand me. They all howled, and he took it over and read it for me. There was no adverse criticism. He considered the story highly successful. He had said last week when he took over the workshop that he was going to have read only the best stories instead of having anything, as we did last semester. He is much stricter than Engle, and I was somewhat afraid I wouldn't be able to produce the quality he demanded, so it was quite a surprise when he liked it.

I have read four times in workshop this year. Nobody else more than twice. It is full of veterans this semester, though, some of whom have published already. It is interesting enough to hear their work. This man Horgan knows what he is doing, and I trust will lead more of us to write publishable stuff. I do not mean in the big money-making fields, howsomever. He is a Colonel, by the way, just got out of the army—big discipline man—insists the writer should write a certain number of hours a day at a given time regularly and without interruption. Which is what I will have to do this summer, as I have to have 20 or 30 thousand words done before September on the novel I will have to do for my thesis.

Went to hear Robert St. John last night. He was talking about how little thinking was required in the higher educational institutions, and he said that he had just been to a place called Georgia State College for Women in a town called Milledgeville, Georgia. "You know what we northerners generally think of southern intelligence and liberality," he said. "Well, here at GSCW, where I least expected to find it, I found real thinking going on." He went on to tell about how responsive the students were, etc. All this was very nice to hear in the middle of Iowa. My acquaintances look on me with new respect. Tell some of the GSCW people what he said. I think they should know he is advertising the place, i.e., they are getting more than their money's worth.

Regards to kin.

Love,

MF

Got your card from Atlanta yesterday afternoon. Such culture!

* * *

Saturday [2 Mar. 1946]

Dear R.

Mrs. Zerby and the dog weren't feeling well last night, so they didn't appear at the seminar, which was perfectly all right.

Several of the people in the seminar who are also in the workshop told me they thought the story read Thursday was the best thing that had been read in there. I hope I will be able to get it in a literary magazine—no pay. Bill Gibson, who writes poetry for *The New Yorker*, gave me the name of the lady he sends his stuff to there. He thought the story was *New Yorker* quality, but didn't think they would take it. He said to send it and let them get used to my stuff coming in, and maybe I could hit what they wanted sooner or later. He said he got straight rejection slips from them for years. Now they use his poetry every two or three weeks.

Louise is poorly.

I was poorly yesterday but am all right today. I think I am doing right well not to be getting all these colds other people have. I eat a lot of oranges, however, and I presume that explains it.

Just got your letter of Wednesday. I certainly am glad I'm not in Atlanta—from my point of view, it sounds nightmarish, but I know you all are enjoying it. Tell Gussie I appreciated her card a lot. Now, I just don't have time to write her. I have to work much harder this semester than last.

Tomorrow we are going to see *Spellbound*.

The weather is delightful, and I'm appearing in my "drear beer" coat—that is what they call it around here, as it is a light beer color.

Now about these peanuts. Unless you positively don't want them, I am sending them back in the cookie box you sent Valentine's. They are getting in the way here, and you like peanuts. They are very good, but they make me sick.

Advise if you want them. Regards to kindred. *Send sidewalk pictures, please.*

> Love,
> MF

\* \* \*

Sunday [3 Mar. 1946]

Dear R.

What about this fasting business? According to the Rt. Rev. Meinburg, at 7:30 this A.M., those from 21 to 60 will be expected to enjoy only 1 full meal during the day in the penitential season of lent. That's OK; but now how much can you eat for the other two? Can you drink milk in between meals? Kindly give full particulars for my state in life. This will not apply to me until the latter part of March so there will be plenty of time to get it straight by then.

Louise and Ruth and I are considering getting a quart of Scotch at the local liquor store and then filling our private tonic bottles therefrom. Now what kind is the best to buy? Also, which is the least expensive?

Have you heard anymore about that wildcat that "preys on human flesh" etc. that I read about in the paper? I am interested in that.

Afraid I will have to wash night clothes today. At least them you don't have to iron. It is very springish here.

Regards to aunties.

> Love,
> MF

\* \* \*

Monday [4 Mar. 1946]

Dear R.

Gloria phoned her dentist to try to make an appointment for me. The lady is going to call me if she has any cancellations. I think I have a cavity, and I aim to get it fixed, but not at the dental school.

I didn't get any card from Sister from Savannah. Where did she address it to? I wouldn't be adverse to hearing from her now, if she cares to write from Milledgeville, you may tell her.

You are too fortunate to have one of the Garner footnotes enamoured of you. Since when has all his improvement taken place?

Yesterday I thought I was going to get a cold, as I sneezed a half hour or so, so I took a Dr. Cline cold pill, and today I am well and healthy.

Today the handyman presented himself, so we got the shade fixed in here that wouldn't stay down, and the essential instrument in the bathroom stopped from leaking.

Regards to all kin.

    Love,

    MF

\* \* \*

### Tuesday [5 Mar. 1946]

Dear R.

Just got your letter of Saturday and enjoyed hearing about my O'Connor kin. Peculiar about the John O'Connors. Sorry you didn't get to have dinner with Uncle at the Country Club, but don't feel too bad about it. We can't all be social successes.

Taking Duchess to the picture show sounds like a risky venture. Mrs. Hodges must be quite a girl.

A spring broke off my typewriter, so I have to take it to be fixed; also get a new ribbon. They fix it the same day, which is helpful.

Louise has sprinkled moth balls all over the room because she has heard they keep mice away, and the next room has had visitors of that variety.

Regards to aunties.

    Love,

    MF

\* \* \*

### Wednesday [6 Mar. 1946]

Dear R.

Engle was supposed to be back yesterday, but he postponed his return for another week, so I doubt I will ever see that fellowship. I may talk to Horgan about it at my next appointment. He being new probably couldn't do anything about it, though.

The lenten services are numerous here—Monday, Wednesday, and Friday nights and Sunday afternoons. I probably won't get to them, but will get to mass in the morning.

Louise is enjoying one of those hacking coughs.

Tomorrow we get our grades.

Just got your letter and will look forward to seeing the sweater and the jacket. They sound awful nice.

Nothing is settled about going to St. Louis. We will probably do just as well to stay here and study. Louise is trying to get her thesis done, and Ruth has a bunch of term papers to do, and I don't have any waste time, myself. I will go over to Cedar Rapids on the interurban and buy myself a head rag and a pair of socks and call it a day. Never fear about my economising on food. I haven't lost any weight. Can you eat oranges between meals when you are supposed to be fasting? I get awful hungry between supper, which I eat at 5:30, and bedtime, which is 10:30 or 11:00. I always fortify myself with crackers or something.

Is Dr. White coming, and if so, when?

Are your apartments rented?

It has entered upon the rainy season here.

Regards to whom it may concern.

> Love,
> MF

* * *

Friday [8 Mar. 1946]

Dear R.

I went to the dentist yesterday. I told him what tooth hurt and said I wanted them checked for cavities. He scraped around and then started putting those little X-ray things, like Dr. Rogers uses, in—fourteen of them. Found 6 cavities and said the condition of my mouth was fair. When I left, I asked the girl what I did about paying. She said first they made a diagnosis and then gave you an estimate of how much the work would cost, and she would call me as soon as he looked at the X-rays, and we would make an appointment. All I wanted was to get the tooth filled that was bothering me, but anyway, I asked Gloria if he was going to charge me for all of those little X-rays. "Oh yes," she said, "but only $7.50." That was after they were taken, so there wasn't anything I could do about it. The girl said he would probably find a lot more cavities after he looked at the X-rays. I am just going to have him fill the bad cavities, and when I come home, Dr. Rogers can tend to the rest of them. This fellow seemed to be a pretty good dentist—thorough, at least—but I am sorry about the $7.50 worth of X-rays.

I will probably get five or ten dollars for that story I sold, which I will apply to my dental finance. I am very pleased at getting that story in this magazine. It is a very well-thought-of publication in literary fields—one of the few that pays anything at all. I don't know how much the check will be, but I am sure not over $10—maybe not over $5. I would have been glad to let them use it for nothing. They may print it in their Spring issue, but maybe not until summer. I will get the check when the magazine with the story in it comes out. This may help me with my fellowship. I don't know.

Got two letters from you today. Sorry Mary has departed. Miss Mary sounds pettish these days. The coat is *drear* beer.

Bill Gibson couldn't enclose any note in my story. Stories are *not* sold that way, but on merit. Personal contact has nothing to do with selling a literary story—any other story, for that matter. Only in getting jobs, and I am not asking for a job. I send my stories out without any covering letter at all. Bill Porter says that personal contact business only marks you as an amateur, and not being one, he should know.

Enclosed a letter from Cousin Katie and a card from M. O'Connor.

I will enjoy working on the porch, I am sure. But do not plan to work a la Sallee. Don't go telling people I am coming home to write this summer etc. etc. etc. I don't like that.

Can you eat meat twice a day when you are fasting? You said you were going to get Josephine to send me one of those cakes for my birthday. I would be obliged if you would postpone it until Easter.

The Garners sound ghastly. Regards to same.

> Love,
> MF

\* \* \*

Saturday [9 Mar. 1946]

Dear R.

Am now busy typing my story with the necessary corrections preparatory to sending it back to Kuerker Quinn.

Engle will be back Monday.

I didn't get any letter from you today, but got two yesterday, so I presume that explains it.

It has been snowing for a day here now and is now icy. I have been out twice without mishap. Howsomever, I have to go out again. It wasn't bad going to Zerby's last night, as we went out on the bus, and a man with a car brought us back. The dog was chained to Zerby's chair and sat in his lap during the procedures. Regards to kin.

> [ *No closing signature* ]

\* \* \*

### Sunday [10 Mar. 1946]

[*postcard*]
Dear R.

No stamps, so am using this. Plan to get rid of a lot of peanuts at the house meeting tonight. Am at present at the Union, eating cottage cheese—have become a cottage cheese addict. Will get some more stamped envelopes tomorrow. Regards to kin.

> Love,
> MF

\* \* \*

### Monday [11 Mar. 1946]

Dear R.

Got your two letters of the 7th and 8th today. Hadn't gotten one since Friday.

It is too bad about Mary quitting. Ha. You ought to go to Savannah right now while there's no cook. After all, Miss Mary thinks it would do you good.

Engle is back, and I plan to see him tomorrow, if I can catch him in his office.

Am glad to hear I don't have to fast. I will try to cut down on my superfluous eating, but I get too powerful hungry to go into any professional fasting. The abstinence is OK, as they have fish and scrambled eggs at the Union on Wednesday, Friday, and Saturday.

The snow is thawing out here, and it is sloppy—highly disagreeable.

They have the stations here on Sunday afternoons as well as Friday nights. They have talks on Monday night and novena on Wednesday night. I am going tonight, and I think Louise is condescending to go with me. The talk is for non-Catholics and Catholics about the church. It certainly won't hurt her.

Never have gotten that card from Sister from Savannah. Probably she put the wrong address on it.

Regards to Duchess.

> Love,
>
> MF

\* \* \*

### Tuesday [12 Mar. 1946]

Dear R.

Presume by your today's letter that this should be addressed to Savannah. Know you will enjoy yourself down there and that Mrs. R will enjoy having you etc. etc. etc. *Don't* send me any money to take anybody to supper with. Nobody knows it will be my birthday but Louise, and nobody is going to. Much obliged, but I don't want it. My idea of a happy birthday is one that you forget until the next week. As I said before—I would prefer to have the cake Easter.

We went to the monseigneur's lecture last night, and it was very enjoyable. Louise was too tired to go, unfortunately, so just Ruth and I went.

My radio and lamp won't work. I don't know if it's a fuse or what, but I hope they get it fixed soon. Something is always falling apart.

Am on my way to see Engle now.

My regards to Cousin Katie and Bessie and whomever of my O'Connor kin you may see. I forget there are not many of them left there. Do you plan to see Nell Huggins?

> Love,
>
> MF

P.S. What do they say of Loretta's whereabouts?

\* \* \*

### Tuesday [12 Mar. 1946]

Dear Regina,

The package came yesterday and I opened it—naturally—and was delighted with the underskirt and pajamas and the stockings. I will save the latter for the summer, as I still have the other two pair fairly whole. Since those pajamas don't have to be ironed, I will use them regularly. The underskirt fit exactly—what made you think it wouldn't? Am much obliged and appreciate them.

Louise got herself a permanent yesterday. I don't think it looks so hot.

I didn't feel like going out to the Union last night, so I got a can of vegetable soup and a can of Vienna sausages and put them all in the same pan with a little water and heated it and ate it all. It was most tasty. In fact, I tasted it for several hours afterward.

Today, Louise and I are going to apply for our rooms—she for the summer, me for next year. I am going to apply for the one Connie and Veronica are in now—i.e., the one next to the bathroom. I am also going to apply for the one Gloria is in now. She says she doesn't want the job next year if her people will let her come back without it. I understand they are a very mercenary crew. I doubt if I could get it, but if I did it would be nice, as I wouldn't have to pay for it, wouldn't have to have a roommate, and would have to use the bathroom with only 3 people. The supervisors here don't have anything to do but call the electricians and plumbers. I doubt I could get it, but it won't hurt to apply.

Regards to Cousin Katie and Bessie.

> Love,
> MF

* * *

Wednesday [13 Mar. 1946]

Dear R.

Mailed your yesterday's letter to Savannah, then got your special. Got your Saturday letter today. Glad you are pleased with the sale. Saw Engle yesterday, and he was delighted. Porter seemed much impressed also—particularly as he hadn't liked the story much in the first place. He said he thought I would get around $20. I don't think so, however. Engle said he would help with the fellowship, and I will know in April if I have been granted one. The stipends have been raised to $20 beginning next year, so if I do get one, I will have $5 more a month.

Saw Bill Gibson yesterday and he said he had sent some poems to *Accent*. Now he gets stuff in the New Yorker, but he said places like *Accent* were the places to appear. I looked at some old copies of the magazine, and most of the people in it have published other stories or novels. I am in good company.

In my letter to the man, I straightened out the Mr. business; but not by saying my 1st name was Mary—I simply signed the letter Miss Flannery O'Connor. As far as writing is concerned, the Mary is so much impedimenta. All my writing will be done under Flannery O'Connor. That is what I am called here and that is the way I want it.

As regards the rights, etc.: a story is of no value outside a magazine. Rights do not enter into this.

Also, I don't know when the story will come out or how many copies I can get. This is not the type magazine sold on news corners.

Hope Louise won't have to go to Atlanta and stay with M. Motum. I don't blame her. Why doesn't she stay by herself?

Love,

MF

\* \* \*

Thursday [14 Mar. 1946]

Dear R.

Got your Monday letter and clipping. Whoever is doing the advertising is certainly splashing the place around. I saw Kitty Burrus's picture, which reminds me to ask: do you know if the Corinthian ever came out? Ask Mary Virginia and get her to send me a copy.

Had a talk with Horgan yesterday. He is very nice indeed. Also encouraging.

My radio is bad again. I just don't think I will spend any more money on it. My typewriter also has sprung a few leaks. I am going to have it fixed tomorrow.

You asked was I wearing the blue dress—yes, a great deal. It is the right weight for right now. Although yesterday it was so hot I wore the grey-striped seersucker thing I got in Milledgeville last fall. I need another one like that, and if I see anything I like of that nature, I will get it. If you see any 2 piece seersuckers cheap, you might get it. I don't want any big checks or big stripes etc., however. It is going to be hot as hades in this room at night. We can hardly sleep at night now, it is so hot.

Regards to relatives.

Love,

MF

P.S. You don't seem to be getting my mail too promptly. I don't see why, though, since I mail it at the same time every day.

\* \* \*

Friday [15 Mar. 1946]

Dear R.

Presume you will still be in Savannah so will send this there. How long are you staying? Write me when to address my communications to Milledgeville again.

Just read an article about Paul Horgan. He wrote 5 novels before *one* was published. He told me the other day it was no quick business, as is easy to see.

What I understand is the rainy season has opened upon us here. Tonight we will have to go to the Zerby Derby in the slush.

Trust you will enjoy yourself at the Turner nuptials. Newell's picture looked like Newell.

Louise is suffering from swollen feet and ankles. It seems to be chronic with her.

My regards to Cousin Katie and Bessie.

> Love,
> MF

* * *

Saturday [16 Mar. 1946]

Dear R.

Didn't get your letter today, but got one from Cousin Katie which I enjoyed, and would be obliged if you would tell her so. Also one from Betty Cline thanking me for a spoon I was so thoughtful as to send her. That was swell of me. Is she marrying a Catholic? Pertinent details would be appreciated.

Had raspberry punch at Zerby's last night. He seemed much impressed when somebody told him I had a story accepted by *Accent*.[1] He said it was a very good start and gave me an extra glass of raspberry punch.

It is rainy and disagreeable here.

Know you are enjoying being in Savannah.

> Love,
> MF

* * *

Sunday [17 Mar. 1946]

Dear R.

We are going to see "The Lost Weekend" this afternoon and thence to the stations. What am I supposed to do with this fur coat when it gets hot? They say there is liable to be a cold spell as late as April, but it ought to be too warm for it here in May. Where do I send it?

---

1. "The Geranium" would be published in *Accent*'s Summer 1946 issue.

I am wearing out my socks. It would be lovely of you to send me two or three pairs from Kresses in Savannah. They are much more expensive up here. Size 10½, white.

I eat cottage cheese all the time at the Union now. I understand it doesn't have cream in it. Is that true?

Yesterday I washed all my shirts at the expense of great physical exhaustion. Today I will iron as many as I can stand to. They look just as dirty as before I washed them. Also put clean sheets on my bed and found that the laundry here had left small brown stains here and there on them. The laundry here doesn't clean them, it just stiffens them. I leave them on the bed about 3 weeks. Nobody notices.

Big ants are coming in. Is there anything I can put out to get rid of them? I have found one on my bed and two on Louise's, and I don't want to get bitten and swell up.

Greetings to Cousin Katie and Bessie.

Love,

MF

P.S. Plan to write to Miss Mary today.

\* \* \*

Monday [18 Mar. 1946]

Dear R.

Will be delighted to see the package when it arrives and will open it immediately, no fear. Yesterday we saw the *Lost Weekend*—very gruesome—you might enjoy it.

Am busy here this week doing my philosophy paper on Croce, which I will have to read at Zerby's Friday night. Lord knows if they'll be able to understand me.

Had a letter from Miss Bancroft this morning. She seems rosy.

Write me when to stop sending this mail to Savannah.

I haven't got up the nerve to do my ironing yet.

Louise's ankles are still swollen and aching. I don't think she is too healthy. She gets powerful gloomy at times. Says she is going to the Doctor's if they don't stop.

Hope Cousin Katie and Bessie are well.

Love,

MF

* * *

Wednesday [20 Mar. 1946]

Dear R.

Today I got your letter with Betty Cline's and one from Bessie. Glad you are enjoying yourself.

Yesterday they took our chairs away and gave us new ones. We have a red one, which does very nicely with our spreads but sits hard.

Tonight we are going to one of the university plays—*The Miser*.

It is springish here and I am wearing my seersucker dress—mainly because I haven't ironed any shirts. I think it would be admirable if we all wore croker sacks.

The Dr. is still here. She is a very energetic character and gets on her roommate's nerves, but I think there could be a lot worse in there, myself.

Louise's health seems to be better, but she dislikes her work here, which doesn't make her very happy about the whole thing.

Thank Bessie for her letter and give Cousin Katie my regards.

> Love,
>
> MF

P.S. Have you found out why John and Ann sold their house and why is Elsie going to New York?

* * *

Thursday [21 Mar. 1946]

Dear R.

By the tone of your Sunday letter, you are being entertained extensively. I have an appointment with the dentist for Saturday, when he will start filling the teeth. Will be glad to get them filled, but am not looking forward to the visit.

It is very nice and warm here, and I am enjoying the change.

I actually ironed 3 shirts this day. I consider it a major achievement. The white one is very dirty after not having been got clean several washes, so I think I will send it home and get it done decent one time.

I wrote Miss Mary, but have not heard from her. I inquired after all the little Garners and asked particularly for Uncle. Sweet of me, wasn't it?

When are you leaving Savannah?

My vacation is from the 17th to the 23rd. I should get a lot of work done in that time.

Hope Cousin Katie and Bessie are well. Regards to Mamie.

> Love,
>
> MF

* * *

Friday [22 Mar. 1946]

Dear R.

Saw the lady about applying for the job here, but she said you had to apply for any of them—any house and go where they put you, so I took my name off the list. We have first choice for the rooms we are already in, however, so I can at least get this same one again and will probably be able to get Connie's, since she wants another one next year, and Veronica won't be here. At least I don't have to worry about being put upstairs, which is all I want.

May sent me a copy of Aunt Elizabeth's will to sign. It seems all the legal kin have to sign it before it can be probated.

It is very hot here. This room is terrific at night. Also in the daytime. You may send those two dresses you mentioned in about a month.

Just got your letter with attendant greenery, which I deployed to the trash can immediately. Do thank the lady for her kindness.

Regards to Cousin Katie and Bessie.

> Love,
>
> MF

* * *

Saturday [23 Mar. 1946]

Dear R.

Went to Dr. Boreland today and got two teeth filled. He had five estimates made up, all the way from $21.00 to $98.00 and showed me the different kinds of stuff he could put in it, etc. I told him I wanted the same kind as whatever my present fillings were, and that hit with his $34.20 estimate, so I said OK. That will be the 6 fillings, the 14 little X-rays ($7.50) and cleaning them. He said he could finish in two more times. He is a very slow, thorough soul. Now, I don't know whether that is too much to pay or not, but I don't much think so for all that. How does that go with what Dr. Rogers charges?

I read my paper at Zerby's last night, and it was perfectly understandable. I enjoyed reading it, and I think they enjoyed listening. I didn't finish it, so I will have to next week, but I don't mind, now that they are used to my reading.

Enjoyed Miss Mary's letter you enclosed. I don't see how Duchess is going to stand going to the dentist.

You asked if no one else had sold to Accent. No one else has sold to anything, but B. Gibson who was selling before he came. He hasn't heard from Accent yet about his poems.

Hope you continue to enjoy your Coca Colas in these cocktail dives you and Bessie go to. I am certainly looking forward to a Coca Cola this summer. I haven't had any since Christmas.

Regards to Cousin Katie and Bessie.

> Love,
> MF

\* \* \*

Sunday [24 Mar. 1946]

Dear R.

We have just returned from La Union, where we didn't have such a hot dinner. Some days, they are a little off.

This afternoon, Gloria is having the two ladies who have charge of the Currier Houses over for ice cream—the better to get more out of them for this house. We are all supposed to be on deck.

Louise feels punk.

My teeth don't feel so hot after getting those two filled. Louise says she thinks $34.70 is a lot. What do you think?

The weather is very fine here.

How long are you gonna be in Savannah, and when should I start sending my mail to Milledgeville again?

Regards to Cousin Katie and Bessie.

> Love,
> MF

\* \* \*

Monday [25 Mar. 1946]

Dear R.

Celebrating my birthday today with a slight case of diarrhea—will sit on the ironing board all afternoon and wash head tonight, as it is a necessity. I will write Cousin Katie tonight and thank her for the check. Naturally, I am delighted with it. I really don't think we will get to St. Louis, but I will go over to Cedar Rapids.

I also want to get a raincoat. It rains a great deal here now, and my other raincoat sleeves are slightly below the elbow. I think I have grown both up and across. Incidentally, the check will come in handy for these fillings, but I won't tell that. Miss Mary sent me $10.00 and wrote me a letter, which I enjoyed.

It is extremely hot here.

Glad to find out about the ant stuff, as I found one in bed with me this A.M.—birthday present.

Regards to Cousin Katie and Bessie, and will write them tonight.

> Love,
> MF

* * *

Tuesday [26 Mar. 1946]

Dear R.

Decided I needed a permanent as the rain here lowers my hair, so I got me some cold wave solution from the drug store and followed the directions and I have got me as good a permanent as you'd get at a beauty parlor. I did it last night without assistance. It was easy and I have just been out in the damp and it is still up. It cost $1.45 and looks as decent as Louise's ten dollar one. It probably won't last as long but it serves my purpose. I will send you some of the stuff if you would like it.

Know Louise will enjoy her visit in Savannah.

My diarrhea has left me.

This afternoon, we are going to hear some Catholic priest talk. I think Louise is going, too.

I wore the jacket you sent me today. It did very well indeed.

Regards to Cousin Katie and Bessie.

> Love,
> MF

P.S. I enclose Miss Mary's letter. Now is old Pattie Turner really going to live with us? I don't know but what that will be slightly ghastly. She's not so bad once you get to know her, but she ain't my idea of the all-round roomer.

* * *

Wednesday [27 Mar. 1946]

Dear R.

The socks came, and boy I was glad to see them. I had darned the others until there wasn't anything left to darn.

Enclosed is the picture of Fr. Hannagan etc. for Cousin Katie. Thought she might like to see them.

Louise is poorly today. I am very well.

Enjoyed Louise's letter. I have a mental picture of her in Atlanta. Sister wrote Cleo said Betty's potential spouse was homely. I don't think Miss Cleo has much room to talk, but here Louise says she thinks he's admirable. Peculiar.

Have you ever found out why John and Ann sold their house?

Regards to Cousin Katie and Bessie.

Love,

MF

* * *

Thursday [28 Mar. 1946]

Dear R.

*Tried* to put on that purple dress with the white on it. Too tight. Too tight all over. I must be getting very fat, as it is absolutely impossible to get it on. The dresses you made me in September fit, but that one doesn't. So I'll just have to put it up till I come home and see can you do something about it. Bought me a wash dress today—a grey linen-rayon sort of stuff with an unobjectionable yellow plaid through it, opened down the front, $6.80. Will write Miss Mary that she gave it to me. It is very nice, and ought to be cool.

We may go to Cedar Rapids Saturday.

The maid brought some ant poison over from Currier and put it around these rooms, so we are looking forward to being rid of them.

Got a card (birthday) from Mary Mills. Please thank her for it. Now, I got no time to do that. I found some very nice shields downtown. They cost $.25, but the pins come with them. Would you like some?

My regards to Cousin Katie and Bessie and Miss Josie, if you see her again.

Love,

MF

* * *

Friday [29 Mar. 1946]

Dear R.

Had a telephone message when I came in this morning that I was to call Dr. Seashore's office (Dean of Graduate College), which I did and was told he wanted to see me right away. So, I went over there, and the secretary said he wanted to talk to me about my appointment before he made any decision. Well, we had our little talk, and I am going to get the fellowship!!! He said he would notify me Monday officially, but would tell me now. He is in his nineties, and you wonder if he's going to pass away before he gets the next word out. Now, if nothing happens between now and Monday, I am set for my $20 next year. Very thankful.

I read Aunt Elizabeth's will but I guarantee I didn't understand it. I got that May got everything and I think that she deserved more than that naturally. I didn't see any provision for after her death but it was so cluttered up with wherases and wherefores, I could have missed most anything.

The radiators are off but the heat is on. That is one reason it is so hot here. Don't bother about the fan but you might as well send those summer dresses—the yellow one and the white one you made—*no others*.

The dentist didn't seem to think my teeth were in such bad condition; however, I will ask him what may cause the cavities. I drink milk etc. Nothing is wrong with my health, I assure you.

Regards to Cousin Katie and Bessie.

Where are Suzie and Howard?

Love,

MF

* * *

Saturday [30 Mar. 1946]

Dear R.

Presume by now you are in Milledgeville again, etc. etc. Did you see the bracelet Cousin Katie sent me? I wondered what you thought about it. It was awful nice of her to send it, but I wish she hadn't.

Finished my paper at the Zerby Derby last night. Madame Z. is expecting an addition to the family. He announced that she "was propagating the species and didn't feel so well." The animal didn't appear.

We didn't go to Cedar Rapids. Tonight, Louise wants to go to town and look for a hat. I go along for the ride.

Regards to the Milledgeville crew.

>Love,
>
>MF

* * *

Sunday [31 Mar. 1946]

Dear R.

Eating a late breakfast now at that wretched Huddle place and then will not go to the Union. It is getting too hot here for that fur coat, and I am afraid the moths will attack it. So I wish you would find out about it.

Today I will iron my shirts, and a sad experience it will be.

I washed my hair last night, and the permanent is still in, and with great vigor.

We ain't doing anything but studying.

Regards to kin.

>Love,
>
>MF

* * *

Monday [1 Apr. 1946]

Dear R.

Got your 28th and 29th letters today and enjoyed them. Also Union Recorder, which comes on Monday. I always enjoy that, despite the fact that there's nothing in it, ever. I saw by the last one that the Corinthian was out. I wish you'd get Mary Virginia to send me a copy.

Your Savannah trip must have been quite a round of dinners, cocktails, and cinemas, so I daresay you are glad to be back in Milledgeville with your duties of the earth, etc.

I see by the Recorder that "The Lost Weekend" is going to be in Milledgeville. Tell my Aunt Mary to be sure and see it. I think anyone with her alcoholic tendencies should be sobered by it.

It is not warm but hot here. The furnace is on, and it is right under us. It is terrific.

When the next leaflet missals come, keep them and use them yourself. I say the rosary in church, as my eyes are usually tired and I have to save them for work.

Louise went to church with me yesterday for the first time since Christmas.

Where is B. Cline gonna live after her nuptial venture?

Regards to the lot of my kin.

>Love,
>
>MF

* * *

Tuesday [2 Apr. 1946]

Dear R.

Have an appointment with the dentist tomorrow and will probably get two filled.

Gloria is having such trouble with her eyes that the doctor has told her she'll have to go home. She is much upset. I don't know if she is going or not. It is a shame for her to have to lose all the time since February.

A student—a veteran—was drowned in the river last night while canoeing. They haven't found his body yet. The girl he was with got towed in. She was all right.

Ruth and I think we'll go to St. Louis for two days. I don't know what we'll do there. We may fly. The airport has started up here again, but I don't know if they go to St. Louis. It wouldn't cost any more.

I am off now for a conference with Engle.

Regards to kin.

Love,
MF

* * *

Wednesday [3 Apr. 1946]

Dear R.

Had four teeth filled this morning and feel sorry about the mouth.

The doctor gave Gloria some new glasses, and she doesn't have to go home.

Last night, Ruth and I and some other people went out about a mile on the highway to a place called The Fish Shack, where they were supposed to have fine fried chicken. They served us a half of old hen that hadn't been dismembered. It wasn't so bad, but I wouldn't care to walk out again for it.

It has cooled off a little here. We could sleep very well for a change last night.

They have never found the body of the student who drowned.

How did Louise happen to decide to stay until September? That will be nice for her.

Regards to relatives.

Love,
MF

\* \* \*

Thursday [4 Apr. 1946]

Dear R.

Got your cards from Sea Island and letter today. I am atop the bed, applying an ice pack to my inflated jaw. I went down this morning and let him look at it. He said he didn't think it was an infection—thought he had just punctured a blood vessel with the novocaine, and for me to put ice packs on it and call him up tomorrow. He also said for me to take my temperature, so I bought a thermometer for $1.50. I figured it would be a good investment. It is a flat one and easy to hold in the mouth. I don't have any temperature.

The weather has got cooler here, and there is a strong wind—wind like I ain't never seen before.

Louise is feeling all right these days.

Regards to aunts, cousins, and uncles.

> Love,
> MF

\* \* \*

Friday [5 Apr. 1946]

Dear R.

My face is still swollen, but I went over to the hospital and had my blood count taken, and the doctor said it was normal and there wasn't any infection. He thought it had just been pulled at too much. It don't hurt.

The fellowship confirmations haven't been sent out yet, but I don't think they would have changed their minds, so I'm not particularly worried.

Got your packet of cards from Charleston. They are nice.

When are Sister and Louise going to B. Cline's wedding? I presume it will be at Christ the King's?

The weather is very fine here.

Regards to kin.

> Love,
> MF

\* \* \*

### Saturday [6 Apr. 1946]

Dear R.

Bought myself a pair of shoes this morning and Louise said they didn't fit so I took them back. Everything I have bought by myself I have had to take back. No resistance to sales ladies.

Got a letter from Miss Mary today, which I enjoyed.

We think we will go to St. Louis Tuesday night, the 16th, and come back Thursday night, the 18th—Ruth and I. Don't think Louise will go. Have no idea what we will do there.

My face is still a little swollen, but it is going down. Louise went to Dr. Boreland—the dentist—yesterday, and she thought he was a fright. Said he almost jerked her jaw off. He is not exactly noted for his gentleness, I understand.

I am going over to the Catholic Student Center this afternoon to see Fr. Beiner, as I want to ask him about some reading I am doing in Philosophy. They say he is very nice.

Regards to kin.

    Love,

    MF

P.S. Don't forget to tell Mary Virginia to send me a Corinthian.

\* \* \*

### Sunday [7 Apr. 1946]

Dear R.

Ruth and I are going down and get our tickets today. The fare is $14.60 round trip. We have to go to Cedar Rapids on the interurban to catch the Rocket. We'll leave Cedar Rapids at 10-something P.M. and get to St. Louis at 7:45 the next morning. Veronica is going to Toronto, Canada, to see her fiance, and Gloria is going home with Connie, so Louise will be by herself, unless she decides to go to St. Louis with us.

Went to see Fr. Beiner yesterday, and he was very nice and gave me the desired information.

My face has gone back to its normal shape. At the next visit with this dentist, he will clean them and polish the fillings, and I will be through—for which I will be grateful.

Trust my relatives are well.

>Love,
>MF

* * *

Monday [8 Apr. 1946]

Dear R.

We went down and ordered our tickets today. We decided to get Pullman reservations as it is only about five dollars more. Also, we are going on Easter Sunday night and come back the next Tuesday instead of going before Easter. I don't want to have to worry about getting to church in St. Louis etc. We are writing for our hotel reservations this afternoon. Since Dr. is doing so much for Louise, wouldn't it be handy if he had *you* bring her up to St. Louis for those days. That certainly would be educational for her. I am sure she would enjoy that.

Got three of your letters today and the Corinthian from Mary Virginia.

The laundry lost a pillow case and towel of mine. They are going to look them up.

Sorry Miss Mary is sick but hope her calomel performs its usual meritorious service.

I will write Cousin Katie about going to St. Louis. We are looking forward to it. Trust you have a cook.

Regards to kin.

>Love,
>MF

* * *

Tuesday [9 Apr. 1946]

Dear R.

The three dresses came this A.M. I can wear the white one and the pink one but not the yellow one. Strange. Too tight, too short, and zipper is broken. That was the one I was counting on, too.

I am having my seemingly chronic complaint today—diarrhea—they say it is going around.

I think Nellie's card is so much corn. Do tell her I was charmed beyond recognition. I will drop her a card from St. Louis to that effect myself.

Now about the cookies. Any little nourishment you may choose to ease my burden with will be accepted in all gratitude. But don't send it until Easter since we will be gone for 2 days after Easter and don't want to eat it during lent. If you haven't already sent the candy Miss Ivey sent me, don't send that until Easter either. In other words, the Wednesday after Easter, I shall be open to all food shipments.

Did Duchess ever get to the dentist?

The novocaine, by the way, was necessary for that tooth. It was on the gum and very sensitive. He did not use it for the others.

Regards to kin.

> Love,
>
> MF

\* \* \*

Wednesday [10 Apr. 1946]

Dear R.

Did not hear from you today. Trust you are well. It is cold here again. Don't think I will write Margaret until after Easter about the coat. Broke my one and only glass, so I am on my way to town to buy one so I can have a drink of water. My diarrhea is gone, and I am getting a little cold, but they always go on off.

Absolutely no news. Presume I will hear from you tomorrow.

Regards to kin.

> Love,
>
> MF

\* \* \*

Thursday [11 Apr. 1946]

Dear R.

Got your two letters today and re-enclose your enclosures.

It is snowing here today, but it is still too hot for a fur coat. My other one does nicely. Our tickets came today—$23 round trip Pullman. We had asked for two lowers, but the man got us a "double bed-room," that being the same price. We feel very classy.

My confirmation hasn't come, and I am worried about it. Dr. Seashore retired from service the day after he told me I could have it. I am still expecting it every day, however.

We are going to Zerby's tonight instead of Friday this week—the weather would be a mess.

Veronica leaves tomorrow for Toronto. Louise and Connie are so glad she will be gone for a week or two, they don't know what to do. She is pretty inconsiderate at times. Goes after what she wants, and anybody in her way can get out of it.

Regards to aunties.

    Love,

    MF

* * *

Friday [12 Apr. 1946]

Dear R.

We are going out to Brother Engle's Sunday afternoon to meet Robert Penn Warren. He is a very fine writer and critic.

When we were at Zerby's last night, his steam pipes got out of hook, and he had to dash all over his house turning the water faucets on. The whole place was filled with steam—looked like it was on fire. It's always something out there.

Had liver for dinner and supper at the Union yesterday. They put some kind of a tomato sauce on it, and it is admirable.

It is hot again here after snowing yesterday. There's nothing like this place for unexpected weather.

We got our hotel reservations today—The Mayfair.

Regards to kin.

    Love,

    MF

* * *

Saturday [13 Apr. 1946]

Dear Regina,

Went by the graduate office this morning and inquired as to why my fellowship confirmation hadn't come, and the secretary said none of the English letters had been sent out, as Maxwell was late getting them in. It will probably be sent next week, she said.

Got two of your letters today. None yesterday—two the day before. Are you mailing them irregularly or something?

They are having an art conference here, and I went to a lecture this morning on cartooning. Very good.

Enjoyed the picture of Cousin Doyle-Groves and Mary Turner. What's the new cook's name?

Oh—the tooth. It was the last tooth on the upper left side. He had an awful time filling it, and I don't know if he did a good job or not. *Make an appointment with Dr. Rogers for me in June.* I would like him to look at this guy's work. His estimate for Louise was $72.00. It seems she needs a lot of work done, but he is very vague about it—i.e., vague about what costs what.

Regards to relatives.

> Love,
>
> MF

\* \* \*

### Sunday [14 Apr. 1946]

Dear R.

Your package came last night, and I am sure glad to get the shirts. I can wear that blue one a lot. The other maybe one or two days. The pajamas will also be nice. I had pound cake for breakfast, and it will be gone in short order. Very fresh.

I was looking for those earrings Julia Cline gave me. I was gonna wear them to Engle's this afternoon. Apparently, they are nowhere to be found. In the same box with them was that lavalier thing Cousin Katie gave me and those silver earrings and a couple of other pieces. See if I left them at home Christmas. I don't even think I brought them, but you might look. Ruth lost a set of hers in November. I don't know if anybody took them or not, but they aren't here.

Regards to kin.

> Love,
>
> MF

P.S. The shirts fit exactly.

\* \* \*

### Monday [15 Apr. 1946]

Dear R.

We had a fine time out at Engle's yesterday afternoon. We went out decked in our respective Sunday black dresses and were met at the door by Engle in a yellow sweatshirt.

Everybody else was dressed up however. He served martinis and rum. They sho were tasty. I had martinis—but don't worry, I only had three.

Engle lives way out. Iowa City is really a place of some dimensions. Bill Gibson sold the poems that Accent rejected to Harper's. On the same day his wife presented him with a daughter. He has been selling to Harper's for a long time, however.

I appear in the blue blouse today. The other one goes fine with the skirt you bought at Goldstein's.

The pound cake is almost gone. If you want to send me another one, I wouldn't stand in your way.

Regards to aunties and cousins.

> Love,
> MF

P.S. Just got your letter and clipping. Don't think much of the clipping.

* * *

Tuesday [16 Apr. 1946]

Dear R.

We had workshop yesterday so Robert Penn Warren could criticize. One of my manuscripts was read and one of another girl's. The criticism was very helpful as it was in the case of J. Crowe Ransom. This makes five of my stories that have been read in workshop. I am much pleased with having yesterday's opportunity.

The fellowship confirmation just came. $20 per month and tuition for next year. I am delighted.

Glad to hear Duchess is picture showing and dentisting.

Today I appear in the long-sleeved shirt. It looks fine. I am going to have to move the buttons on the sleeves howsomever, as they are too big (the sleeves not the buttons).

Regards to kin.

> Love,
> MF

P.S. Glad you got the little apartment rented. Who is in the middle-sized one that the Sam Simple Simpsons had? Is Gertie Manchester going to stay? Have you heard any more about old Pattie Turner living with you?

* * *

Wednesday [17 Apr. 1946]

Dear R.

Louise just got a job for next year at Fresno, California for $280.00 a month. She will be a demonstration teacher, and she is delighted. She has been worrying about getting a job ever since she got here. She got the job through the placement bureau here. They say it's a good one.

Will it be the first time Uncle has flown? I dare say he will be full of it.

You asked about the shoes I got—I didn't get any. I got my money back. I am looking for some low-heeled shoes I can wear with stockings. We plan to visit the stores in St. Louis.

I presume this will reach you Easter. Easter Greetings. I sent Cousin Katie some of the same. Extend the same to my kin.

    Love,
    MF

* * *

Thursday [18 Apr. 1946]

Dear R.

Just got your regular letter and air mail edition. I will go to Fontbonne [University] and ask for Mother Mary Paul and repeat my speech. They will probably think I'm nuts. I haven't written Cousin Katie about the bond, as I thought you said wait until it was put in my name or something. I reckon we'll go out to Fontbonne Monday afternoon and get it over with.

The Union is closed during the holidays, so we are eating the night meal out and fixing soup and sandwiches for lunch.

Louise's sister is gonna get married next fall, she wrote her.

We went to high mass this morning. It was very elegant—an extravagance of altar boys in red collars—reminded me of the Cathedral in Savannah. We will by all means go see the one in St. Louis.

Regards to relatives.

    Love,
    MF

* * *

Friday [19 Apr. 1946]

Dear R.

Well, I got me just the kind of shoes I wanted yesterday—8-4A. They are low-heeled black shoes and cost $6.60. It was worth it.

On this day of penance, I am cleaning my corner and washing my shirts. The maid is here washing our windows and woodwork. It is very depressing.

I think I will start sending various and sundry things home. I have collected a lot of stuff here and am not wearing a lot of my clothes, so they might as well not be cluttering things up.

Make the dentist appointment as soon as you can, as I don't want to be waiting all summer.

This afternoon at 3, we have meditations at St. Mary's and tonight the stations.

Regards to kin.

    Love,
    MF

* * *

Saturday [20 Apr. 1946]

Dear R.

Certainly will be glad when the Union opens again. This eating around is not to my taste. The food is right good at Moore's where we are eating, but not like the Union, where you can see what you're getting.

Took my typewriter down this morning and had it fixed and a new ribbon put on. I use a ribbon up in about 2 months.

This room is so clean, it is hard to work in it. I'm not gonna clean it any more.

I think I can store my fur coat at one of the department stores here. I don't know for how much, but it would seem to me to be better to store it here than be sending it back and forth to Washington. What do you think?

Regards to aunties and cousins.

    Love,
    MF

* * *

Sunday [21 Apr. 1946]

Dear R.

Today on account of its being Easter, we are eating at the Rose Room. Went to high mass at 7:30—three priests and a profusion of altar boys. We go to Cedar Rapids tonight on the interurban trolley and take our train from there at 10:30. We get to St. Louis at 8:00 the next morning. Will present ourselves to the good nuns Monday afternoon.

How does Duchess get along at the dentist?

No news. Regards to kin.

    Love,

    MF

* * *

Monday night [22 Apr. 1946]

[*The Hotel Mayfair stationery, St. Louis*]

Dear R—

Well, we went to dear ol Fontbonne. We started out at 2 o'clock. At 5 o'clock, we arrived at Fontbonne. The people here told us how to get there on the streetcar, only they told us wrong. We went on 4 trolleys, got off at the wrong place three times, walked a fourth of a mile, and finally hailed a taxi. I asked for Mother Mary Paul. Oh, they said, she's over at the Mother House—about 12 miles on the other side of town. Ha ha. It so happened they had the Mother House on the phone, so they said I could talk to Mother Mary Paul on the phone. So we had a jolly conversation—i.e., we pulled several words out of each other at irregular intervals. She seemed pleased that I had called and asked for my cousin's health, etc. The name "Mrs. R. J. Semmes, née Katie Flannery" didn't seem to make too much impression on the sisters who were there, albeit I pronounced it at least a dozen times, using a different inflection on each try. They were very very pleasant to us, however—called a taxi for us to get back in town. I left my card—also my gloves, but was too thankful to get away to go back for them. By that time, we both felt like battle fatigue cases. Fontbonne, I am told, is very pretty. I was too tired to look myself. On the way out, we passed the Cathedral and so went in. It is very beautiful. Last night, we went to see *Dragonwick*, which stunk. This morning (it is now Tuesday) we are going to the art gallery, and this afternoon to the stores. The hotel is O.K. We are on the 17th floor, but the view is not so hot.

The double bedroom was the nuts. It has a washbowl that folded into the wall and a throne that looked like a chair. We had a highly superb time in it and took a number of pictures of it, which may or may not come out. There was an upper and lower in it. We leave this afternoon at 5; get to West Liberty at 12; take a train from there to Iowa City at 1 and get to Iowa City at 2.

We have been eating here at the hotel, and the food is good.

I got your two letters yesterday at the desk and enjoyed them. Hope C. Garner is feeling better by this time.

Regards to kin.

Wrote to Cousin Katie an account (not so heavily loaded with invective) of the Fontbonne expedition.

> Love,
> MF

* * *

Wednesday [24 Apr. 1946]

Dear R.

We got in this morning at 2:30 after a decent trip. We had reserved seats in the parlor car. Yesterday in St. Louis, we went to the art museum. It was very fine—we had our dinner there. In the afternoon, we went and looked in the stores. There was nothing in them. I wanted to send you and Cousin Katie something from there, but I didn't see anything.

In half an hour, I am to go to dear Dr. Boreland to get my teeth cleaned and fillings polished. Louise went yesterday. She said he nearly killed her, but I think she is satisfied with the work.

Got your letter today and enjoyed.

It is hot here.

The cakes have just arrived. They sho look good, and as soon as I come back from the dentist, I'll start in on them. Highly obliged.

Regards to kin.

> Love,
> MF

* * *

Thursday [25 Apr. 1946]

Dear R.

Got your letter and enclosures of Sunday night. Have just been down to Strubes Department Store. They will clean, store, insure for $300.00, and come for my fur coat for $9.00. I think that is reasonable and would rather do that than send it to Margaret. Then it will be right here for me next year when I want it.

I am still going to town on my pound cake, also several other people are doing the same.

My regards to Mary Thomas, if she ever comes over.

I will write Cousin Katie about the bond.

I would like to get the skirt, but I don't have any tape measure, and as there are just about four more weeks to stay up here, I might as well wait. What I need is a seersucker suit, but I can't find any.

Regards to kin.

Love,
MF

* * *

Friday [26 Apr. 1946]

Dear R.

We went to workshop yesterday, and one guy came in with a check for $200.00. He had sold a story to Esquire. So we all went and had beer at the local joint immediately. It was his first story. $200.00! I reckon he could afford to pay for the beer.

I wrote Cousin Katie this morning and thanked her for the bond.

They are going to come for my fur coat tomorrow—clean, glaze, value for $300.00 for $10. Pay in the Fall when you take the coat out. It is at the best department store in town—they send the coats to Chicago, however.

Tonight we go to the Zerby Derby. I am working on my 2nd paper for it.

Regards to kin.

Love,
MF

\* \* \*

Saturday [27 Apr. 1946]

Dear R.

Went to Zerby's last night, and the place smelled so doggy I could hardly sit through it.

Trust the little Gs are entertaining you hugely and that the hurricane shades are intact. Glad their Ma is mending.

We have had to have the heat turned on again here on account of it's getting chilly, so now we are burning up again. Always something.

Regards to my kin.

Love,
MF

\* \* \*

Sunday [28 Apr. 1946]

Dear R.

Bought myself some dried pears and soaked them in water and they are very decent. No more pound cake.

We are going to the picture show this afternoon to see *Tomorrow is Forever* or some such thing.

I think I will be home on the 28th of May, as I have no exams. I haven't got my ticket yet, howsomever. I will have to work 6 hours a day *at a regular time* this summer to finish this thesis. Nothing is gonna interfere with this regular time.

Trust Cousin Garner is doing well and the little Garners lodged respectively in the hurricane shades.

Love,
MF

\* \* \*

Monday [29 Apr. 1946]

Dear R.

Got a letter from Cousin Katie today, which I enclose. I thought the pictures lousy but will write Bessie to the contrary. Where were they taken? I think the one of you and Bessie is a howl. That's just like Bessie.

I thought I told you that I forgot to mention my kinship with Mother Gabriel. By the time I got to Fontbonne, I couldn't remember my own name. Yes, the trip was worth the effort. If we make any money next year, we plan to go to Denver. We probably won't make any, though. Ruth is mighty good company.

The Bishop of Davenport is here and celebrated the mass this morning. On the way out, we heard a little kid from St. Mary's school say, "You know that bishop— he's a swell guy." St. Mary's is a very nice parish, and we enjoy the services.

We saw *Tomorrow is Forever* yesterday and it stunk.

Trust you are well. Regards to kin.

Love,

MF

*  *  *

Tuesday [30 Apr. 1946]

Dear R.

I got both your Friday night and Saturday night letters today, both postmarked the 27th. Crazy service.

Now I was downtown this morning and I saw a hat and it looked just like you and I am going to send it to you. If you don't like it you don't have to wear it. It is for Mother's day. I will probably mail it in a couple of days, so you can be on the lookout. I have never bought a hat for anybody before. I paid $10.00 for it but it really has quality.

I wouldn't want to room with Ruth Sullivan next year. I will wait and take what they give me.

Use the missals yourself.

You may relay my sympathies to Mrs. Garner orally if you will. I got no time to send her a card. Regards to the rest of my kin.

Love,

MF

P.S. I am surprised Louise doesn't like my bed. I think it's admirable. Does she ride the horses much? Four girls from here went horseback riding Sunday morning, and one horse ran away, and they every one fell off and inflicted injuries of varying degrees upon themselves.

*  *  *

Wednesday [1 May 1946]

Dear R.

Did not receive the customary correspondence from you today. I presume because they both came yesterday. Who do you get to mail your letters? Miss Fanny?

Can I get her back from Annie Bruce this summer, by the way? Or is she in the freezer locker?

The weather here is punk.

I am worrying how to pack the hat I bought you, but I will send it as soon as I can find a box. I think you will like it, and I am sure it will go with anything.

No news. I had creamed eggs at the Union today.

Regards to kin.

> Love,
>
> MF

\* \* \*

### Thursday [2 May 1946]

Dear R.

Got your letter about the coat today, which is slightly too late, as the coat is already in.

Do you all have the little Gs all day—just for meals or what? It must be hellish. How long is Catherine going to be in the hospital?

It is still chillish here. I reckon I will be wearing these skirts and sweaters up until the time I come home.

Am now on my way to workshop. I dare say we won't go beering today, as $200.00 checks don't come in often.

Regards to kin.

> Love,
>
> MF

P.S. Enclosed is the stub of my social security card. Will you kindly put it *where you will know where it is*. I have the other half, but I don't want to lose both of them.

\* \* \*

### Friday [3 May 1946]

Dear R.

At workshop yesterday, Engle had my revision of the story that was read for Robert Penn Warren read. He had a cold, so a guy known as "The Brush" read it— the one sold the story to Esquire. It is very fortunate for me that Engle is so interested in my stories. This makes the 6th time my work has been aired, and each time is most valuable. I am pretty sure that when I get this story finished, I'll be able to get rid of it. Engle thinks it is very fine, or will be when I get through with it.

It is freezing here and raining and we are cold, as the heat is off. I trust it will let up in a matter of days.

We will have to go to Zerby's in the slush tonight, I reckon. I am going to cut the ironing board this afternoon, as I don't relish crossing the river.

Regards to kin.

    Love,

    MF

* * *

### Saturday [4 May 1946]

Dear R.

Got your letter and clipping about Mother Mary Maurice. It was too bad I didn't get to see her.

It is still cold here, but we've got the heat turned on again finally, which means it will warm up immediately and leave us burning up.

It is certainly too bad about the 2 GMC [Georgia Military College] students. Something like that happened to a whole fraternity house at Dartmouth a couple of years ago, I am told.

Duchess sounds like she is getting along royally.

The spring issue of Accent is out, but my story won't be in until Summer or Fall. Regards to my kin.

    Love,

    MF

* * *

### Sunday [5 May 1946]

Dear R.

Out of envelopes. Could you send me a box of kleenex? Now on way to Union. Saw *Adventure* yesterday. It was as sorry as they come. Weather now decent again.

Regards to kin.

    Love,

    FO'C

* * *

Monday [6 May 1946]

Dear R.

Cold again today. This place is the nuts. I am mailing your hat tomorrow, and I think it will get there by Mother's Day. If not, know that it is on the way. I may send a couple of mine in with it to get them out of the way, but you will know which is yourn. It really cost $25 originally, but I found a feather missing, and they gave it to me for $10.00.

I will ask about the English Dragoon tomorrow at Herteens. I think they gave me a knife—or maybe a knife and a spoon.

I think the hat in the picture is too old for you, myself. The one I'm sending is red and gold and a lot younger looking. Louise don't like it much, but I don't think much of her taste.

Regards to aunties and cousins.

    Love,

    MF

P.S. I plan to leave here Friday the 31st if we have a workshop on the 30th. If not, I will come on the 27th.

* * *

Tuesday [7 May 1946]

Dear R.

Inquired about the silver—to wit: knife $4.25, fork $4.67, teaspoon $2.92. All they have, however, is a butter spoon or butter knife or some such business for $3.13. If you want me to get that and send it to Mary Virginia (from me or from you or from me and you or what?)—write me pronto. As it's the only piece they've got, and other people get married and graduated around here.

Well, I mailed the hats today—one of mine, yours, and another little package in it. You may have to buy a particular dress to go with the hat, but do like you please.

That was certainly too bad about the Shouse child and the boys at GMC. The Recorder doesn't have much in it but such as that these days.

Trust Louisa and Mary Virginia enjoyed themselves in Atlanta at the Doctor's party. Am very thankful I wasn't there.

Weather still peculiar around here.

Will expect to see Duchess and Mrs. Hodges up here any day now.

    Love,

    MF

P.S. Mary Virginia's pattern is sho fancy—roses, pansies, nasturtiums, and pinks, whew.

* * *

Wednesday [8 May 1946]

Dear R.

The suit came last night before your letter about it. I certainly do like it, and it fits. The skirt if anything is too tight, not too big, but I can wear it. I put the buttons on the jacket and that fits perfectly. That kind of suit is quite the thing around here, and I have wanted one. I went downtown this morning and bought me a black blouse to go with it. They were all from $5.00–$7.00, so I decided not to get one, but found a very nice one indeed at a Jewish establishment for $2.70. So I am well taken care of. I tell you, I am no thin character, if that skirt had been any tighter, I couldn't have worn it.

I think I am coming home on the plane. With the strikes, the trains are somewhat unsteady up here, and also I think I might as well express my trunk, as I don't want to fool with it in Atlanta or have Louis and Doctor have to. The airport here has opened up, you know, and they are trying to get my reservations for me for the week of the 27th. If they can get them, I will leave here at 10:30 in the morning and get to Atlanta at 6:30 that afternoon, with an hour's wait in Chicago. All of which sounds admirable to me.

Your coat sounds nice. I am delighted with the suit.

Regards to aunties and cousins.

    Love,

    MF

* * *

Thursday [9 May 1946]

Dear R.

Packed me a box of clothes last night and will do the same with a bunch of books tomorrow, and will express them sometime in the near future. It is hard to find wrapping paper. You can't buy it. If you don't object, I will send these boxes collect, because then I won't have to stay here and wait on the man to come get them.

Certainly do hope these plane reservations come through. The people at the airport here are very nice indeed. I wouldn't be going but to Chicago on their line, yet they will try to get me tickets with Eastern from there to Atlanta.

Have a conference with Engle this afternoon. Also workshop.

It is jolly Louise has Mary Virginia and her little boys to play with. I must be off. Regards to kin.

> Love,
>
> MF

Oh, the laundry returned me a pillowcase for the one they lost. It looks like an ex chicken feed sack.

* * *

Friday [10 May 1946]

Dear R.

The weather is filthy wet here today, and I understand usually continues so about this time.

Engle read a section of a new revision of that same story of mine yesterday. He thought it was better. I don't think anybody much cares whose stories are read most, as the criticism is generally uncomplimentary and not too polite, and most of them don't take it too well. Engle has a great time making fun of people, but I like him. He don't say anything behind your back he wouldn't say to your face. He told me yesterday he had to talk hard to get me that fellowship—that Mr. Schramm was very much opposed to my having it. They say Mr. Schramm will stick a knife in your back the minute you turn it. He had told me he would be glad to help me get it, and then he opposed it. Very funny. Engle wouldn't say why; he just said, "Well, you're in the English Department now, and you don't have to go see him (Schramm) anymore." Which I won't.

Don't worry about fixing my bed. It suits me all right the way it is. I hope there is a table I can type on around somewhere, though. If not, I want one of those $10 Sears Roebuck jobs.

> Regards to kin.
>
> Love,
>
> MF

* * *

Saturday [11 May 1946]

Dear R.

Your special came last night, and I was happy to see it. I took the things out the box and refilled it with books and wrapped it up again, ready to express—after which exertion I sat down and ate a pound cake. I certainly do like those dates— they are better than any candy you can buy, I am convinced. The kleenex will help a great deal. Louise has been using TP for in-house nose conditions, but she don't like to be seen in high society with it.

Ruth's plane reservation was confirmed yesterday, and I am hoping mine will be Monday. I figure it will cost me from fifteen to twenty dollars more to go by plane—including expressing the trunk, but coming home a week earlier, I save about ten dollars anyway. I figure I can attribute the rest to education. Of course, I may not get the reservations in the first place, but I hope I can.

Regards to kin. It's been snowing in one part of Iowa but not here. Bessie's letter was most Bessie-ish.

Love,
MF

* * *

Sunday [12 May 1946]

Dear R.

Today I appear in the check suit. It fits admirably, but I think you will have to let the sleeves down when I get home.

We are going to see "Whistle Stop" this afternoon. Ate soup in for dinner and will eat supper out.

Do you roll Duchess to the dentist and just wait till somebody comes along to tote her up the stairs? It sounds gruesome.

Didn't hear from the airport yet, but hope I will tomorrow.

If I come on the train or the plane either, why don't you meet me in Atlanta? I sho hate to have to spend the night there. I would have booked the flight through Macon, but couldn't.

Am I going to have to go see Cousin Katie this summer? I don't want to take any more time off from this thesis than is absolutely necessary. I don't mind going for a couple of days if I have to. The thesis is going to be the devil to do, and I am not too capable of doing it, so I got to work awful hard.

Regards to kin.
>Love,
>MF

* * *

Monday [13 May 1946]

Dear R.

Will get the butter thing for Mary Virginia tomorrow and will see can I find another piece at the other jewelers. If so will send it to you, but I doubt if I'll find it.

I haven't heard about the plane ticket, so I doubt if I'll get it. If I come on the train, what about expressing the trunk anyway? If not, how does it get from Atlanta to Milledgeville, as it will probably come in a couple of days after I get there—advise.

As far as I'm concerned there would be absolutely no value in a membership to the Country Club. I don't like their dirty pool and I look forward to eating all my meals at home.

"Whistle stop" was putrid.

It is amiable of Brother Morris to uphold his obligations these days.

I enjoyed wearing the checkered suit yesterday. I reckon I will wear it home.

Regards to uncles and cousins.
>Love,
>MF

* * *

Tuesday [14 May 1946]

Dear R.

I went to the jewelry store this A.M. to get the silver for Mary Virginia. Well, they had a lot of it. I didn't know exactly what to do. It was all expensive, looked like to me. So I got a salad fork and a butter spreader and sent them both to you. They totaled $7.25. Now, I think that's an awful lot of money. I figured you could send the salad fork ($4.00) from you and me and work the butter spreader off on Louise and Sister. They must be gonna give her something. So, they are on the way to you. I trust that was the proper thing to do. I hate to spend that much money. I don't see why we couldn't give her the one piece together.

I went to the station and ordered me a train reservation for the 31st. If the plane one comes through I may take it, but I don't think it's coming through. That train will be the Dixie Limited—same one I came on Christmas. I won't leave here until 9 o'clock in the morning and will only have an hour's wait in Chicago.

Hope Sister takes the butter spreader. Regards to kin. Or you might save the other piece until she gets attached, and then you wouldn't have to buy anything.

Love,
MF

\* \* \*

Wednesday [15 May 1946]

Dear R.

Got your letter of Saturday today and am glad you liked the hat and the earrings. I thought they were both nice of their kind, but I was worried about the hat. These people started telling me it was a lousy thing to do and so forth. They are the kind send roses and all that truck, but I didn't pay too much attention as I figured you would enjoy it. What is this womanless wedding business?

Know you are glad to be rid of the Garner angel children.

The other night some character called me and said he'd just got here two weeks ago from Athens, Georgia, and a friend of his told him I was here from Georgia, and he'd like to go beer drinking that night. Which offer I declined. He then said could he come at two o'clock the next afternoon, which I agreed to. He came. He was a pitiful character. I don't think he had much sense. He wanted me to call up a Hilda Wirick he knows in Milledgeville when I go back and tell her I saw him. I never heard of any such person, but told him I would if I could find her in the book. Like I said once, the people you meet from Georgia are 3/4 of the time that class of people—just because most of them in Georgia are. Too bad. This poor creature's name was John McCrea from Moultrie, Georgia.

Regards to kin.

Love,
MF

\* \* \*

Thursday [16 May 1946]

Dear R.

Well, yesterday they called me up from the airport and confirmed my reservation to Atlanta for the 28th. The fare is $4 more than Pullman and they feed you. The trip takes eight hours from Iowa City. I wrote Louis to get me a hotel reservation for the 28th. Since you know when I'm coming home, will you get me a dentist appointment? I am not happy about one of my teeth—at all.

Yesterday I bought me a laundry kit—a cardboard thing you send wash through the mail in—and I will send my dirty sheets and stuff in it the morning I leave.

Enjoyed Mrs. Semmes's letter.

Regards to kin.

> Love,
>
> MF

\* \* \*

Friday [17 May 1946]

Dear R.

By all means, move the desk of Miss Mary's out. I'd like the typewriter desk in there if you are sure you aren't going to use it. What will you use? I don't want to take it away from you. If you do put it in, put it where it's cool, if there's any such place. I am looking forward to being in a room of my own for a while. I have been more than lucky in having Louise for a roommate, but 2 in a room is 2 in a room.

That was certainly funny the way Louise acted about the car. Why is she sleeping in Sister's room now?

Perhaps she told Sister first, and Sister told her not to tell you. That would be like her, you know. Personally, I don't care about learning to drive this summer—avoid confusion if I don't. Is Louise going to stay all summer, and are Catherine or Frances coming down?

A friend of mine wants to use my little stove for the summer. She has a one-room apartment. I don't know will I let her have it or not. They don't think this place here will be open this summer, and if not, Louise will have to find a room and won't want to fool with it. Edna, the maid, said I could pack it in the attic here—which may be best. I don't know. I feel sorry for poor Louise if she has to move out.

They are losing a good dean at GSCW.

Regards to kin.

> Love,
>
> MF

Tomorrow Ruth and I are going to walk out to the airport and pay for my plane ticket. If I don't like the sound of it after I ask them some questions about it, I won't pay for it and will take the RR reservation. I think I will come on the plane, though.

* * *

Saturday [18 May 1946]

Dear R.

At Zerby's last night, Mr. Swanson, one of the members of the class, shifted his weight slightly in his chair, whereupon there was a terrific crash, and Mr. Swanson was sitting on the floor in a pile of kindling wood. I didn't know a chair could break into so many pieces. It's always something out there.

The wrapping paper came yesterday afternoon, and I am much obliged. It should come in most handy.

Louise will have to move out of here, as this house is going to be closed. I think she will go to Currier. It will be an awful nuisance for her to have to move.

I have no objection to staying at the hotel by myself. I just didn't want to have to stay in Atlanta any longer than necessary. I will be out of there on the early bus.

Am delighted Cousin Katie is coming to Milledgeville. I will write her and suggest it.

I reiterate—nothing is going to interfere with my thesis this summer. I'll choose my own form of play.

Regards to kin.

    Love,

    MF

For pete's sake, don't spend the money to come to Atlanta to stay at the hotel for the night with me.

* * *

Sunday [19 May 1946]

Dear R.

Went to the airport yesterday and bought my plane ticket. It cost $45.00. The train ticket is $39.00. I also have a train reservation which I don't have to pay for until the 28th. So if the plane is too late leaving here for me to catch the other plane in Chicago, I can go pay for my RR ticket and wait three days and come on the train. So that is that. I don't think the plane will be late. He said it usually wasn't—but I like to be on the safe side.

The weather here is punk.

Regards to kin.

    Love,

    MF

* * *

Monday [20 May 1946]

Dear R.

I have just come from Dr. Boreland's. I had this yellow spot on the gum underneath one of the teeth he filled, and it was pretty sore and a little swollen this morning when I got up, so I thought maybe the tooth was abscessed. The day before, I thought it was just a gum boil and put merthyolate on it, but that didn't do any good. Anyway, he took an X-ray and said the tooth was all right, he felt sure. He burned the spot and said that if it didn't get better to come back. I want Dr. Rogers or Zateau to be looking at my teeth the 1st week I am there. So please see about an appointment.

I must busy myself this week packing my paraphernalia up. I am going to try to get the trunk off Saturday. The airport just called me to say that my plane is leaving 17 minutes earlier—that will make it much easier for me to catch the other in Chicago, so I am pretty sure I won't have to come on the train.

Louise's party sounds awful silly. Why did Lou Tigner have to cook the meal? Enclose two letters I got today.

Regards to kin.

    Love,
    MF

* * *

Tuesday [21 May 1946]

Dear R.

I got both your Friday and Saturday night letters this A.M. The mails are getting pretty speedy, what.

When I get in Atlanta Tuesday night, I will be dead tired. I certainly hope they will let me go to bed in peace. Also listen: I am not going to be going to Atlanta any more this summer. Dr. may think he has to invite me with Louise to be polite, but I'm telling you now I ain't going. If I had a job at the fuse plant I couldn't get off and believe me what I'm doing is more important than that. It is the habitual business of writing *everyday* for a *certain length of time at a certain time* that gets you anywhere. I have made a success of this year I think, and what I do next year will depend on this summer. You don't know how much.

Enjoyed Cousin Katie's letter. Maybe she will get up in July. I wrote her and asked her why she didn't come in June.

My mouth is still under the weather but I think it is better than it was yesterday. Regards to kin.

> Love,
> MF

* * *

Wednesday [22 May 1946]

Dear R.

Didn't hear from you today, I presume since I got two letters yesterday. Always hate to get two in one day, as there is never one the next.

Tonight we are going to a play.

My permanent is about gone. They don't last much longer than two months, but also don't cost but $1.45.

My jaw is clearing up OK, but I still want the dentist appointment.

Louise is going to move to Currier for the summer.

No news hereabouts. I go to see Engle tomorrow.

Regards to kin.

> Love,
> MF

* * *

Thursday [23 May 1946]

Dear R.

You need not send any earrings via Louise to Atlanta as I will have no evening dress with me.

Also, as I have said before, I have no intention of following Louise's social pattern this summer, so be so good as not to impose it on me.

Yesterday, I got a box of ice box cookies from Frank, Josie, and Frank Jr., which I thought handsome of them.

I enclose a clipping about Paul Horgan, which I think interesting.

How long will Agnes, Frances, and Catherine stay?

We go to Zerby's tonight for the last time—which is OK by me.

I am off for a conference with Engle.

Regards to cousins and aunties.

> Love,
> MF

# Academic Year 1946–1947

During her second year at Iowa, Flannery's letters generally become shorter and less chatty than her first year. The Flannery in these letters is one focused on work, honing her craft, and finding a job. Many letters describe the placement agencies that Flannery contacts, dreading a future of teaching, hoping for an opportunity that will allow her to continue focusing on her writing. The contacts she makes during this period become invaluable resources both during her graduate school career as well as in her future writing career. One of the agencies she contacts, for example, is recommended by Robert Penn Warren, who during this time had just finished his tenure as the Consultant in Poetry to the Library of Congress (later termed U.S. Poet Laureate) and would publish his Pulitzer Prize–winning novel, *All the King's Men*. She also works with Allen Tate, one of the group of Vanderbilt academics who self-identified as the Agrarians and with whom Warren had collaborated on the 1930 manifesto *I'll Take My Stand*. About Tate, Flannery notes that "My admiration for him is extreme" (23 Apr. 1947).

Both Warren and Tate would continue to be important mentors to Flannery, instrumental in helping her find literary representation, for example. Tate's wife, author Caroline Gordon, would be a close friend and correspondent throughout Flannery's writing life, providing significant feedback on Flannery's early short stories (see Flanagan, *The Letters of Flannery O'Connor and Caroline Gordon*). Flannery's characterizations of the writers she is meeting are often notable, especially in the way that she describes them for Regina. When recounting meeting poet Robert Lowell, for example, she describes him first as "the Catholic convert," and only second as "this year's Pulitzer Prize poet" (5 Oct. 1947). By the end of the academic year, she graduates with a master's in fine arts; she has also won the prestigious Iowa-Rinehart Award and is planning to return in the fall to continue her work with her mentors at Iowa, supplemented by a fellowship.

It is also during this time that Regina inherits the family farm, Andalusia, from her brother, Dr. Bernard Cline, who originally purchased the farm in the early 1930s as a weekend getaway from his home in Atlanta. Hiring workers to operate the farm as he expanded his acreage, Cline trained his sister to keep the books for what by the 1940s was a growing, productive farm. When Bernard Cline died in 1947, he left the farm jointly to his sister Regina and their brother, Louis. Regina and Louis expanded the operation, managing two hundred acres of pasture and several hayfields while keeping the rest of the property for timbering. As Louis continued to work and live in Atlanta, the day-to-day operations of the farm fell primarily to Regina in the 1950s and 1960s. After Louis's death in 1973, Regina became the farm's sole owner until her death in 1995 ("Andalusia").

As noted in the introduction, Flannery expresses concern for the difficulties she expects her mother to face in taking on the management of the farm. In one letter, she says she hopes that the farm will not increase her mother's worries (1 Feb. 1947); two days later, she writes that she hopes Regina will be able to make the farm pay—"that is, come out even"—and suggests that Regina might rent out the house (3 Feb. 1947). I have argued elsewhere that these letters encourage reading the farm women in Flannery's stories in a more sympathetic light than they typically have been read.

However, the academic year is not without its amusements. It is also in this group of letters that the so-called mayonnaise letters appear. While the entire *Dear Regina* collection evinces Flannery's preoccupation with food, these letters from the fall of 1946 showcase her gustatory interests in a special light, especially how much she enjoys mayonnaise with pineapple and Triscuits. These letters in particular have been a favorite of the scholars who have read them, notably David A. Davis and Caroline McCoy.

* * *

Chicago [Thursday, 19 Sept. 1946]

[*postcard*]

Train got in here at 11 and I was fortunate enough to be able to change my 5 P.M. Rocket ticket for one at 2 P.M. Will get to Iowa City at 6 P.M. Very fortunate, I must say. Called Mrs. C and the usual conversation ensued. Rode to Atlanta with a former Miss Myrick, whose name was a Hawkins and lived on the farm—Andalusia at that time. She remembered an outdoor kitchen there. Enjoyed lunch etc.

     Yours,
     MF

* * *

Friday [20 Sept. 1946]

[*Hotel Jefferson stationery, Iowa City*]

Dear R.

Presume you got the card from Chicago saying I was going to catch an earlier train. Got in here at 6 P.M., which was much better than at nine. Saw about my room immediately. Am in the one next to the bathroom where Connie was last year. Ruth arrived this morning by plane and is ready to go back—homesick. I presume she will be better satisfied tomorrow. My prospective roommate's bags have arrived, and we see by them that she is an ex-WAVE—Ensign.

I am now in the throes of getting the trunk delivered. It was supposed to be here at 3 and it hasn't come yet.

Apparently, Mrs. Curtis has been in a bad way—in bed all summer and can now walk only as far as the hospital.

There are two Quonset huts in the backyard here and numerous ones in numerous backyards of University houses. I would hate to have to live in one.

Not but about eight people in this house as yet.

Next week, the Iowa City restaurants are supposed to close—on strike! We can eat at Currier that week, I understand. Went to the Union and the prices have gone up a great deal, it seems to me. From 2 to 5 cents on every item.

Had a letter from Miss Bancroft waiting for me here. A friend of hers is getting her Ph.D. at this university, so I hope to see her. She lived with Margaret Sutton, Miss Bancroft wrote. Have not seen Jo Hunt.

Regards to my kin.

MF

\* \* \*

Saturday [21 Sept. 1946]

Dear R.

I couldn't be more satisfied with the roommate. She is about 32, an ex-WAVE Ensign and of studious disposition. She has her own radio, typewriter, lamp, and clock, does not care about curtains, and empties her own ashtrays after use. She is from Des Moines, and in the WAVES was stationed in Miami. Knew a lot of WAVES who trained in Milledgeville and said they all liked the place and hated the weather.

This room is not as hot as the other one, and I will need another blanket. I also need about a dozen coat hangers P.D.Q.

Got the trunk yesterday afternoon. The bottle had oozed a little on the towel but had not broken. Don't think more than a spoonful was lost.

Have started my delicatessen in the window again. Plan to have milk delivered every other day.

The extension cord is essential and I am enjoying it.

There is only one girl so far in the room we had last year. She has pink and blue plush rugs sitting on the floor. Disgusting.

The room rent here has gone up $25 a year. Everything has gone up.

I am off to visit the A&P.

Yours,

MF

The roommate's name is Sarah Dawson.

\* \* \*

Sunday [22 Sept. 1946]

Dear Regina—

Last night I dined with Miss Nutter in her apartment—beans, bread, tomatoes, and I brought a pint of ice cream. She is very poor, so I thought I better contribute something.

The young ladies next door have moved in—plush rugs, et al. They seem harmless. My roommate looks like Mrs. Lester, if you can fancy it, only thin and not stooped. I have three pictures left in that roll of film, and I may get to take her picture.

I called Engle up yesterday about some work. He said he had been down to Urbana (where *Accent* is published) and that they were very pleased with my story and wanted to know where I was so they could send me copies—evidently didn't get my card. He said he would write them to send me my copies, so don't go writing down there. As soon as I get one, I'll send them to you.

Milk is 16 cents a quart here. Last year, it was 12.

I presume Louise got off yesterday.

Don't send me any blanket yet, but I want the coat hangers.

Regards to mine Aunts Mary and Catherine.

> Love,
> MF

The roommate refers to the bathroom as—the head.

* * *

Monday [23 Sept. 1946]

Dear R.

Found out yesterday in the conversation that my roommate worked with Lady Marjorie Handwork in Washington. And did not care much for same.

I have written Cousin Katie, Stella Semmes, Louis, Miss Bancroft. Trust that is satisfactory.

Have not seen Jo Hunt. There are 10,000 students here, and she is not listed in the book.

I am only going to have three classes—most of the work will be done at home, reading and writing.

Walked into a store today and got 6 Coca-Colas. I have to have my stove fixed before I can use it. The plug is bent or something, and it won't go into the wall. I wish I had bought that one in Hendersonville, but no matter.

Union Recorder came.

This girl I room with was telling me about the dairies and dairy help around here. They get around $350 or 400 for what Mr. Bond is doing. They have degrees in dairy work etc. Very ritzy.

We have the heat on today.

It is too bad about poor Katherine.

Regards to kin.

> Yours respectful,
>
> MF

* * *

Tuesday [24 Sept. 1946]

Dear R.

Got your letters of 21st and 22nd today. Looked in the Recorder again and found the clipping—which I had overlooked—and am enclosing it.

Another ex-WAVE from Milledgeville training lives in the hut in the backyard. There are about 16 girls to each hut (about the size of our dining room)—no place to put their clothes—public bath. I would have come home if that had met me.

The young lady next door (of the plush rugs) is very wealthy and impetuous. She gave us a dozen apples and pears for some reason yesterday—painted the University furniture in the room white (not supposed to be done)—scattered DDT powder liberally in the bathroom to get rid of the silverfish. (If your towel was in the way that was too bad.) She has a car and drove us to supper yesterday.

They have turned the heat on, and our room is very hot now.

Ruth and I plan to go to the Newman Club tonight.

Glad Miss Louise and cat got off and in the company and by the hand of males.

Do I have to write Katie Mac? I mean, is it an absolute necessity? I got so much to do, I don't know how I'll do it all.

Card from Cousin Katie.

Regards to kin.

> Love,
>
> MF

The trunk was in good condition and the books were packed too tightly to rattle.

* * *

Wednesday [25 Sept. 1946]

Dear R.

Did not get your letter today—I presume because I got two yesterday. If you mail them the same time each day, they should come consistently.

Got my stove fixed and it works fine—cost 35¢. Went to the Newman Club and gave them two bucks that I hated to part with. I won't be able to go to the meetings.

Saw *Accent* yesterday. I am in very good literary company in that issue—Katherine Anne Porter, a distinguished writer, and Austin Warren, a very fine critic, a couple of recognized poets, etc.

If any manuscripts or letters from quarterlies come for me, I want them as soon as possible, as I need them.

I am going to get somebody else to type my thesis, as I don't have time. Will probably cost me $25.

Regards to kin.

> Love,
> MF

What about chickens? Is the one that was ill still here?

We had a house meeting last night. The young ladies this year seem to be more personable than last.

I *need* those coat hangers but no blanket.

* * *

Thursday [26 Sept. 1946]

Dear R.

I find I will need the following books that I have at home:

1) Writers of the Western World—big blue book, in bookcase in ante-room
2) English Literatures Vols. I and II—not the exact titles, but these are two large, dark red books—probably in the bookcase in my room
3) Principles of Literary Criticism—a bright blue book—large.

I am sorry to put you to this trouble, but it is well I have the books and won't have to buy them. I have to do a great deal of reading.

What does Mary Virginia know about Latin? I imagine she would make a good Spanish teacher.

Am still anxious for the coat hangers.

It is nice to be able to open our own door and have the milk sitting there every other day. I don't find things too expensive, as my tastes are simple.

Have not seen Jo Ann Mills.

Add to those books Brewster: Modern English Literary Criticism—a regular size dark blue book.

Visited the A&P today and returned with prunes.

We have our room fixed conveniently, and it is certainly better than last year.

Regards to kin.

> Love,
>
> MF

P.S. If it wouldn't make it too heavy, include Our Heritage of World Literature—big blue—heavy.

* * *

Friday [27 Sept. 1946]

Dear R.

The coat hangers came yesterday, and I was mighty glad to see them and have now hung up my clothes. Also will be using the shoes and rain hat shortly. It is very warm here—no coat or sweater required yesterday or today. You say you are sending the blanket—I presume you might as well send it, as I might possibly need it later in the winter.

The roommate of the plush-rug-kid next door is exceptionally nice. We eat together frequently. She went to Cornell and is from Iowa.

Went to buy some eggs yesterday and couldn't find any. The meat is generally small and tough, but I had good fish at the Union today. The Union remains my favorite eating place.

I have dinner at 11:10, supper at 5:00. This to avoid the huge lines.

Regards to my assortment of kin.

> Love,
>
> MF

* * *

Saturday [28 Sept. 1946]

Dear R.

Spent my morning at the A&P whence I returned with a can of crushed pineapple and a can of Vienna sausages. Also got some eggs today which are very scarce. If you could see your way clear to sending me a bottle of homemade mernaise (sp?) sometime I would be mighty thankful. I have some mustard but it's just too strong. The Vienna sausage is terrifically hard to get, too. I have tomatoes in my room now.

The roommate is off at a football game, she being a big outdoor girl.

Would you get Dr. to give you a prescription for some drops for eye strain. Now I am not straining my eyes but naturally they get tired by the end of the week.

My roommate goes to bed by 10 every night which is nice—a lot of times she is there by 9:30.

Was surprised that the cartoons are already on the wall. Are they on cardboard and tacked up or are they on the wall itself? Why don't you go look at them?

Send me John Sullivan's address as I forgot it and want to write to him.

Had a letter from Mary Boyd. She makes reservations for Delta. Likes the work. Regards to kin. No blanket yet.

> Love,
> MF

\* \* \*

Sunday [29 Sept. 1946]

Dear R.

The blanket came yesterday, and it turned cold yesterday, and it felt more than welcome. I am glad you sent it on.

The roommate and the girl next door and I are going to walk out in the country this afternoon. They seem to know their way around.

Ruth and I et in the Rose Room last night—very classy. It cost a $1.20 but it is worth it occasionally.

I hope to take the pictures this afternoon.

How are the poor Garners?

Regards to kin.

> Love,
> MF

\* \* \*

Monday [30 Sept. 1946]

Dear R.

We walked five miles out into the country yesterday and enjoyed it—very pretty territory. Glad you enjoyed old Beuna's function. What did you get? I understand that in the September 23rd Life, there are some pictures of Paul Engle and family—haven't seen them, but thought you might like to. You might find somebody with a copy of that issue.

Thought Catherine's letter somewhat pitiful.

If it would just be "nice" for me to write Katie Mac, I can't do it. Can't do anything not absolutely necessary.

Know you are glad to be rid of the cat.

I now fix my egg and cream of rice in same pan at same time. Very handy.

Dare say you will enjoy faculty reception.

Amazed that you got so much for the clarinet. The accordion is not worth $35 in my estimation. Will write Sister and K as soon as I can.

I am looking forward to the home made mernaise and think it is awfully nice of you to want to send it to me. A 12 oz. jar will do. I am saving the pineapple for it.

It is getting cold hereabouts.

> Love,
> MF

* * *

Tuesday [1 Oct. 1946]

Dear R.

I am between writing you and eating my lunch—mushroom soup in one bowl, a tomato, sliced hard boiled egg and six prunes in the other. I top this off with a peanut butter sandwich and a cup of coffee. The milk is in the soup. Very fine.

Glad you enjoyed the faculty reception. If brother Wells feels I am reflecting anything on the school, I wish he would be looking out for a job for me and I *do not mean at GSCW*. He travels to different colleges in the southeast and hears of places. You might mention that the next time you see him. I would want work in English in a college.

I understand the picture in Life is just of Engle's infant, so you wouldn't be interested probably. She is a cute little girl, but from my view of her a hellion.

I haven't bought anything in the nature of a sweater yet, but I need a light (weight) one and may get it.

The pipes in this room pop all night, but I presume I will get used to it. Like this room much better than the one last year, anyway.

Regards to kin.

> Love,
> MF

P.S. I am due to get two more manuscripts.

* * *

Wednesday [2 Oct. 1946]

Dear R.

Glad the books are on the way. The coat hangers, hat, and shoes came all at the same time.

I don't care who you sell the accordion to. I can't imagine Catherine or Frances possibly wanting it (a gift of it might have a slightly different complexion, of course) but if that is the way Doctor wants to waste his money, sure, sell it to him.

The cartoons sound interesting. How many were there? Do they look like the originals?

I bought me a light weight grey sweater yesterday for $3.98. It is very pretty except the buttons. ◯ They are that size and there are 7 of them. It is a very light grey. Do you got anything better? If so, you might send them.

Had a card from Cousin Katie saying they were going to leave Monday. I don't suppose Miss Mary is going to see her? How is humor of the same? I mean to write her as soon as I can.

Connie is fine and in the back room.

Regards to kin.

    Love,

    MF

I tore a pair of my nylon stockings. Do you want me to send them to you?

* * *

Thursday [3 Oct. 1946]

Dear R.

We went out to some place on the road last night for supper and had fried chicken. It was punk. The Union is still the best and the cheapest.

Go to Workshop this afternoon and always enjoy that.

Sorry Miss Bessie is in the hospital. I will endeavor to write her today but you may believe I have more than enough to do.

Edna tells me the meat I've been eating she feeds to her cat. It is potted sandwich stuff you know—made of tripe, trimmings, and cheek. Delicious!

Am certainly looking forward to that mernaise.

Tried that grey pearl button that you put on the brown-checked skirt on the sweater I bought but it was a little too big so don't send any like that.

Regards to kin.

    Love,

    MF

* * *

Friday [4 Oct. 1946]

Dear R.

Highly disappointed about the mayonnaise. You can't buy it here *anywhere*. Hope you will reconsider.

I wanted J. Sullivan's seminary address. Please send.

Dr. sent me two prescriptions. I will have the eye one filled today.

It is very hot here. Fortunately we have gotten the heat turned off.

The books haven't come but I hope they will today or tomorrow.

The roommate is going home this weekend and she thinks she will hitch-hike as none of the bus schedules suit her.

Couldn't get much out of Miss Williams's letter because couldn't read it.

I generally can't get to bed by 9:30. But we have our beds at different sides of the room, and she doesn't mind my light. An altogether agreeable character.

    Love,

    MF

* * *

Saturday [5 Oct. 1946]

Dear R.

The books came yesterday after noon and I was glad to see them, and appreciate your getting them off so soon.

Spent a few minutes in the A&P this morning but only came off with some Dreft. No mayonnaise anywhere. Bought me a bread box from Sears Roebuck for .81¢ because I want to keep the rats out of my food.

The roommate decided not to hitch-hike because she couldn't find anybody to hitch hike with her and being a person [of] delicate sensibilities, she didn't want to do it by herself.

Also, Barbara, the girl next door, has gone to a wedding in Davenport, so just the plush rug kid and I are here.

Had a very handsome stew at the Union today.

Uncle sounds like his usual self. How is your eldest sister and her attitude toward you?

I would be interested to hear Miss Pagett's reaction to the wonderful Mr. Williams.

Regards to kin.

> Love,
>
> MF

P.S. I wrote Miss Bessie Thomas a few kind words. Cancel the debt.

* * *

### Sunday [6 Oct. 1946]

Dear R.

It is very nice to have the room to myself every now and then and I hope the roommate will spend many weekends at home. She is a very fine girl, I think. She had to work her way through college.

The plush rug kid rode me to church this morning as I didn't have time to walk. Last night she gave me a lot of coffee candy which she got in Cedar Rapids during the day. It was delicious and if I get over there, I am going to try to get some and send you. I would like to send some to Cousin Katie also.

Ruth and I think we may go over there this week sometime. There is a second-hand bookstore there that may help us.

Found a can of sliced pineapple yesterday afternoon. Don't plan to open my pineapple until it gets cold. Would also like to wait on some mayonnaise. Maybe Louis could get some for me? It would be a help indeed. I found a place where I can get 100% whole wheat bread and I am enjoying it.

Regards to kin.

> Love,
>
> MF

* * *

### Monday [7 Oct. 1946]

Dear R.

Got your two letters today and the enclosed papers, all of which I enjoyed. The Macon News seems to be a GSCW supplement. The cartoons must be terrifically light not to show up any better than they did. Mr. Williams looked like he needed a lace collar and a hair ribbon. Send me more of those papers.

I am on my last half-box of kleenex. I sneeze when confronted with soap, wool, and numerous other necessaries; i.e., I need more kleenex, and haven't seen any around here.

Sunday afternoon, the roommate returned with her mama and sister from Des Moines. Very nice-looking, substantial people. She brought back a stove like mine and a percolator, and numerous articles of food.

I generally eat two meals in and one out per day. I haven't lost any weight but presume I have gained some.

Does Joan like the school any better?

I know the deck of cards with dear little Bo Peep must be lovely.

Regards to kin.

Love,
MF

*  *  *

Tuesday [8 Oct. 1946]

Dear R.

I am sitting on the porch waiting for the postman to bring the mayonnaise. That is mighty fine. Every time you see any extra can, you can get it. This should last me about 3 or 4 weeks, I dare say. Glad you sent the blank from the Yale Review, as I took a year's subscription. I had to buy $6 worth of books today for my seminar; but I reckon that just goes under the general heading of education.

When I send the torn stockings, I will also send the pair Agnes gave me—which are too small. That leaves me with only one pair, so if Louis brings any more, I need a pair.

Wrote Cousin Katie Sunday. Had a letter today from Miss Bancroft, no news in it.

Regards to kin.

Love,
MF

*  *  *

Wednesday [9 Oct. 1946]

Dear R.

The mayonnaise came just in time for dinner and I must say it is superb. Man! Now please get me some more because it just isn't around here. The chicken dinner I will probably save for the weekend. It looks delicious. I haven't seen any of it around here. That mayonnaise tastes just like homemade. I plan to open my pineapple now.

Last night the plumbing went to pieces and the upstairs works backed down into ours and overflowed. The plumbers arrived at 1:AM and stayed until 2. And it is working again. That happened last year about this time.

The buttons on the long sleeve blouse will do for the sweater—don't add much to it, but they will do. I'll use it like it is until Christmas, when I'll bring it home and let you put them on; I don't have time to sew.

Am eating some kind of canned liver spread that is lovely—pate de foie gras. Did Duchess's fall scare her?

Wish I could be eating some of those chickens.

Regards to kin.

> Love,
>
> MF

P.S. Is Mary Virginia still teaching?

* * *

Thursday [10 Oct. 1946]

Dear R.

Broke my rosary beads into another piece today. Is there an old pair around the house you could send me? I tried to get a pair here, but there is nothing under 5 bucks. All I want is something like a 25¢ pair that they had in the back of the church in Milledgeville. If you could find something I would appreciate them, as I don't like to read my prayers when I have all this other reading to do, so I say the other. Kindly have them blessed before you send them if they aren't already. Would appreciate them soon.

Send the ballot if you like and I will try to get it fixed the proper way, etc.

How did Miss Mary take Lizzie's third degree re Mrs. Garner's spiritual vagaries?

Distressed to hear about Gene. Tell him to kick himself in the chest with an ax and maybe he'll feel better.

How long is Doctor going to be in Chicago? Too bad he couldn't come over and see this place.

That mayonnaise is mighty fine.

Regards to kin.

> Love,
>
> MF

\* \* \*

Friday [11 Oct. 1946]

Dear R.

Engle was away on a lecture tour yesterday so his new assistant conducted the workshop and read two of my stories. He didn't know they couldn't understand me so after I had read a couple of sentences he had to take it over. They argued about them pro and con for two hours, the usual procedure.

Went to the A&P today and got myself a head of lettuce, also found pineapple juice. I never see salad dressing or mayonnaise; but I am enjoying that you sent me I mean to say. It is mighty fine.

Am enclosing this alumnae thing. It will cost me 10¢ more if I send the check from here, so will you send them a check—note that it says make payable to Sara Bethel. I will be much obliged. It is cold today for the first time but not cold enough yet for the fur coat. I won't send for it until necessary because it won't be good for it to sit around in this hot room. Our closet is directly over the heating apparatus in the basement.

We are having the 40 hours this weekend. (St. Mary's)

Enjoyed Cousin Katie's letter.

Regards to kin.

Love,

MF

P.S. John Sullivan's letter was in my room. I think on the long table. Kindly look.

\* \* \*

Saturday [12 Oct. 1946]

Dear R.

We went to see "Till the End of Time" last night and it was certainly lousy. That was the first time I've been this year and I reckon that will be the last until something decent comes along.

Everybody is on their way to the football game, so I'm looking forward to an afternoon at home undisturbed.

Had half of the can of chicken dinner just now and I mean that's classy business. It sho was tasty. I will have the rest for supper—conserved meantime in a *glass* jar in window—since you can never get anything to eat on these football Saturdays at the Union on account of the terrific lines.

Trust you enjoyed yourself in Atlanta. I doubt now if we will get to Cedar Rapids. I don't know.

Enjoyed the papers.

Will be glad to advise Aunt Mary on any of her housekeeping difficulties.

Hope you can get the kleenex.

Regards to kin.

> Love,
> MF

\* \* \*

Sunday [13 Oct. 1946]

Dear R.

The roommate went to the football game with a cold and came home with a worse one. She is the variety what catches everything. I don't think I will catch it, as I am very healthy these days.

Tonight we are all invited to the other graduate house to meet the young ladies there. It promises to be dull, but I generally go where invited.

Ice cream has gone up 2¢ a pint.

It is cold and rainsome here and before long I am going to see about getting my big coat. The other still feels comfortable with a suit under it. I am enjoying pineapple sandwiches mightily.

Regards to kin.

Regards to Mrs. Logan.

> Love,
> MF

\* \* \*

Monday [14 Oct. 1946]

Dear R.

We went to the function of the other graduate house last night. They have two girls from France, one from India, one from Hawaii. The Indian, who wears her native garb all the time here, demonstrated how it went on and the Hawaiian did some native dances. After which there was ice cream and cake, which I enjoyed.

The roommate has a friend whom she is inviting here for dinner tomorrow. She plans to have creamed tuna fish. I am to provide the fruit, Barbara next door something else, and we four will eat together. I don't know how she is going to get the tuna fish fixed. She ain't got any flour; but that's her worry.

Got your Thursday letter from Atlanta today. Hope Louis will be able to get the mayonnaise and kleenex. The mayonnaise is a great help.

Regards to relatives.

Love,

MF

* * *

Tuesday [15 Oct. 1946]

Dear R.

We have just finished our fancy dinner with the creamed tuna fish. It didn't exactly cream, but it tasted mighty fine. The guest brought a pumpkin pie. I furnished lettuce and canned apricots. Just before dinner, I got an angel food cake from Frank and Josie. Haven't tasted it yet but it looks fine.

The chokers and kleenex haven't come, but I appreciate them. 10½ size stocking.

There is a nest of pigeons over our door. They make various interesting noises and are now falling out of the nest daily.

Edna cleans up the plumbing mess. Fortunately, the plumbers don't come through here.

Duchess must be spending most of her time on the floor these days. Tell her to watch out for pins.

I am certainly enjoying the mayonnaise. Am anxious to see the chokers.

Regards to kin.

Love,

MF

* * *

Wednesday [16 Oct. 1946]

Dear R.

The kleenex and chokers haven't come yet but I am looking forward to seeing them this afternoon.

The roommate is going to Des Moines (home) tonight and won't be back until Sunday, so I will have the jernt to myself. She has gotten fouled up with her veterans pay or something and has to go see about it.

Know Miss Mary is going to enjoy her trip (suppose you will too). Too bad you didn't get more chickens this summer.

I would rather have cookies like last year—plain with raisins—that would be mighty fine. I could use about a cup of that sugar in a little cloth sack, for my liquor, you know. (I have used it twice) (two teaspoonfuls).

Regards to my kin.

    Love,

    MF

\* \* \*

Friday [18 Oct. 1946]

Dear R.

The chokers came yesterday with the kleenex and both are appreciated. I like both chokers—the plainest better I believe, although I have things that both will go with. Put polish on them this A.M. The rosary beads and the crackers came this morning. I wish the crackers could last as long as the rosary beads. I am much obliged for all your sending.

You should see me eating my dinner now. I have a half head of lettuce and a can of sardines—very fine—the stewed apricots, a bowl of asparagus soup and numerous small items to remind me that life can be beautiful. Do you know where I could pick up a small electric dish washer?

They haven't sent me the *Accents* yet but they are busy people.

Enjoyed Cousin Katie's letter.

Regards to kin.

    Love,

    MF

P.S. These are the finest sardines I ever ate—7¢ a can—Admiral—great big ones.

\* \* \*

Saturday [19 Oct. 1946]

Dear R.

Found me a jar of mineral oil salad dressing today and promptly bought it. It doesn't taste bad and is better than nothing. I haven't finished what you sent me by any means—I give it about two weeks more.

There is nothing going on around here. I expect the roommate back tomorrow night and that will be plenty soon enough.

I went to see about my fur coat yesterday and it was there. They said if I would bring in the ring that was off the front of it, they would put it on. I don't imagine they will charge me much, but I remember the trouble you had getting it on last year, so I reckon anything will be cheap. They'll send the coat up next week. It looks just like it did last year to me.

Trust my Aunt Mary had a fine time at Mrs. Tarleton's.

Regards to Mrs. Logan.

> Love,
> MF

* * *

### Monday [21 Oct. 1946]

Dear R.

Didn't get to write you yesterday. Sunday is always a hard day, and I had given out of my stamped envelopes, postcards, stamps etc. Yesterday the roommate, her mama, sister, and prospective brother-in-law all trooped in and made themselves at home. It is hard for me to know what to do with myself when they arrive. Also, I don't think the brother-in-law ought to be brought back to use our bathroom, but there's nothing I can do about that.

Had a letter from Cousin Katie today. She wants Peter's address, but I don't have it. I guess she wrote you about Dan O'Connor going to get married after Christmas.

Glad to get the manuscript. There is still *one* out which I want, however.

Too bad about the duck. Hope you kill the other before the dogs do.

Nothing doing around here but work.

Regards to kin.

> Love,
> MF

* * *

### Tuesday [22 Oct. 1946]

Dear R.

It was a great surprise to see that box and all that food. Brother. Particularly delighted with the sausages, chicken dinner, mayonnaise, dates, salad dressing, and kleenex. Also the sugar. Many grateful utterances for it all. I will write Gussie.

This morning at A&P, I found some vanilla and butterscotch pudding, which I plan to brew up.

I have an appointment at 3 this afternoon at the barber's to get my hair cut—it is too long on top to be managed easily. Trust he will do a decent job.

Bought myself some mineral oil today, as I had a little pain in my side—all right now. Couldn't get anything with vitamin D added—they had never heard of such anywhere. I got Squibb's, however, so it should be all right.

The weather here has certainly been handsome so far.

Regards to my kin.

That food. Brother. How did Gussie get that mayonnaise? Man.

> Love,
> MF

* * *

Wednesday [23 Oct. 1946]

Dear R.

Have just finished a handsome lunch of chicken dinner (1/2 can), eggs, green peas, prunes, and butterscotch pudding. Mighty fine.

The phone here is Extension 8465—however, I don't believe in calling that distance unless you got something to say. If I ever sell another story, I might call you. I know you will enjoy the phone in your room. Is the number the same? I presume it is an extension.

I was delighted with the barber's job. He was very nice indeed and knew his business. Only charged me 25¢. Cut the top down so it didn't have to be pinned up—didn't bother anything else.

How did Doctor enjoy his Chicago trip? Miss Mary her Atlanta trip?

Where is Tony Hardy coming from? Does Joan like GSCW any better now? I am beginning to wonder, will I take the plane or the train at Christmas. Every time I think of the trip last year at Christmas, I get pale. I reckon I will take another chance on the train, though.

Regards to kin.

> Love,
> MF

* * *

Thursday [24 Oct. 1946]

Dear R.

The package hasn't come yet, but I am again looking forward to it this afternoon. It takes packages a long time. I had letters from Miss Josie O'Byrn and Miss Bancroft today.

Bought me some dried apricots and cooked them this morning with the pineapple juice I had left over from the can of pineapple, since I didn't have any sugar. I mean they taste mighty fine.

I had to lend the roommate six dollars to get home with. Her government checks have been tied up, and that was what she had to go home to see about.

The weather is wet and cold here again.

Be sure to see that none of my manuscripts came when you were in Atlanta, which Sister might have stuck somewhere, also letters. Those manuscripts have been out a long time.

Glad you got the beads. I thought all the blessings were the same. Sorry you have had to send so many packages. It looks like every week I have been after something else.

Wish Doctor would come over here on the Rocket and see this place, but I reckon he is back in Atlanta by now.

Regards to kin.

    Love,

    MF

* * *

Thursday [24 Oct. 1946]

Dear R.

Well, on my way out to a class this A.M., I passed Jo Hunt. I got her telephone number and will call her sometime. She works in the President's office and looked very well. I don't know when I'll get to call her up.

Wrote Gussie and Mary Virginia the thank-you letters today.

Next Saturday is a big football day, and the roommate's kin will arrive at 11 and have dinner (in this room), and thence depart for the game. I plan to spend the day in the library.

The weather here today is wet and rotten. I reckon it's an indication of the winter coming.

Finished my chicken dinner today—mighty fine.

The house is having a party tomorrow night. Very social people this year.

Regards to kin.

    Love,

    MF

* * *

Friday [25 Oct. 1946]

Dear R.

Nothing doing around here but people worrying about is it going to rain for their football game. The roommate has bought pies, coffee, and so forth to serve her kin. I won't come in until I know they're off. She is going back to Des Moines with them for the weekend. I enjoy having such a traveling roommate.

Enjoyed seeing the pictures of Mrs. King's daughter. They must be has money.

Bought me some instant Sanka today, as I can't sleep drinking the other at night.

Regards to kin.

> Love,
> MF

* * *

Saturday [26 Oct. 1946]

Dear R.

I am hiding out at the library now until the football fiends get out of our room. I hope they will be gone when I get back.

Enclosed are the pictures. I think they are very good ones. I am going to have a couple more of the ones of Cousin Katie and Miss Josie and you made and send them to them.

At the party last night, some innocent little boy and I played bridge for three hours with two Jewish gentlemen who were sharks. We beat them by a good many points. It was very funny.

Got two of your letters yesterday so presume I won't get one today.

Made me up some vanilla pudding this morning and put some chopped up dates in it—mighty fine.

Regards to kin.

> Love,
> MF

P.S. Send the Florencourt picture to them the next time you write them.

* * *

Sunday [27 Oct. 1946]

Dear R.

Got home yesterday at 1 o'clock to find Sarah's brother and cousin ensconced in the chairs and Sarah gone off to the game. Saw them through the door, so I went on back to the library. They had left when I came back at 1:45. Returned at 5, so out I went again. I was powerful glad when they went on off to Des Moines. Sarah went with them and will be back tonight. Barbara has gone home, too. The plush rug kid having a family reunion in the next room. Her mother is very nice and gave me a piece of cake.

I will be glad when all this football mess is done with. It is a lot of crooked rot. I have never seen so many drunk people as after it yesterday afternoon. Sarah said there were sharks in town selling tickets to it for $50 a piece.

How did Doctor enjoy Chicago?

Weather is still most pleasant around here.

Regards to kin.

> Love,
> MF

* * *

Monday [28 Oct. 1946]

Dear R.

Had half a can of vienna sausages for dinner with vegetable soup—very fine.

Too bad about the duck. If he doesn't get happy at Daniel's, send him out to Miss Fannie's.

Nothing doing around here but work. Sarah came in at 10:30 last night and Barbara at 12. They don't bother me coming through at night to the bathroom.

Have an appointment with Mr. Klonsky, Engle's assistant, this afternoon. He is going to work with me the first part of this semester. He seems to be a good critic.

Regards to kin.

> Love,
> MF

* * *

Tuesday [29 Oct. 1946]

Dear R.

Got your Friday and Saturday letters today, both postmarked 26th. How do you work that business? I prefer to get one a day.

The hair ain't bangs—it's just shorter. I have ordered some Accents through the bookstore, so keep your shirt on.

What does Betty Semmes look like? I never liked her much. Will see about the bank statement.

I am working every minute these days and enjoying it and don't need to go to any football games.

I didn't get a Recorder this week.

Regards to kin.

    Love,

    MF

* * *

Wednesday [30 Oct. 1946]

Dear R.

Didn't get any letter today. Yesterday they sent me two *Accents*. I will mail one to you and the other to Cousin Katie. The bookstore is going to get me ten, so don't be passing yours around promiscuously. I won't be able to get them off today or I doubt tomorrow, as I am struggling to get a paper in.

It is turning cold now.

Sarah only has one friend coming to the game next Saturday, and that will be the last one played here, so I am very thankful.

There is a book in one of those bookcases, either the one in my room or the anteroom, that I want. It is called Modern Literature or Contemporary Literature or something like that. Anyway, look inside it and see if T. S. Eliot's poem: The Wasteland is in it. If it is, I would like you to send me the book. I am pretty sure the poem is in that book. The book has short stories and poems in it, and I think there is a jacket on it. I will have to pay $2.50 for the poem if I don't get it in the book I have. I have already had to spend $10 for books this semester and have some more yet to come. So I would like to save this.

Regards to kin.

    Love,

    MF

* * *

Thursday [31 Oct. 1946]

Dear R.

Hope Doctor gets to call up as it would be nice to talk to him. Have wrapped the *Accents* up and will mail them tomorrow after church.

It has gotten so cold that today we had to turn the heat on in the house. I don't reckon it will be long before winter gets here. I asked at a department store about long drawers, but they had sold out.

How is the duck doing at Darnell's?

No news around here. I am going to see "Anna and the King of Siam."

Regards to kin.

    Love,

    MF

* * *

Friday [1 Nov. 1946]

Dear R.

Tell Miss Mary I enjoyed the clipping.

I think I will have them send my coat up tomorrow as it is sho nuf cold now. Also wet today—generally disagreeable. I presume they will have a sloppy game. Sarah is having a friend arrive at 10 A.M. from Des Moines.

Miss Nutter is still here; also Ruth. Gloria is supervisor. She leaves in February, and I think Sarah is going to try to get her job, as she needs the money. That will mean a new roommate for me.

I didn't get my Recorder this week. How come?

What ails Darnell?

Regards to kin.

    Love,

    MF

* * *

Saturday [2 Nov. 1946]

Dear R.

Got an airmail letter from Miss Hallie asking for something for the Corinthian, so I sent her something. Everything around here has gone off to the football game, so I have the prospects of a quiet afternoon.

Visited the A&P today but didn't get anything spectacular. The stores close for the football game.

The plush rug kid took us to ride last night—very interesting.

They were supposed to send my coat up today, but they didn't. It cost $9.50.

When is Uncle going to visit his spouse? I think I will come on the 13th.

Regards to kin.

> Love,
> MF

* * *

Sunday [3 Nov. 1946]

Dear R.

Sarah is having a friend to supper for sandwiches tonight, so that is something to be bothered with. I hope the friend leaves early so I can study. It is sometimes hard to get anything done.

Now please make an appointment with Dr. Rogers for me. Do it this year please. You will save both time, trouble, and money. I will be home by the 18th at least. I think I will come by the 13th, but don't make the appointment but for after the 18th, as I may change my plans. Make it with Dr. Zateau, if you'd rather.

Nothing doing around here. Regards to kin.

> Love,
> MF

* * *

Monday [4 Nov. 1946]

Dear R.

Got two letters from you today as usual and two Recorders, both the same issue. What ails them?

Got my coat now, but it is not quite cold enough for it. I hang it on the outside door on a hook instead of in the closet.

Made me some applesauce today out of canned pie apples. Most tasty.

I wish you would let Miss Hallie read the story in *Accent* if you get a chance.

Must be off to see Brother Klonsky—Russian Jew, I presume—very fine.

Regards to kin.

> Love,
> MF

\* \* \*

Tuesday [5 Nov. 1946]

Dear Regina,

The box yesterday was a great surprise and certainly handsome. The kleenex are a great help, also the stockings. I will enjoy the pineapple and chicken dinner and sausages—my! I now have enough mayonnaise to last into the spring. Everybody has enjoyed the candy, which I passed around.

Got two letters from you today, so presume there won't be one tomorrow. Dare say you are glad Aunt Tarleton has went whence she came. How long did the agony last?

Too bad the poem isn't in the book. Out goes $2.50 more.

Wrote Cousin Katie today. Am still trying to get to writing Bessie.

Regards to kin.

Love,

MF

P.S. One of the girls in the house knows Dr. Dolan—says he is a wonderful doctor.

\* \* \*

Wednesday [6 Nov. 1946]

Dear R.

Did not hear from you today, as I got two letters yesterday. Doctor has not called, so I presume he didn't have time.

If you get any more of those perfumed things send them to me. I use them for bookmarks and when I misplace the book, can smell where it is. Handy.

I wrote Bessie today; glad to have that over with. Hope I won't have any more people to write.

Still not cold enough here for the fur coat. Don't believe the winter is going to get here. I mean to call Jo Hunt tomorrow. I really don't have time.

Regards to kin.

Love,

MF

\* \* \*

Thursday [7 Nov. 1946]

Dear R.

Didn't get any letter from you yesterday or today. Hope nothing ails you.

Sarah was sick all night and is sick today. She says it is enteritis. She plans to go home Friday, so I hope she gets to go. I also hope I don't get what she's got. But I am very healthy. I hope she hasn't got the flu.

The weather is cold and damp.

Nothing doing but work.

Regards to kin.

>Love,
>MF

\* \* \*

Friday [8 Nov. 1946]

Dear R.

Sarah is still sick but over her fever and nausea—recuperating, I dare say. She isn't going home, unfortunately. The nurse from Currier came over to see her last night and said she had that enteritis. I feel fine.

Dare say you are wearing the *Accent* out.

The $9.50 for the coat was the storage charge, and (.50) charge for sewing the hook on it, i.e., you pay when you take it out. I don't think that was so bad.

Had a can of smoked fillet of herring for my entree at dinner—very fine.

Coming home the 13th will only be coming a week early and since the deal costs 75 bucks, I think I ought to make it pay. It costs me approximately 10 dollars a week to live here.

Regards to kin.

>Love,
>MF

\* \* \*

Saturday [9 Nov. 1946]

Dear R.

Doctor called last night, as I presume he has told you, but I was at supper. I traced the call and called him this morning and talked to him a couple of minutes. He said he would see you tonight.

Was supposed to dine with Miss Nutter this evening but she canceled the invitation, as she had an invitation to go to Cedar Rapids.

Sarah is up today and staggering around. It looks like snow.

Thought Anna and the King of Siam was poor.

Enclose a letter from Cousin Katie.

I doubt seriously whether the little Garners will be remembered by me on the 16th. Don't you think that's straining it a little?

Regards to kin.

> Love,
> MF

* * *

### Sunday [10 Nov. 1946]

Dear R.

Sarah is still poorly. Can't keep any of her food down. Certainly hope the rest of us are spared. I feel fine.

It is sho nuf cold today, and we presume it's going to snow. I would like to have that good lamp in my room at home, here. I think it might pay in the long run. I don't know how you could send it easily. Please advise.

Nothing doing hereabouts.

Regards to kin.

> Love,
> MF

* * *

### Monday [11 Nov. 1946]

Dear R.

Waited for the mail today and then realized that it was Armistice and it wouldn't be delivered—therefore, I should get three letters tomorrow.

Ate the can of chicken dinner today, and it was mighty fine.

Pretty cold here, but I still haven't had to wear the fur coat. Hate to think of what it's going to be like in a couple of weeks around here.

Sarah seems to be all right now. She is going to go home sometime before Thanksgiving and get her car and bring it down here for a few weeks. Said she would take us out to one of these German colonies, which should be interesting.

Regards to kin.
> Love,
> MF

* * *

Tuesday [12 Nov. 1946]

Dear R.

Got 4 of your letters today—quite a haul. The appointment at the dentist is OK. I will be there on the 13th, I am pretty sure. Going down to get my ticket sometime soon.

What did Dr. Beiswanger think about the story—I thought you said you showed it to him.

I couldn't read Doctor's letter.

Haven't read the articles yet.

I must be off to the A&P.

Regards to kin.
> Love,
> MF

* * *

Wednesday [13 Nov. 1946]

Dear R.

No letter from you today but the enclosed from Bessie. It is warm again here, and I am powerful glad and feel I can venture out to stock my larder for the winter. We are on our way to the market.

Ruth and I are entertaining Miss Nutter tomorrow night at one of the local hash houses. She has asked us to her place a couple of times, so this is the payoff.

Barbara thought she was getting the flu last night, but she took the proper precautions and now she feels all right. I trust. I feel fine. I hope I don't come down with anything on the 12th.

Regards to kin.
> Love,
> MF

\* \* \*

Thursday [14 Nov. 1946]

Dear R.

I went to the 10¢ store today and all that junk was just too cheap, also too dif-ficult to get wrapped properly—also, you didn't tell me what the occasion is—was—birthday, Thanksgiving, what? Anyway, I didn't get them anything. If you want to get them something from the 10¢ store at home and tell them it's from me, what's the difference?

I mailed Duchess a little package this morning that I picked up at the grocery store. Sarah eats them, but I hadn't seen them before and thought Duchess might enjoy some. Maybe you have them at home, but I never saw them.

Forgot to enclose the letter from Bessie, I see—which I will do today.

Sarah started cooking hamburgers for her dinner today. Put them on in a glass skillet, which immediately exploded all over the room. I think the glass was cold or something. She cleaned the glass up and is now eating the hamburgers, having cleaned the glass off them and cooked them on Barbara's sandwich grill.

She is going home tomorrow for the weekend, so the place should be quiet—no radio. Ugh, that radio.

Regards to Darnel.

Love,
MF

\* \* \*

Friday [15 Nov. 1946]

Dear R.

Engle has invited a few of the workshop people to have dinner at the Jefferson next Wednesday with a Mr. Selby—a novelist and publisher connected with Farrar and Rinehart. He asked a couple of us for two stories each which Selby will read and, I hope, talk personally to us about. I am happy that he invited me. It should be interesting, and these are the connections that will help someday. At present I am busy getting my two stories ready.

Reckon Uncle will enjoy himself while Miss Mary is off. Is he going home for the Yuletide with his spouse? Or is said spouse coming to him?

I thought May Cash was going to live in Atlanta? How does she look?

Regards to kin.

Love,
MF

P.S. Who is Dorothy Woods's victim?

\* \* \*

### Saturday [16 Nov. 1946]

Dear R.

Sarah got off yesterday, so it is very peaceful with no radio etc. Ruth has gone to Chicago for the weekend. She said she was going to call Peter up and tell him hello. It is raining here and cold again, so I reckon this is the last of the decent weather.

They tell me if you want to buy shoes before they go up, you had better do it now. I may get a pair if I can find what I want.

I was out with Klonsky yesterday, and he says Selby is *the* publisher himself of Farrar and Rinehart and has a lot of money to give away. Hope I get to talk to him personally.

Glad you are sending the lamp. Hope it is not too hard to send.

Had a letter from Miss Hallie thanking me for the stuff and returning the postage.

Regards to kin.

    Love,

    MF

\* \* \*

### Sunday [17 Nov. 1946]

Dear R.

We are expecting Sarah to bring her car home with her. Barbara tells me that you can buy fine wool material very cheaply at these colonies around here so when Sarah takes us, I am going to look at some. They have the mills there or something. I need a wool dress and I might buy the material for it. Would you like some for yourself?

We had chicken at the Union today—very fine. That is certainly the cheapest place to eat.

Sarah's cousin manages the largest A&P in Iowa, and she plans to go there this weekend and pick up some groceries. Very handy.

Wore the fur coat today and felt like a medium-sized monster but very warm.

Trust the Garner function was a success.

Regards to kin.

    Love,

    MF

\* \* \*

Monday [18 Nov. 1946]

Dear R.

The three packages came today, and I was powerful happy to get it all. I have the lamp set up and in operation. It is really a fine improvement. By the time I was through unpacking it and establishing it, I was so hungry I opened the chicken a la king and ate it—all. Whew! That's fine stuff—plenty of chicken in that. Will enjoy the rest as much.

Sarah didn't bring her car, because it turned suddenly so cold and she didn't want it to sit out, so I don't reckon we will get to Amana until after the winter.

Enjoyed Louise's letter—typical Florencourt stuff—what?

I am going down to get my ticket Thursday, I think. Can't take any time off until this Selby business is over.

That is certainly a shame about Viola. How did you hear about it? What was wrong with her?

Who is renting your apartments now?

Regards to kin.

> Love,
> MF

\* \* \*

Tuesday [19 Nov. 1946]

Dear R.

See in the paper where there will be a coal shortage if J. L. Lewis gets excited about the labor situation and that the trains will be cut down as to passenger service. I am thinking about the plane again. Don't know what I'll do, however. If I get a plane, I am going to get one to Macon so I won't have to spend the night in Atlanta. Ruth is going to Chicago with me.

Had a note from Edith which I thought mighty nice of her. Saw Florence's thing—very nice.

Gloria is sick today. Everybody is getting fluish it looks like. I feel fine.

Just listening to the radio—says if strike, last 80% of railroads will be cut off. Oh well.

Regards to kin.

> Love,
> MF

\* \* \*

Wednesday [20 Nov. 1946]

Dear R.

On my way to the Jefferson to eat with the workshop people and Selby. Hope he gets here.

It was Ruth, not Gloria, and I who took Miss Nutter out. I seldom see Gloria (thank the Lord). She is still sick.

I bought a $10 Knox hat for $3 at a sale yesterday. It is brown and plain and very nice.

———

Just returned from dinner. Selby's plane grounded in Moline, so he won't be here until tonight, and we are invited to a party for him again after the workshop meeting tonight. Liquor party, I presume. Engle has a very fine stock of that.

Regards to kin.

    Love,

    MF

\* \* \*

Thursday [21 Nov. 1946]

Dear R.

Certainly hope Dr. Nippert can say Ben Harrison doesn't have the lupus; however, I imagine they can do more for it now than 5 years ago.

Engle had us out last night after the workshop for drinks, and I had a very fine time. Selby didn't get in until too late to read our manuscripts but asked that they be sent him so Engle says he will do that. I liked Selby very much.

Have gone on and gotten train reservations as the plane connections to Macon are poor and I fear it is too late to get them for Atlanta. Selby was held up for 8 hours at the Chicago airport because of fog.

Thank Miss Mary profusely for the pictures which I think are good and enjoy sporting around.

They say it's going to snow here.

Regards to kin.

    Love,

    MF

P.S. I gather Duchess didn't like the Cocoa Wheats? The way they tasted, that is.

* * *

Friday [22 Nov. 1946]

Dear R.

No letter from you today as I got two yesterday. Had a letter from Cousin Katie, however, and she said she was sending me a box for Thanksgiving, which I think handsome of her.

I called the airport today and have asked for plane reservations for the 13th just in case. I don't know whether they can get them for me. At any rate, I feel safer doing it with the coal strike started. I could get to Chicago without any trouble, as the Rockets are diesel trains, but Dixie Limited is a steam one, so would probably be stopped. If I get the plane reservation out of Chicago, I will go to Chicago on the early Rocket and thus save $5, as the plane fare from Iowa City to Chicago is twice as much as the railroads, although the two are the exact same from Chicago to Atlanta.

Sarah is going home Wednesday and [will] stay over Thanksgiving. I should get a lot of work done.

Regards to kin.

Love,
MF

* * *

Saturday [23 Nov. 1946]

Dear R.

We are in Cedar Rapids and I bought a pair of shoes—$8.95—imitation skin and very nice—said terminates my purchases for the year. I think eight dollars was cheap for them.

Connie has the flu now.

What are they going to do about Ben, since they don't know for sure if it's the lupus?

We have to be off to catch the electric train back.

Regards to kin.

Love,
MF

* * *

Sunday [24 Nov. 1946]

Dear R.

We were powerful tired when we got back from Cedar Rapids, what with wearing those heavy coats. I get tired twice as quick when I wear it. The lining in it, by the way, is beginning to slip and show at the bottom. I presume something will have to be done about that soon.

Today it is hot again and going to rain. I will almost be glad when it gets cold and stays that way.

Connie is all right now. This flu gets them for about two days, it seems.

Regards to kin.

    Love,
    MF

* * *

Monday [25 Nov. 1946]

Dear R.

This going home business is a rare mess. I can get plane reservations and train reservations and have to pay for whichever I decide on by the 29th. Both are a risk—if I give up one and the other goes down at the time I get ready to go, I am out of luck.

The plane reservation, if I pay for it, is to Atlanta—gets there at 8:30 P.M. or something around there, so I guess I would have to have a hotel room. I hope the strike will clear and I can come on the train, as I don't want to be stuck in Chicago if the weather is too bad for flying. I am going to get a Chicago paper and try to find out if the Dixie Limited is expected to continue running.

By the way, you don't worry about getting a non-stop flight—you worry about getting a flight.

Will be delighted to get the box with the usual contents. Don't know where I will eat my Thanksgiving dinner.

Fixed my fur coat last night—the lining and the things that hook it.

Regards to kin.

    Love,
    MF

* * *

Tuesday [26 Nov. 1946]

Dear R.

Visited the A&P today and found some brussel sprouts (fresh) that were so old they had reduced them to 10¢ a box, so I bought a box and fixed them for my dinner. Oh, they were mighty fine.

Last night we killed a mouse.

Sarah is feeling poorly, but I certainly hope she goes home tomorrow as planned. Barbara is going home, too. It will be very quiet and conducive to work.

Still don't know what I'll do about the trip home. Guess I will buy both train and plane tickets and then cancel the one I don't want. You have to cancel them 24 hours before they are for, if you want to get your money back. I should know by then. I can't find out from the papers whether the Dixie Limited is still going. Please ask Louis to find out and drop me a card—else I will have to call Chicago. Do this soon, kindly.

Regards to kin.

Love,

MF

* * *

Wednesday [27 Nov. 1946]

Dear R.

Got your box and Cousin Katie's both today. My word! Between the two of you, I could eat until spring without going to the A&P. I will enjoy the cookies particularly. Cousin Katie sent me two jars of rum soakies, a box of FFV cookies, benne candy, almond nuts etc. I imagine she had a good time getting it together. I think I'll keep some of it for Duchess.

I am on my way to the railroad station to purchase my ticket.

Peculiar about dear Lois Hatchet. Is Mrs. Hatchet going to get to go to the wedding?

We (Ruth and I) were supposed to dine at Miss Nutter's tonight, but she called, she has a cold—so it is postponed.

Must be off. I am certainly going to have a fine Thanksgiving with that chicken a la king and those cookies and pineapple and all of it.

Regards to kin.

Love,

MF

Sarah leaving this afternoon.

* * *

Thursday [28 Nov. 1946]

Dear R.

It is very peaceful around here today. Sarah left yesterday afternoon; she was driving with the plush rug kid about 40 miles up the road and was going to hitch-hike from there. Barbara left last night.

A good many of the people went to Cedar Rapids for dinner, but I prefer to stay here and work and eat chicken a la king.

Yesterday when I got in from buying my ticket ($56.50 round trip) I found a cake here from Frank and Josie—a big one. It looked like somebody had played football with it on the way, but it tastes fine. I think it was very nice of them to send it.

Last Thanksgiving, it snowed here, but today is warm enough for my light coat. Regards to kin. I am certainly enjoying the cookies.

 Love,
 MF

* * *

Friday [29 Nov. 1946]

Dear R.

Got your Sunday and Monday letters today and enjoyed. You seem to get my mail quicker than I get yours, or maybe it is just the way you date them.

Went to Cedar Rapids with Sarah and Barbara when I went.

Too bad about Katherine Cline and her poor health.

Glad you got invited to the Hatcher ceremony. Dare say it was a howl.

Nothing doing around here but work. I am enjoying the peace and quiet.

Regards to kin. Is Uncle still in Atlanta? Will he be home for Christmas?

 Love,
 MF

P.S. Enclosed that clipping you asked for which I have forgotten to do previously.

* * *

Saturday [30 Nov. 1946]

Dear R.

The enclosed I got from Eberharts today. What is it all about? I didn't say any-thing to her about wanting any miniature for you. I think they are silly and par-ticularly if you've already got a picture. If you want me to get the thing, however, send me back the bill and I'll send her a check. If not, please call up and say you don't want it—unless they've already made it and I certainly can't remember telling them to do any such thing, which I think would be ridiculous.

Billie must be nuts. The more I read the thing, the more it looks like they've already made it—and I see .50 charged for Mrs. Hines's print. Pay for that anyway. I am puzzled by all this.

Had a sore throat yesterday, but bought some merthyolate and it is all right today. Tried all over town to have Doctor's gargle filled, but they say they (the doctors) don't use that combination around here and none of the places had the hydroliptol to put in it. However, the merthyolate took care of it and at less expense.

Regards to kin.

    Love,

    MF

I read that thing again, and it certainly looks like they have already made it. Just find out and if they have, send the bill back to me and let me pay it, as I don't care to have them think you pay for your own Christmas presents—although I didn't know that was what I am giving you. Hmp.

* * *

Sunday [1 Dec. 1946]

Dear R.

Nothing doing hereabouts. My 10 copies of Accent came last night. I am sending one to – Agnes – Margaret & Ben – Frank and Josie – Frank and Ida – and will bring the others home. I thought I might give one to Mary Virginia if she would like to have it and one to Mrs. Hines. I see I got too many copies.

I trust you have attended to the Eberhart business. I certainly don't recall telling her I wanted any miniature.

I am enclosing a little picture of Engle out of the Chicago paper. Thought you might like to see what he looks like.

Regards to kin.

    Love,

    MF

* * *

Monday [2 Dec. 1946]

Dear R.

Sarah brought her car back this time, so we are going out to the Amanas some-time this week. I doubt if we get to the wool place, however. If I ever see a cheap, reduced wool dress, I will just get it.

It seems we are entertaining again tomorrow for dinner here—some of Sarah's friends—bacon is on the menu, I believe.

The Hatcher wedding sounded very Hatcherish—also the Garner party very Garnerish. Hope nothing radically wrong with Madame G.

Has turned terrifically cold here, and Sarah predicts snow before the week is out.

Regards to kin.

Love,

MF

* * *

Tuesday [3 Dec. 1946]

Dear R.

I see on the outside of your letter that you did not ask Louis about finding out if the Dixie Limited was running. Will you *please* do this. Naturally if I could find out in any more direct way I would—the station here does not know, as I asked them before I asked you. The only way I can find out is to call Chicago, which is not satisfactory. Please find out and write me.

I paid for the plane reservation today. I have both now but will have to relin-quish one or the other 24 hours before leaving. If I have to fly, I will get in Atlanta at 8:15 P.M. Friday 13 and presume will need a hotel room, but would rather *much rather* take a night bus to Milledgeville, if there is such. Since that will probably be 7:15 Atlanta time, perhaps I could.

Naturally, I won't bring two coats home or any unnecessary clothes. I will have to bring my typewriter, as I will have to write a couple of hours a day.

Sarah is going home this weekend. She drove me to the airport, and it was a great help. We are going to the Amanas Thursday. Regards to kin.

Love,

MF

* * *

Wednesday [4 Dec. 1946]

Dear R.

Was most amazed to hear about Mr. Wood. How did he do it?

Papers say today that 50% of the passenger travel will be cut beginning Sunday. I am mighty glad I have the plane ticket. Of course, if the weather is bad, I will be out of luck there and will have to come back to Iowa City I suppose. Hope Darnell gets where she wants to go.

The weather is fine again here. It is amazing, but there have not been over 10 cold days since I came and no snow.

Went to see "Green Years" last night. It was punk.

Enclose letter from Miss Bancroft.

Regards to kin.

> Love,
> MF

* * *

Thursday [5 Dec. 1946]

Dear R.

You better be careful how you invite non-Catholics to hear missionaries you haven't heard yet. Some of them have mighty small minds and represent the church poorly.

Tonight we are going to the Amanas—Sarah, Barbara, Ruth, me, and a WAVE that was in Milledgeville—Jean French. They say the food at these places is very fine—famous over the country.

The strike looks bad, and I am glad I have a plane ticket.

Went to a lecture last night with Ruth and Klonsky and then to the tail end of a concert. Some pianist, very good.

It is so warm here, no coat is necessary.

Regards to kin.

> Love,
> MF

P.S. Why is Jane Patterson going to live in Milledgeville? Where's her husband?

* * *

Saturday [7 Dec. 1946]

Dear R.

Got your special today and am obliged to you. I will call Chicago anyway to make sure before giving up the plane reservation. They are talking of having the University run through the Christmas holidays, i.e., no holidays. I will come home as planned unless they decide to do this before the 13th.

Glad Mrs. McCullar liked the story.

How is Katherine Cline's health? You never said how they found her.

Nothing doing around here but work.

I met Jo Hunt's husband the other day but have not had supper with them yet. Don't have time.

Regards to kin.

 Love,
 MF

* * *

Sunday [8 Dec. 1946]

Dear R.

Will call and cancel my plane reservations tomorrow. Am mighty thankful John L. decided in this manner.

Have been reading about the Winecoff fire. It must have been a terrible thing.

I will probably send my laundry kit with a pair of shoes and a sweater or something in it. Don't know when I'll get to that, however.

Regards to kin.

 Love,
 MF

* * *

Monday [9 Dec. 1946]

Dear R.

Had a letter from Louise Trovato today. She likes her work but not California. I never have gotten around to writing John Sullivan, so haven't heard from him.

Thought the Frances letter enclosed in yours was most Florencourtish.

Think Miss Mary was mighty nice to bring us dresses and will tell her so when I get there.

Yesterday it was so hot here, you didn't need a coat. Is wet and cold today. I am hoping I will avoid the sinus this vacation.

Regards to kin.

Love,

MF

* * *

Tuesday [10 Dec. 1946]

Dear R.

It will not be necessary for anybody to meet me in Atlanta. Ruth and I plan to have a look around in Chicago, as I'll have about eight hours if the train gets there as scheduled.

That letter of Cousin Katie's sounded as if she had two copies of my story. How is that?

The weather here is very fine.

Regards to kin. I will not write you again.

Love,

MF

* * *

Tuesday [7 Jan. 1947]

Dear R.

Got here last night around ten. Train from Atlanta was 4 hours late, so I was glad I had the 5 o'clock reservation, but came to find at 5 o'clock when I got to get on the train that there was no such car as they had given me a seat on—they had left a numeral off the car number or something. They finally let me on; also Milton, who was at the gate but with no reservation.

Ruth came in this morning on the plane. It is not so cold here.

I called Mrs. Curtis up and talked to her and looked the Mrs. Bowden up, but she was not in the book.

I am powerful tired after all the train riding and plan to rest.

Regards to kin.

Love,

MF

\* \* \*

Wednesday [8 Jan. 1947]

[*On "Miss Mary Flanner O'Connor" notecard*]
Dear R.

Feel somewhat rested after the trip and am back to work. If Gloria graduates, Sarah will be supervisor and a friend of hers, another ex-WAVE, will move in with me. It will be a nice arrangement if it works out—all depends on if Gloria graduates in February.

My laundry case has not come yet. I went over to the education placement bureau today and made an appointment to talk to the head of it about job possibilities. Will see her tomorrow.

I trust you are in Savannah. I am sending the card to Milledgeville, however, instead of the letter.

The weather is very nice here.

Regards to Cousin Katie and Bessie.

     Love,
     MF

\* \* \*

Thursday [9 Jan. 1947]

Dear R.

Got your letter today and enjoyed it; yesterday the laundry case came—with a hole in it, but nothing was lost or damaged. I reckon it has seen its best days.

I have recuperated from the train travel now. I wrote Doctor and Louis and thanked them for their kindnesses etc. in regard to my arrival and departure etc. I will write Miss Mary as soon as I have time and tell her I had a nice time at home—which I did.

My bottle in the suitcase only leaked about a tablespoon, and that onto the kotex I had wrapped around it, so most of the contents are good for my winter use.

I saw the head of the placement bureau today. She seemed to think there would be no trouble at all in getting a teaching place of the kind I wanted. She said the salaries for where I would have to start would be around $2,400 a year. She said that was low, but it suits me. In fact, I doubt if I'll be able to get that much. I am applying at a couple of colleges in New York City and a couple out here and a couple in the Southwest.

You will be happy to learn that I have had another story accepted—this for an anthology put out by the James A. Decker Press and edited by one Alan Swallow of the University of Denver. The volume comes out in May. I will send you the letter when I get through with it. This is a very good thing. The story accepted is called "The Barber," and it will appear in the first volume of "New Signatures."

Regards to kin.

>    Love,
>    MF

* * *

Friday [10 Jan. 1947]

Dear R.

Will enclose the letter I got about the story but *please send it back return mail* as I will need it when Engle comes back, which I hear is next week. I doubt if he goes to GSCW.

It is slushy here with melting snow but very warm. I am to dine with Miss Nutter this P.M.

You had better watch out if your mouth continues sore; however, those things made my tongue feel peculiar. Ruth was taking them when she came back. She said if you took too many of them, you made yourself immune to penicillin. Her papa is a druggist.

Nothing doing here but work.

Regards to kin.

>    Love,
>    MF

* * *

Saturday [11 Jan. 1947]

Dear R.

Our plumbing backed up last night and the plumbers came and did something to it and today it has backed up again. Always something falling down around here.

Weather is very warm.

Sarah's father is very sick these days and in danger of dying. They have taken him to the mental hospital in Knoxville.

Sent my laundry out Tuesday and got it back today. Sent some pajamas and this time they didn't shrink.

Too bad about Madame Hodges and Jr.

Regards to kin.
>Love,
>MF

* * *

[Sunday 12 Jan. 1947]

[*On "Miss Mary Flannery O'Connor" notecard*]
Dear R.

Sunday, when nothing goes on, so I will use these fancy items. Turning pretty cold today. Plumbing back intact, but for how long, I wouldn't know. They say there are roots in the pipes. Trust you all are well. Regards to kin.

>Love,
>MF

* * *

Monday [13 Jan. 1947]

Dear R.

Got your two letters today and enjoyed them. You seem to be becoming a card shark of parts.

I am going to the A&P this afternoon to get my winter provisions so I won't have to go that far away from home again until spring when I presume it will thaw.

There are several of us who have to have application pictures taken, and we are going to the University photographer, where we can get it done more cheaply.

Found 4 Union Recorders here when I came but did not get one today. It may come tomorrow.

Hope Mary Virginia doesn't get stuck in the post office.

Plumbing has not acted up again so far. Do you still have the colored girl? Regards to kin.

>Love,
>MF

* * *

Tuesday [14 Jan. 1947]

Dear R.

Got your Friday and Saturday letters today and two January 9 Recorders. Enjoyed your letters and one of the Recorders. What is all that Carrington Woods business? Hope it won't decrease the value of your apartments.

I found Betty Patterson's address in my pocketbook where May had given it to me—3832 McArthur, Jacksonville.

Sarah did not bring her radio back with her, so we don't have as much music, which pleases me no end. I don't think the girl who will have the room with me next semester has one. It is very springlike today. The frying pan hasn't come, but I will be happy to see it when it does. I may buy some bacon or something now. Spam, I reckon, would be better.

The barber who cut my hair for 25¢ didn't have anything to do with the story. Regards to kin.

> Love,
> MF

* * *

Wednesday [15 Jan. 1947]

Dear R.

Got your airmail today and am much obliged for your sending the letter back. The girl who will, we hope, get this room is a friend of Sarah's—we eat supper with her at the Union every night. She is an ex-WAVE and all right. She works, and I am hoping will not be around much.

Amazed that the Garners are moving into that dump. I remember Miss Mary saying "but of course they wouldn't want to be out in Emris Heights or Penndale!" What does she think about this deal?

The books published in '47 by the Swallow Press are just the books they already have to publish. It doesn't concern me.

Herman [Talmadge] is headlined in the Daily Iowan today. Regards to kin.

> Love,
> MF

* * *

Thursday [16 Jan. 1947]

Dear R.

No letter from you today, I presume because of that airmail yesterday.

Today Sarah is in bed with the misery (cold) and Gloria is in the hospital with it. Gloria was to take her comprehensives and oral examinations tomorrow to graduate, and now she is in the hospital. We presume they will give them to her when she gets out, although I don't know.

Ate my individual date pudding for dessert this noon and put Gerber's pineapple pudding over it for a sauce. Hit won't bad.

I am going to have my application picture struck next week. They don't charge but 50¢ at the University photographers.

I have started drinking tea instead of coffee and think I like it better.

Still can't picture the Garners in that trap. What do they say about it?

Regards to kin.

    Love,

    MF

* * *

### Friday [17 Jan. 1947]

Dear R.

The skillet came just before I was fixing my lunch, so I had scrambled eggs. It is certainly a nice one and will alleviate much of the cramped conditions of mine utensils. Where did you get it?

Enjoyed Cousin Katie's letter. Too bad about Fred Doyle.

Saw Engle yesterday—he didn't get to Milledgeville. Said he passed through Waycross and wondered if Milledgeville was anywhere around.

Sarah is over her misery, but Gloria is still in the hospital.

Regards to kin.

    Love,

    MF

* * *

### Saturday [18 Jan. 1947]

Dear R.

This morning water started dripping through the walls where somebody had spilled a lot on the floor upstairs, but it is cleaned away now.

The weather is very fine here. No snow, no ice, no rain—clear and not too cold. Mighty fine.

Ruth either broke or sprained her wrist yesterday ice skating. She has it in a cast now.

When is Catherine Garner going to have this operation? Do you think you will be nursing little Garners?

Know you will enjoy having Mary Ann around.

Must be off. Regards to kin.

> Love,
> MF

P.S. I am going to buy me a can of Spam this afternoon.

* * *

[Sunday 19 Jan. 1947]

[*On "Miss Mary Flannery O'Connor" notecard*]

Dear R.

Sundays ought to use these things up. Nothing going on hereabouts. Ruth will have to have her arm in a cast for 2 weeks. Weather here so fine you hardly need a heavy coat. Regards to kin.

> Love,
> MF

* * *

Monday [20 Jan. 1947]

Dear R.

Unfortunately, I didn't save those papers. I don't know if the thing about the party was in it or not. It has taken to snowing here and to getting terrifically cold, and they say it will be this way until the middle of March. Gloria came home from the hospital Saturday afternoon after having just had her last (21st) penicillin shot. She washed her hair and sat up late and thereupon the next day was ready to go back to the hospital; however, she didn't. And is walking about today spreading her germs behind her.

How long do the Garners think they will have to be in that chicken house before they get to Carrington's Woods?

When are you going to Savannah?

I saw some buttermilk at the store the other day. I am going to try it, and if it is good, I think I'll get it instead of sweet milk.

Regards to kin.

> Love,
> MF

* * *

Tuesday [21 Jan. 1947]

Dear R.

Sho wish I had some of those shrimp Cousin Katie sent. I eat a lot of scrambled eggs now that I have the skillet. Haven't bought any bacon yet, but I plan to as soon as I eat up the Spam I have.

It is 5 above today, and I mean cold. I had to go out this morning, but I don't aim to do it again until supper time. Last night the wind went at 50 miles an hour.

When do the Garners move into this shack they're renting?

Regards to kin.

    Love,
    MF

* * *

Wednesday [22 Jan. 1947]

Dear R.

Enclosed is the picture I had taken at the University place. I don't like it, but I may go on and use it, or again I may have it taken over. What do you think?

Don't know why my letters don't get there on Saturday night. One day I put it in my pocket and forgot to mail it until the next day. That might have been it.

Sarah is going home this afternoon and [will] stay until Tuesday.

Why should the Garners expect even to get milk from the farm now they plan to leave it?

Has Mary Virginia been working in the library for $1 a day?

Regards to kin.

    Love,
    MF

* * *

Thursday [23 Jan. 1947]

Dear R.

Glad you like Mary Ann. How long is she going to be with you?

Sarah got off for home last night. They have taken her father to the sanitarium. He is pretty bad off, I gather. Martha Bell, the new roommate, will start moving in next Saturday. She is a nice girl and doesn't smoke, so I hope the room will quit smelling like tobacco. It is hot again here—first one thing and then another.

Is Doctor going to get you the car anytime soon?

I wondered if I could ask Ruth to come home with me a few weeks after school in June. I would like very much to have her. She would be no bother. ?

Regards to kin.

    Love,

    MF

* * *

Friday [24 Jan. 1947]

Dear R.

This should hit about at the time of your birthday. Happy birthday.

Yesterday I broke my coffee cup, and this morning I went downtown to get one. There is a shortage of them apparently, as I went to 3 10¢ stores and 4 hardware stores and couldn't get one. I finally ended up with a sugar dish—it is shaped like a cup, has two handles and a top, but it does very well.

By the way, did I tell you that the light shade is a great help. I hope you were able to get another one. If not I'll send this back.

Got a withholding statement from the University saying they had paid me $150 last year and had not withheld anything. I gather I don't have to file anything since my year's accumulation will not total $500. So nice to be poor.

Barbara went home, too, so there is only myself and plush rug kid in this half of the house.

Regards to kin.

    Love,

    MF

* * *

Saturday [25 Jan. 1947]

Dear R.

Ate at the Union this noon for a change and had apple fritters—never had tasted such before. They weren't anything but fried muffins with an occasional piece of apple in them, but very nice.

Gloria just came back from taking her oral exam which she passed, so she will graduate. So much for her around here. She has a job in Kansas City.

Nothing doing but work.

Regards to kin.

    Love,

    MF

* * *

[Sunday 26 Jan. 1947]

[*On "Miss Mary Flannery O'Connor" notecard*]
Dear R.

Nothing doing hereabouts today but work. Weather spring-like. Sarah away. Regards to kin.

Love,
MF

* * *

Monday [27 Jan. 1947]

Dear R.

Presuming that today was your birthday, I went to mass etc. in your behalf. Sarah got back last night. Enjoyed your two letters I got today. I would like such a jacket no end—preferably the black if available, and would consider wearing it anytime it was sent. When next you send me something, I would be obliged if you would enclose some of that cinnamon sugar Bessie gave me. I didn't have room to bring it. Glad Cousin Katie is sending me the missal, and I would be obliged if you would forward them.

When are the Trawicks taking north, and who has made Marie the grandma— Mable or Dorothy? That is too bad for you all about Willie going. Does he look forward to it?

Your activities in behalf of that hunting expedition sounded somewhat rugged. I dare say you earn that $50 a month. I think it would be just too mean for words to expect those poor Garners to pay a week's rent on their shack when they could just as easy stay with you. Gad!

Among other things, I had 3 scrambled eggs for dinner. Very fine. Regards to kin.

Love,
MF

* * *

Tuesday [28 Jan. 1947]

Dear R.

Was of course most astounded to get the letter about Doctor. By the way, that paper Mrs. Semmes sent you is very appropriate for such notices. Presume there will now be questions as to the farm, etc. Went to mass etc. for him this A.M.

After school in June, Sarah is talking about going to see a friend of hers in Atlanta (in her car), and if it comes through, she would drive me and Ruth home, via St. Louis, Memphis, Birmingham, and Atlanta. It would be a great thing if it comes through. I don't know for sure if Ruth can come, but I plan to ask her.

Sarah will drop her mother off in St. Louis to visit friends. Something to think about, anyway.

Regards to kin.

    Love,

    MF

* * *

Wednesday [29 Jan. 1947]

Dear R.

Didn't get any letter from you today; presume because got two yesterday. Will be glad to get the box with the puddings and sausages—hasn't come yet.

Today is blizzardish with much wet snow etc. Don't know if I will have the nerve to go out and mail this. Have not been out all day.

If Sarah is going out, she will do it.

Regards to kin.

    Love,

    MF

* * *

Thursday [30 Jan. 1947]

Dear R.

Got your Sunday night letter today. I would imagine Louis would be cut up. Can't imagine his staying any longer in that Bell House trap. What is he going to do?

Had my picture struck again today, this time in a black blouse, so I hope it will be better.

There is 10 inches of snow here and it is most disagreeable outside although not too cold but very slippery,

The sausages and puddings came yesterday, and they look mighty good.

Have not yet got the letter you said you sent a copy of to me that you wrote to Agnes. I dare say this will be much a blow to them.

Regards to kin.

    Love,

    MF

All the trains and planes are tied up in these parts on account of this storm. Most disagreeable.

\* \* \*

Friday [31 Jan. 1947]

Dear R.

Got the copy today of your letter to Agnes. I know you all must be mighty tired after all this. You had better remember your own health.

Do not have any application pictures made of those pictures Billie Everhart took. I am applying for a *teachers* position, and none of those are at all appropriate. If this next one is no good, I will go somewhere else. I enclose Sarah's and Barbara's application pictures because I thought you might like to see what they look like. Put them up somewhere for me.

The moving takes place tomorrow, so I don't reckon I will get any work done for it. The girl's last name is Bell. She is an anemic-looking soul, but she works and I am hoping will be gone a lot of the time.

It has quit snowing here, but the snow is piled up all over the place and most disagreeable as far as I am concerned.

I now buy buttermilk instead of sweet milk. I think it is very good.

I think it rather lousy of the Tarletons to bring their hound. Hope they didn't stay long. Who is Father McGrath, and where was Father Toomey?

Hope Louis is better.

Love,
MF

\* \* \*

Saturday [1 Feb. 1947]

Dear R.

I wrote Sister today and I trust the letter will be considered appropriate, it being on white paper. I got yours telling about the will and I think it very fine of him to leave the better part of the estate for Katie's benefit. I hope the farm will not increase your worries. Much moving, cleaning up, etc. going on today. Most disagreeable. Martha will not sleep here until Tuesday, as she is paid up where she is until then. Plumbing backed up again last night, but we are used to that by now. In a few days, it will be necessary for me to iron some shirts—something I haven't done since coming back.

Regards to kin.

Love,
MF

* * *

Sunday [2 Feb. 1947]

[*On "Miss Mary Flannery O'Connor" notecard*]
Dear Regina—

Moving not yet over but plumbing fixed. Weather improving slowly. New semester begins tomorrow—same work. Regards to kin. Enjoying pudding greatly—better without any sauce at all.

    Love,
    MF

* * *

Monday [3 Feb. 1947]

Dear R.

Got your two letters today. Is Louis staying with Dr. Fowler or is he back at the Bell House? It must be a joy having Uncle around again. I hope you will be able to make the farm pay—that is, come out even. I dare say you will rent the house?

Opened the canned turkey today for dinner and had a most handsome sandwich out of part of it.

How are the Garners making out in their shack?

It is some warmer here and not snowing—very slushy out.

I wrote Cousin Katie and thanked her for the missals.

Regards to kin.

    Love,
    MF

* * *

Tuesday [4 Feb. 1947]

Dear R.

It is much below zero here today and miserable. I went out once because I had to, but I ain't going again.

The second pictures I had taken at the University photographers were so bad they didn't even make me pay for them. Ruth's were poor, too, so we have made an appointment at a place in town to have them taken tomorrow—which will cost us $5 (for the 12 prints), which I dislike, but I don't know anything else to do.

Bought the paper for my thesis yesterday, and Barbara is going to start typing it this week. Five copies of it have to be made. The paper cost me $3.50, and I reckon it will be around $20 or $25 for the typing, as it is 125 pages long. I think the University pays for the binding. I am at least thankful that it is finished.

Martha Bell and trunk arrive officially this afternoon.

Regards to kin.

> Love,
> MF

* * *

Wednesday [5 Feb. 1947]

Dear R.

Enclosed is the clipping from the Recorder. Too bad about your being Mrs. Conner.

Our damnable plumbing backed up again last night. They ought to be prosecuted for charging us $15 a month for these rooms.

At one thirty today we go to have our pictures taken. The man says he makes from 4 to 6 proofs, so we are at least hoping to get something decent. I had two dresses, that black blouse, and the big sweater cleaned, and they charged me two dollars. Isn't that right high?

Hope you all have a cook.

Weather still terrifically cold, but the wind has died down, which makes it not as bad.

Martha Bell established here now. She is a nice girl and much less talkative than Sarah, which is easier on my work. Also, she has not brought her radio, for which I am most thankful. Altogether, I have been extremely fortunate in what I have gotten in the roommate line.

Regards to kin.

> Love,
> MF

* * *

Thursday [6 Feb. 1947]

Dear R.

It is certainly too bad about Ben, but I don't gather what they mean by "inactive." Is it inactive for good?

Snowing again here. It may take longer to get the mail, on account of the railroads that are slowed up with these storms.

We had our pictures taken yesterday and get to see the proofs Monday. The person who took them was a Chinaman, a Mr. T. Wong. He is supposed to be good, and he seemed to know what he was about. We hope, anyway.

How long is Mary Ann going to stay?

Regards to kin.

> Love,
>
> MF

\* \* \*

### Friday [7 Feb. 1947]

Dear R.

Just finished a can of sardines and a couple of eggs—mighty fine. It is about 5 below. I have two classes every Tuesday and Thursday, none any other days so I stay at home and go out only to mail these letters and to eat supper. I don't reckon you will be getting mail on schedule. They say this will keep up a couple of weeks.

Glad you ordered the jacket. Is it coming straight here or to Milledgeville?

Am very pleased to have this Martha Bell here. She is much quieter than the other one. Ruth got the cast off her arm yesterday. Nothing doing around here but work. Regards to kin.

> Love,
>
> MF

\* \* \*

### Saturday [8 Feb. 1947]

Dear R.

I don't take a bath in that tub until after Edna has cleaned it. She does it thoroughly.

Didn't mean to imply any lack of enthusiasm over your having the farm. I think he knew you were the only one in the family who could and would handle it like it ought to be done; however, my doubts are simply in the line that it may increase your worries without increasing your pocket book. It always seemed to be eating up his. I presume if you are going to cut it down to such an extent, however, you will be able not to lose anything on it. The reason Miss Mary hasn't said anything is because she doesn't like the added independence this gives you. What did Madame Tarleton think? What are they going to do with their portions of land? I don't imagine they like your being executriss [*sic*] of it.

Still mighty cold but the wind has died some and that helps. Fell down yesterday twice but didn't hurt myself.

I wouldn't like having all those letters to write.

Regards to kin.

> Love,
>
> MF

* * *

Sunday [9 Feb. 1947]

[*postcard*]

Dear R.

Nothing doing hereabouts on Sunday but church and dinner. Weather some improved. Have not fallen down again. Regards to kin.

> Love,
> MF

* * *

Monday [10 Feb. 1947]

Dear R.

Got your two letters and one from Cousin Katie, telling me it is 32° in Savannah. At this point, I would be inclined to consider 32° summer.

I wouldn't fool with the Garners for milk, either. Do you think Mr. Bond was glad to see them go? What does the inside of their hut look like now they are in it?

Today we go to see what Mr. Wong made of our ugly faces. For 5 dollars I think it ought to be something worth the effort. If there is one I like I will have it made for you as I do not like those concoctions of Billie's.

How is Miss Mary?

There is a new man in the workshop working with Engle and Milton. He is from Nashville and I will be under him for the rest of the year which I will enjoy I'm sure. He is a novelist—Andrew Lytle.

Regards to kin.

> Love,
> MF

* * *

Tuesday [11 Feb. 1947]

Dear R.

Got your letter with the checks and the chewing gum. Chewing the latter at present. Don't send me any money. If I need any I will write a check for it but I don't think I need any and there's no use getting a lot in this bank and having to transfer it to wherever I am next year. I have had to buy a good many books and the thesis business and the 5 dollars for the pictures. About the pictures: only one can be used and so I will have the application pictures made from that one and send you one and if you like it, I will have a bigger one made from it. Waste of money.

Temperature has gone up a few degrees, and it is a great relief. It is 13 above today and feels like spring.

Regards to kin.

    Love,

    MF

* * *

Wednesday [12 Feb. 1947]

Dear R.

Nothing doing around here but work. The snow is thawing, but by the time it gets thawed good, it will start again. Too bad about Joan and the house. I don't imagine you would like Mary Anne using your phone, but it looks like it might be easier to tell her than to lock the door every time you went out it.

I am going to make a trip to the A&P today, since it is not so cold, and stock up. Regards to kin.

    Love,

    MF

* * *

Friday [14 Feb. 1947]

Dear R.

The box came and I was delighted with it. I fixed one of those bouillon cubes for breakfast and was having a fine time with it when I realized it was Friday and had to throw it down the drain. I got some bouillon cubes here before Christmas but they were not much good. Would you send me some more of the beef-liver ones? I haven't tasted the chicken yet. Cooked up my canned apples with the cinnamon sugar and then used the apples as a sauce over a pudding. Very fine. Will enjoy all the rest of it as much. Got a valentine card from the Frank Clines.

When I get my application pictures, I will send one to Annie Bruce and suggest she hang it in Miss Fannie's quarters. Very fine of her to offer her services. I reckon Miss Mary would have thought she just wanted to be in the midst of things.

It is getting cold here again.

Hope too that you all will be able to make something off the farm, and include that petition in my novena.

Martha Bell is going home for the weekend.

Regards to kin.

Love,

MF

P.S. When you get around to sending me the bouillon cubes, I would be obliged if you would include a tube of that Worcestershire Salt Toothpaste, as I can't get [it] up here.

* * *

Saturday [15 Feb. 1947]

Dear R.

Ate the chicken dinner for lunch and some of the potatoes—all very fine. Plan to have a pudding in the middle of the afternoon. Got your letter and one from Margaret O'Connor saying they liked The Geranium and were sorry to hear about the Doctor.

I think it is fine Mr. Bond is doing so well. Hope it lasts. Is Mrs. Bond still spitting in the fireplace?

When is Madame Garner planning to have her operation? When Julia comes, will she stay with you all and her spouse or at the shack?

We took Sarah to dinner last night for her birthday and gave her a whistle as a present. Cost 10¢.

Does the farm keep you any busier now that you have charge of it?

Regards to kin.

Love,

MF

* * *

Monday [17 Feb. 1947]

Dear R.

Got one letter from you today and the Recorder. Usually get two. The fact that it is Lent already seems amazing. About this fasting—ask Father Toomey again. The Monsignor here said for breakfast you could have a piece of bread and a drink but that you could really have 2 or 4 pieces of bakers bread because there was no food value in it. He is very nice and everybody likes him. It is still clear here and I am going to the A&P while I have the chance. I like those beef liver extract cubes very much.

That looks like an old boy Rosemary Patterson attached herself to. What's his business?

I was invited to Miss Nutter's for supper last night—milk and crackers and I took a pint of ice cream.

Regards to kin.

> Love,
> MF

The cook sounds handsome.

* * *

Tuesday [18 Feb. 1947]

Dear R.

The jacket came yesterday, and I am delighted with it. It is nicer to wear than a sweater because it is so light and loose. I am highly obliged. You ought to get you one. I will only have to tighten the sleeve bands.

I reckon Agnes feels somewhat out of it way up there, and I know she enjoys your letters. She was always waiting on the postman when I was there.

We get the pictures tomorrow, and I will send you one.

Trust Miss Mary is well.

> Love,
> MF

* * *

Wednesday [19 Feb. 1947]

Dear R.

Enclose the picture. Write what you think about it. I reckon I can have a larger one made if you want it. Prefer it myself to what you have at home, but I'm not going to get one made unless you're going to keep those colored pictures under cover.

Why is it hard to rent the farm house? Don't people want places anymore.

I got the bill for that call I made to Milledgeville. It was only $1.15 and I was amazed.

Regards to kin.

> Love,
> MF

* * *

Thursday [20 Feb. 1947]

Dear R.

Enjoyed your letter and John's which I return. How was May Cash?

It looks like it is going to snow here again. They say this is the worst month for such goings-on. I trust Louis is better. You may inform him that my experience with low blood pressure has been that the least exertion the better. Trust you still have the cook. Nothing doing here but work. Regards to kin.

> Love,
> MF

* * *

Friday [21 Feb. 1947]

Dear R.

Mr. Lytle read one of my stories at the workshop yesterday. Both he and Engle thought it a fine story. It was.

Nothing doing around here. We have two masses in the morning now; one at 7:25 and one at 8. I go to the earlier one usually. Tonight we attend a lecture.

I may want you to send that application picture back as I am joining an agency in Chicago that may want them. We have to give eight to this placement bureau. I am hoping the one in Chicago will not require so many. This agency was recommended to us by a Mr. [Austin] Warren, a well-known critic at present here at this University. He is writing us (Ruth and me) recommendations for both places. We were very fortunate to get a recommendation from him, as his name carries weight.

Regards to kin.

> Love,
> MF

* * *

Saturday [22 Feb. 1947]

Dear R.

Is Miss Mary going to Savannah? I didn't get from your letter if she was or wasn't. How long will you stay when you go?

Had to buy myself two pair of socks today as all mine are wearing out.

Sarah has gone home for the weekend, and Barbara is having company. I am able to work much better now that Sarah is on the other side of the house. She talks a great deal, but this Martha Bell is writing a thesis and doesn't have time for such.

I am enjoying the jacket greatly. Nothing doing around here. Regards to kin.

    Love,

    MF

* * *

Sunday [23 Feb. 1947]

Dear R.

Getting mighty cold here again, but I hope that the worst of the winter is over. It couldn't get much colder than it was a few weeks ago.

Nothing doing on Sunday. We go (Ruth and I) to the high mass at 10 and thence to Smiths, a restaurant, to eat.

Wrote Dr. Taylor today for a reference. If you ever see him sometime after Tuesday, you might mention I appreciated him doing it for me. I also have one from Engle, Austin Warren, and Paul Horgan in New Mexico now. They should all be good references. I reckon you better send that picture back.

    Regards to kin.

    Love,

    MF

* * *

Monday [24 Feb. 1947]

Dear R.

Got three of your letters today. I must have forgotten your letter that Sunday. That is usually a hard day around here. The cubes haven't come but I will be glad to see them, also the puddings and toothpaste.

Do you mean that Catherine's talking may have made the place hard to rent? Or does Uncle talk?

You needn't feel sorry for Miss Nutter. She gets plenty.

About the washrag—do you mean Gussie's mother? I would like to know whom I'm writing to before I do it. That was most handsome of her, by the way.

When did George Harper die? I think that was quite a blessing.

You needn't send the picture back, as I heard from the Chicago agency and I can send them one picture and get 25 made from it for $1.25, which I think very reasonable. The way this agency works—if they get you a job, i.e., if you accept one they introduce you to, you pay them 5% of your first year's salary, e.g., if they get you a $3,000 job, you pay them $150. Of course, it is worth it if they can get you the right place. If they can't, you pay them two dollars for their trouble. If I get a job through the Bureau here it won't cost anything; however, they say this bureau is not very good, and since Warren suggested the other, I don't think it will hurt to join it.

Hope the Duchess is better.

Love,

MF

\* \* \*

Tuesday [25 Feb. 1947]

Dear R.

The box came while I was eating my beans so I also had a pudding. It all looked mighty fine and I will have a great time eating. Enjoyed those papers you included and would like to know how you are enjoying the "Marvelous Medal Novena." Was there a correction of it the next day?

I hope Louis is better. If he goes to May's, he should stop by here.

How did you get to the "bone yard"? I would like to see that myself. What are you going to do with the horses?

It is sort of dribbling snow around here but nothing to speak of.

Ruth's brother has planned his wedding for the 7th of June. She is supposed to graduate on the 7th, and she is also supposed to be in the wedding. There was some mix-up, but they have already engaged the church etc. I don't know what she will do. I suggested if she didn't come with me she could come later in the summer. She doesn't know how it will work out.

Hope you get somebody for the farm house. Does Uncle ever go out there now? What does he do with himself all day? Regards to kin.

Love,

MF

\* \* \*

Wednesday [26 Feb. 1947]

Dear R.

Didn't get any letter from you today. I presume because I got three Monday. Peculiar.

Martha Bell uses this solidified brilliantine on her hair after she washes it and I thought you might like some. So I bought you a jar. She puts it on her hair when her hair gets dry—rubs her fingers over it and then along the piece of hair she is putting up. I will send it to you in a couple of days. I'd like to try it myself before I send it. If you think Miss Mary would like some I'll send her a jar.

I got my grades today—they were all As. I was gratified, not that it makes any difference, but they look well on the record.

I am cooking apples. Regards to kin.

> Love,
>
> MF

* * *

Thursday [27 Feb. 1947]

Dear R.

Was gratified to get your letter today since didn't get one yesterday. Do you mail them at the same time every day or what? Glad to hear Louis is better. How did Duchess get?

How long are Mary Virginia and Lizzie going to be in St. Louis? Why doesn't Mary Virginia come up to see me? It's just a day's ride.

Hope you are finding a renter by now for the farm house.

Nothing doing around her but work. Regards to kin.

> Love,
>
> MF

How did Joan Herdy ever get?

* * *

Friday [28 Feb. 1947]

Dear R.

Enjoyed your letter and Cousin Katie's. Is Louis living with Cleo now or what? Too bad he is still sick.

Nothing much doing around here. I find the eating harder during lent. I try not to eat between meals but I understand you can have fruit juice even when you are fasting. Will you find out if you can have bouillon cubes on days that are not days of abstinence. Also can you have meat at the small meal a day on days that are not days of abstinence. The monsignor here said you could cook things in meat, but I never get it all straight.

Hope Mrs. Semmes's maid is ugly enough for her to keep. What about you all's cook? Regards to kin.

> Love,
>
> MF

* * *

Saturday [1 Mar. 1947]

Dear R.

Got your letter, one from Miss Bancroft, and one from Cousin Katie, sending me the leaflet of the Sacred Heart, which I was glad to get.

Surely Miss Bancroft is going to stay with us this summer? If not, why not?

Last night for supper I had baked lobster tails; cost $1.50 for the dinner, but were mighty fine. Lost them at 1:30.

I like the hair stuff I bought for you and will send it Monday.

It is snowing here again and is most disagreeable.

Saw a dog get run over today.

Regards to kin.

    Love,

    MF

* * *

Sunday [2 Mar. 1947]

Dear Regina,

Nothing doing around here on Sunday. I am going to eat one of the chicken a la king cans today. Mighty fine. I can't fancy Duchess not eating between meals. Does she holler for food all day or what?

Bought myself a jar of Sal Hepatica today to get rid of whatever lobster is still crawling around in me. It was mighty good while I was eating it, however.

Hope Louis is better. Cousin Katie writes that Sister is very low in spirits. That is too bad. Is she ever going to Savannah to see Cousin Katie?

Regards to kin.

    Love,

    MF

* * *

Monday [3 Mar. 1947]

Dear R.

Got your two letters and the paper and a copy of the Corinthian from Miss Hallie today. Enjoyed. I have got the package of stuff for you wrapped up and will get it mailed today or tomorrow.

The head of the English department called me in today and offered me another fellowship for next year if I would still be working on my degree then. As

I would not, I thanked him kindly for his interest. I thought it was very nice of him.

Snow is melting again and it is very slushy.

I will write Mrs. Bloodworth.

Regards to kin.

> Love,
> MF

* * *

Tuesday [4 Mar. 1947]

Dear R.

Got two letters from you and one from Sister which please inform her I enjoyed. Tell her I will write Miss Bancroft, expressing my satisfaction that she would be present this summer.

Hope you and Gussie had a nice time in Atlanta. I wrote Mrs. Bloodworth I trust an acceptable note.

I saw that in the paper about Miss Margaret Oakey being maid of honor. I wondered what bush they hid that child of hers under.

The apples are canned but not sweetened or flavored. I just heat them with some of that cinnamon sugar in them.

Glad you and the Lindseys are exchanging courtesys. Does Miss Meeks still sew now that she has married the blind man?

Regards to kin.

> Love,
> MF

* * *

Wednesday [5 Mar. 1947]

Dear R.

Got your letter from Atlanta today and enjoyed. Trust you got your business finished.

The weather is springish today, and I hope that is what it means. We have some off time for Easter in a month. Ruth and I might go down to Chicago for a day or so depending on how our work is coming. I don't know.

We are having hot water heater trouble today, and the hot water will be off all afternoon. They are not going to use this house for graduate students next year. They shouldn't use it at all, in my estimation.

Glad you all like your colored girl. Regards to kin.

>Love,
>
>MF

\* \* \*

### Thursday [6 Mar. 1947]

Dear R.

Got your airmail letter today. I am not fasting but try not to eat between meals. Glad you all had a nice trip.

They have installed the new hot water heater and sent a man yesterday to fix our window, which he said can't be fixed. We have to put tin cans under it to keep it open. This room has five doors and two windows in it.

Ruth Sullivan had a bat in her room last night and had to sleep in the parlor. Regards to kin.

>Love,
>
>MF

\* \* \*

### Friday [7 Mar. 1947]

Dear R.

No letter from you today I presume on account of the airmail yesterday. It is sho nuf springish today and I hope that means it continues so.

Barbara is typing my thesis now and expects to have it done by April. I think she will charge about $10.00.

I have not joined the agency yet and do not plan to until April or May, i.e., until I see what the one here turns up. I am also going to write letters around myself to places I would like to be.

Nothing doing here but work.

Regards to kin.

>Love,
>
>MF

\* \* \*

Saturday [8 Mar. 1947]

Dear R.

Enjoyed your letter and Cousin Katie's. You seem to have took a christening streak. How come this popularity on the part of the Kinneys for you?

The weather here is decent now and I feel more like working. I hope it will stay this way.

What do you hear from Agnes? Do you reckon any of them will come down this summer? I am looking forward to seeing Miss Bancroft.

Regards to kin.

>Love,
>MF

\* \* \*

Tuesday [11 Mar. 1947]

[*On "Miss Mary Flannery O'Connor" notecard*]

Dear R.

Still haven't got myself any envelopes so will make this do today. Nothing doing here anyhow but work. Let me know soon enough when you are going to Savannah so I can mail the letters there. Glad you liked the brilliantine business. Regards to kin.

>Love,
>MF

\* \* \*

Wednesday [12 Mar. 1947]

Dear R.

Sending this airmail as requested. That was too bad about losing the calf. What about renting the house? Do you reckon it will ever get rented? Strikes me $50 is right high, too.

Glad Cousin Katie liked the picture. The rainy season has opened upon us here—disagreeable but much better than the ice.

What is Loretta doing? You might find out since you're in Savannah. I will write Mrs. Logan if I can find the time and think of something to say to her. Glad you like your dress.

Regards to Cousin Katie and Bessie.

    Love,

    MF

P.S. Maybe I should be using white paper when writing you in Savannah?

* * *

Thursday [13 Mar. 1947]

Dear R.

That is certainly too bad about Joan breaking her vertebraes. I will try to send her a card. She seems to have a hard time, poor girl.

I doctored upon my fur coat yesterday—sewed the lining in it again. It was ripping all over the place.

My story *The Geranium* was reprinted in the Arts Forum Issue of the U of NC Women's College literary magazine. They chose 13 stories out of 139 or so, and those stories are going to be discussed by critics at this forum, it seems. Engle sent it in. I didn't know anything about it.

Still raining here. Regards to Cousin Katie.

    Love,

    MF

* * *

Friday [14 Mar. 1947]

Dear R.

Got your Monday letter today. Think that was very silly what Sister wrote Agnes about Catherine's getting the hotel job. Those places are supervised, and nothing would cure her of wanting to do such things like the work involved in doing them. I would be a waitress before I'd be anybody's secretary myself although Lord spare me from either.

The placement bureau called me about an opening at a teacher's college in Wisconsin, but I was not interested. They said Dr. Taylor's letter had come in.

That is too bad about Gussie being in the hospital. Has Mary Virginia ever got back from New Orleans?

I trust you are having a fine time in Savannah. Why don't you go to see Emma? I would like to hear how she is.

I have given out of bouillon cubes and I wish when you get home you would send me 5 or 6 packages of the beef and liver extract ones. I find them superb for that tired feeling.

My regards to Cousin Katie and Bessie.

Love,

MF

* * *

Saturday [15 Mar. 1947]

Dear R.

That is certainly too bad about the Bonds. I thought the first wife had remarried or something. Where is Mrs. Bond going to?

It is snowing all over here today and like to keep up. Most disagreeable. I thought this kind of weather was over.

Martha Bell's sister is coming for her today so she will be gone over tonight and tomorrow. I always enjoy such rests. However, it is most agreeable having her for a roommate, as she leaves at 8 o'clock in the morning and isn't back until after supper, when I am usually out. So much nicer than the last one.

I thought there were several cases in the attic. If you can't find one, I'll look here.

Regards to Cousin Katie and Bessie.

Love,

MF

* * *

Sunday [16 Mar. 1947]

[*On "Miss Mary Flannery O'Connor" notecard*]

Dear R.

Nothing doing here but work. Weather improved. Martha Bell [will] be back tonight. Regards to all.

Love,

MF

\* \* \*

Monday [17 Mar. 1947]

Dear R.

Got two letters from Milledgeville and one from Savannah today, so presume I won't get one tomorrow. Too bad about Joan. Sarah went home Friday, and yesterday her sister called that she got the flu that Friday night and wouldn't be back until Wednesday or Thursday. She gets sick a lot.

I will be mighty glad to see the puddings and cubes. They have not come yet but may get here this afternoon.

Hope you get to see Loretta—also Emma. I would like to hear how Emma is—or if Emma is.

I presume you people are parading today, etc. etc. Nothing doing here but work. My regards to Cousin Katie, Bessie, and Mamie.

    Love,
    MF

\* \* \*

Tuesday [18 Mar. 1947]

Dear R.

No letter today but will look for one tomorrow. The boxes came and I was mighty glad to see those reinforcements. Mighty glad.

Talked to Engle today. A fine critic, name of Allen Tate, is coming in April, and he wants him to see my stuff etc. I hope he has another party.

It is snowing again—most disagreeable.

Hope Cousin Katie and Bessie are well. I plan to write Miss Mary.

    Love,
    MF

\* \* \*

Wednesday [19 Mar. 1947]

Dear R.

Got your Saturday letter today. You seem to be seeing all the people there are to see—i.e., have seen them, as I presume this finds you back in Milledgeville. I trust affairs at the farm kept over your departure.

Sarah has not come back yet. I hope she stays away until she is sho nuf over it, as I don't want to get it. A lot of people here have it, but I drink much fruit juice and hope to avoid it. It doesn't seem to last over a day with most of them.

Paul Horgan is the one, yes. I haven't read that story and didn't know he had one in there. It was probably just a potboiler, however, because he generally writes for good magazines such as The Yale Review, which don't use Good Housekeeping formulas.

It has mercifully stopped snowing and for the next 24 hours will be slushy.

Regards to kin.

> Love,
> MF

* * *

### Thursday [20 Mar. 1947]

Dear R.

Why did Mrs. Semmes decide to give you a hat? Didn't she like your present stock? Am glad she liked the dress you gave her, I have forgotten it.

Sarah must still have the flu, as she is not back yet.

We went to see a Russian movie, *The Stone Flower*, yesterday. It was in Russian with English subtitles. It was very dull, but the technicolor was unusual—new process or something.

I dare say you are glad to be home.

Regards to kin.

> Love,
> MF

* * *

### Friday [21 Mar. 1947]

Dear R.

Sarah got back last night. She looks bad. The two in the next room both have colds and sore throats. I, however, remain in perfect health.

Did I write you that Ruth's brother is changing his wedding to the 14th? That won't give Ruth time enough to come home with me, but I hope she will come later in the summer. I am afraid the poor girl is not going to graduate. Engle told me yesterday he didn't think she had a chance. She doesn't have enough stories for her thesis, and unless she gets them in a month, it is pretty doubtful if they will give her the degree. Would be obliged if you would pray that she gets them written.

Sending the Duchess three boxes of incense sticks. If you burn the black ones in the dark, they glow.

The weather is most disagreeable here.

I won't hear anything about the reading at NC. Engle said they liked my work. Regards to kin.

> Love,
> MF

* * *

Saturday [22 Mar. 1947]

Dear R.

Got your Tuesday letter today containing Sister's and picture of you to Margarite. What I want to know is, how did you know that was you?

I imagine it will be good to get rid of Mrs. Logan myself.

Barbara is better and up. She had fever last night but none today. The weather is improving. I imagine you got sick of all that Pink House and hotel food in Savannah.

I don't think we will go to Chicago now, with Ruth so pressed to get her work done. I think I will buy me a pair of shoes if we don't go.

Martha Bell is going home for the weekend again today.

Regards to kin.

> Love,
> MF

* * *

Monday [24 Mar. 1947]

Dear R.

Got your Wednesday and Thursday letters today—the Wednesday one missent again to Sioux City. Ruth just brought your package back, and I think the blouse is mighty pretty. I will reserve it for Sundays and holy days of obligation. It looks like it would be easy to iron. The mirror is most handy and fits my tube of lipstick. I will saw on the candy come Sunday.

It is snowing again today and most disagreeable. Nobody has the flu here now.

I hope those incense sticks I sent the Duchess were not all broken up. I heard them rattling a little as I bid them off.

Regards to kin.

Love,
MF

* * *

Friday [4 Apr. 1947]

Dear R.

When Sarah comes back I will tell her. You might write me a letter in which you simply say that it will worry you too much for me to come home driving with only two people in the car and that I can't do it—i.e., a paragraph without any mention of not hurting her feelings, something I can show her, as I cannot show her your previous communications. I have no desire whatsoever to come home driving with her.

I am still enjoying the cookies and have eaten all the date ones up.

Rainy and disagreeable here. Regards to kin.

Love,
MF

* * *

Saturday [5 Apr. 1947]

Dear R.

This place is very morgue-like these days and I like it very much. Met Miss Nutter on the street last night so brought her home to a peanut butter sandwich, and then took her to the stations with me.

It has been raining here ever since Wednesday, and I presume will be raining tomorrow.

I have almost finished the cookies and will enter upon the date roll at noon today.

Since it is too late to send the nuts for Easter and she probably has more than is good for her anyway, I will wait until later to send Duchess the nuts.

Regards to kin.

Love,
MF

\* \* \*

Sunday [6 Apr. 1947]

Dear R.

Will honor the character of the day by using white paper. Dined with Miss Nutter after church and am just before taking off for dinner at the Jeffersons. It is very windy and cold but dry so far today.

The date roll is mighty good.

I am wondering what is to be done with this fur coat this summer. I don't know that I'll be anywhere near the Chicago area again, so I don't see any use sending it there again. I probably won't know where I'm going to be next year until around August; therefore, will you find out if Dairron's or JP Allen's stores them over the summer. I would be surprised if they didn't.

Nothing doing around here. Regards to kin.

    Love,

    MF

\* \* \*

Monday [7 Apr. 1947]

Dear R.

I found the strap so settle your mind. Do you want me to send it to you or something? Thought you might like to see the clipping. The dress you are sending sounds handsome, and I will enjoy it. I meant the amount of work necessary to graduate. There are examinations attendant upon this degree, you know. The examinations come on the 22nd or 23rd; after that I will have time to start sending stuff home.

Amparo has just brought a box back—a huge cake from the Frank Clines. It looks beautiful and isn't torn up at all this time. They certainly are nice to me, I must say. I must say.

I am looking forward to riding this summer. Perhaps you would let me work out there some—I mean write, not hoe.

All these people will be back tonight. I have enjoyed the vacation.

Regards to kin.

    Love,

    MF

\* \* \*

Tuesday [8 Apr. 1947]

Dear R.

Got your Friday and Saturday letters today. Don't bother about sending any more of the big stick things unless you already have, as I won't have any occasion to give one to anybody.

There were several of us in this house over Easter.

That is a shame about Mr. Bond leaving, but I presume there are plenty of good people who want that kind of work. Are you advertising like you did before or what?

Glad you are enclosing shields with the dress. Am anxious to view it.

Ruth has not come back yet. Do not discontinue your prayers for her. She doesn't realize how bad her situation is.

I liked Barbara's mother very much. She looked something like Ivy Carpenter.

I told Sarah you were too nervous about the proposed trip for me to make it. She said she thought she'd make it anyway, and I said if she did, she'd have to come to Milledgeville anyway, and she said she would. I think her feelings were hurt, but I got enough business of my own to worry about without being concerned.

When is Miss Mary going to Savannah?

Regards to kin.

> Love,
> MF

\* \* \*

Wednesday [9 Apr. 1947]

Dear R.

The jodhpurs and the dress came yesterday. I like the dress very much, and it fits fine, with the exception of it being too blousy here and there and too long; however, I am not going to do any sewing on it myself. You can do it when I come home, and for now, I will wear it like it is. I will wear it with a black belt, I think, as the colored one doesn't fit and I don't think looks as good as a black one, anyway. I like it very much and am obliged to you; also for sending the jodhpurs.

Would have enjoyed talking to you Sunday. Although I don't think much of the long distance call as a medium of social communication.

Engle's oldest had an appendicitis last night but I think is doing all right now.

I had the letter from the girl about apartments. Naturally, I couldn't give her much information.

Nothing doing around here. Regards to kin.

> Love,
> MF

* * *

Thursday [10 Apr. 1947]

Dear R.

No letter from you today, I presume because I have got two in one day twice this week.

Nothing doing around here but work. The weather very poor. When is Miss Mary going to Savannah?

I have a little cold and have borrowed somebody's liquor book and plan to go down today or tomorrow and get me a fifth of something. Bourbon if they've got it. It's rationed here.

I hope you are being successful in your search for a farm man.

Regards to kin.

> Love,
> MF

* * *

Friday [11 Apr. 1947]

Dear R.

Got your letter with enclosure to show Sarah, which I will do. Cold much better.

Too bad about Mrs. Logan and her flu. Is she still leaving you in the summer? I read in Time Magazine that John L. Lewis may keep the mines tied up for two months. In which case, I will fly home again.

Tate comes Monday week and stays a week. I am hoping Engle will have a function for him. I am working now to complete a longer thing for him to read.

Hope Miss Mary enjoys her trip. Regards to kin.

> Love,
> MF

\* \* \*

Saturday [12 Apr. 1947]

Dear R.

Got your letter with Bessie's enclosed. Ain't she silly?

There is a big parade here for army day, but I didn't go. I presume I saw enough parades in mine early youth.

Amparo is moving into another house to live with a sick girl from her country, so the plush-rug kid is going to move in with Connie, and another—a new girl—in with Barbara. It will be very nice, I think, as the new person seems more considerate than the plush-rug kid.

Glad you are getting plenty of letters and hope you will get the right people in the end. Presume you are trying to avoid the Crisliff type again. Are your apartments rented?

Regards to kin.

Love,

MF

\* \* \*

Sunday [13 Apr. 1947]

[*On "Miss Mary Flannery O'Connor" notecard*]

Dear R.

Ruth and I dining at Miss Nutter's tonight. Weather fine. My assortment of spring clothes in operation. Regards to kin.

Love,

MF

\* \* \*

Monday [14 Apr. 1947]

Dear R.

Enjoyed your two letters. Forgot to mail your card yesterday, but will not send it on as there wasn't anything on it anyway.

That is too bad about Willis. Why didn't you tell me you thought he had it, and I would have looked sooner. That was nice of Mary Virginia to bring you the perfume.

I presume Sister is in Savannah now. Will or did Cleo stay and bring Master T when she brought the nurse? I presume she also brought the hound?

Regards to kin.

Love,

MF

\* \* \*

Tuesday [15 Apr. 1947]

Dear R.

Got your letters of Friday and Saturday. The man from Dublin sounds good. I hope he is if you take him. Looks like you ought to look at more than two before you decide, however.

Is the nurse you are getting from 9:30 to 5:30 black or white?

Was talking to Engle today, and he says he wants to have some of us out to his farm one of these weekends. I hope he gets around to it.

Ruth at present plans to come down to see me after her brother's wedding on the 14th of June. I hope she can.

What do you hear from Uncle?

Regards to kin.

> Love,
> MF

\* \* \*

Wednesday [16 Apr. 1947]

Dear R.

No letter from you today. I got two yesterday. This afternoon I am going to see "Henry V," the English film Laurence Olivier made from the Shakespearean play. It is costing me $1.85 but I think it is something worth much more.

It is *snowing* here today. I was most amazed, as I thought we were shut of it for the coming months.

Hope you have gotten your man for the place. Will be interested to hear.

Martha Bell is in the throws [*sic*] of writing her thesis and so stays home a lot and types but doesn't worry me. She is certainly nice to room with.

Regards to kin.

> Love,
> MF

\* \* \*

Thursday [17 Apr. 1947]

Dear R.

Got your letter with Mary Virginia's picture in it. She looked her usual, silly self. Do you want it back? I don't have any place to keep it, and I thought maybe her parent would want it. Anyway, I will stick it in this letter. The Garners' place looks like it might be in the middle of the woods.

Your activities on behalf of Janet were most charitable, and I hope you get the money back. I think Dr. Baily is a stinker. Why didn't you deal with the BMH?

The weather is very fine here again.

Regards to kin.

    Love,

    MF

* * *

Friday [18 Apr. 1947]

Dear R.

Mighty happy you have got a man for the place and a good one; also that your financial status is holding its own. I hope my financial status will have picked up by next year, too.

Weather variable these days; very blowy withall. I was wondering if John Cline Jr. was located anywhere near that Texas City that got blown up to such an extent.

There is nothing doing here but work. I have to write six hours a day and don't get time for much else.

I begin to think now Ruth will make it on her thesis, but it isn't sure yet.

Regards to kin.

    Love,

    MF

P.S. Martha Bell liked the date roll so much she wants the recipe. Do you mind sending it?

* * *

Saturday [19 Apr. 1947]

Dear R.

Hope you enjoyed your pasture tour and took it all in. Maybe you ought to take a Ph.D. in pastures or something.

Raining and most disagreeable here today and everyone working themselves out. Sarah went to Des Moines for the weekend, and it is always easier to work when she is out of the way.

When is Miss Mary coming back?

Is this nurse black or white, red or yellow, and where did she come from?

When does your new man move in?

Regards to kin.
>Love,
>MF

\* \* \*

### Sunday [20 Apr. 1947]

[*postcard*]

Dear R.

Nothing to fill up this card with ever on Sunday. Weather improved, and we are all working for one thing or another.

Regards to kin.
>Love,
>MF

\* \* \*

### Monday [21 Apr. 1947]

Dear R.

Sorry you are having nurse trouble and hope Darnel gets back shortly. Had a card from Cousin Katie today from Charleston. Mighty glad you found those things I thought I had lost. I don't know how they could have got where you found them.

Barbara finished my thesis last night. It came to 102 pages, and I reckon will cost 10 or either 20 dollars. I don't know how she figures on charging per page. It looks mighty nice.

We go to hear Tate tonight, hear him three times tomorrow, twice Thursday, and will have an appointment with him Wednesday or Thursday, I trust.

Weather admirable here now. Regards to kin. That was fine that Duchess went to Holy Communion. How did it come about?

>Love,
>MF

\* \* \*

### Tuesday [22 Apr. 1947]

Dear R.

You can write Ruth if you've a mind to, but it's not necessary, she says—she knows she is welcome. As for entertaining her, I am not going to entertain her. Now get that please—no little tea. No nothing. She is going to bring her typewriter, I presume. Maybe we could ride a couple of times or something. She says she can just stay a week, but I imagine she will stay two.

We enjoyed Tate last night and got three hours of him this afternoon.

Have you found out anything about the fur coat business?

Regards to kin. Glad Donelle is back.

> Love,
>
> MF

P.S. Ruth plans to be married in August—a Mr. Finnegan who teaches at Notre Dame, but don't say anything about it if you write her.

* * *

Wednesday [23 Apr. 1947]

Dear R.

Have just talked to Tate for a half hour and will talk to him again Friday. My admiration for him is extreme. He discussed a story of mine with me and is reading the first 4 chapters of the novel [*Wise Blood*] I am working on. He said among other things that I was a born writer. He is going to try to help me get a fellowship at Vanderbilt next year. I would like nothing better than that. I am to write and see if I can apply, and then write him, and he will use his influence. He was at Vanderbilt a long time as one of its leading lights. He said he thought there would be no trouble about getting the novel published if I finished it, but if I taught somewhere, it would be extremely difficult to finish it; therefore, Vanderbilt will be the answer, *if* I can get the fellowship. Kindly do not discuss this with anybody or say I am writing a novel, but pray that I will get the fellowship at Vanderbilt— that it hasn't already been given. Imagine it is a thousand dollars or so. I think it would be very fine to be at Vanderbilt.

What does that mean about there being pus on her kidneys? Is that serious, permanent?

Regards to kin.

> Love,
>
> MF

Hope your man is all he is supposed to be.

* * *

Thursday [24 Apr. 1947]

Dear R.

We are all working on the Vanderbilt deal. It just depends now on whether the thing has already been given. I wrote the man (Prof. Donald Davidson) yesterday applying and sent him examples of my work this morning. Tate wrote yesterday and Engle is writing today.

I hope that if we are too late for this next year, I can be considered for the year after. No one applying could have better recommendations than I am having. The Lord seems always to send somebody. Last time, Dr. Beiswanger—this time, Tate. Of course, I am not counting on getting it. I think, myself, it is pretty late; but I will get one year after, if I don't this year, I am sure.

Who is this Blanche, and where did she come from? Is the Duchess still sick?

You might be making a couple of novenas about the Vanderbilt business now that you've got the man on the farm settled.

Regards to kin.

    Love,

    MF

P.S. Don't tell *anybody* about the Vanderbilt thing, *please*.

* * *

Friday [25 Apr. 1947]

Dear R.

Got your letter and one from Annie Bruce, which I appreciated. No, I haven't written Mag Steinbridge. I will do it as soon as I can. You can tell her I appreciate the spoon and want to write her. I do well to write you every day. There is no help for working as hard as possible right now. I will also have to write long hours this summer.

I have another appointment with Tate on Sunday, and then he will be off. I may hear next week whether it was too late to apply at Vanderbilt or whether I have a chance.

Obliged for the recipe, which I will give [to] Martha Bell.

Can't get the Barrington Hall office anymore, so have started mixing the regular coffee with egg and pouring boiling water over it. It is fine.

I presume from the card that Agnes has got the people out of the upstairs and has her tribe moved in.

If you see Annie Bruce, ask her where she got the idea I was going to New York? Regards to kin.

 Love,
 MF

* * *

Saturday [26 Apr. 1947]

Dear R.

Too bad about the trained nurse. I hope she has not gone for good.

What did my last bank statement say? I don't know how much I've got in the bank but now that it is hot I am eating two meals a day out and of course it is more expensive. I have plenty of money I am sure, but I don't know whether I will have enough for my ticket home also.

If I come on the train, what happens about the trunk? How does it get to Milledgeville?

Hope to hear something about Vanderbilt next week—at least whether or not I have a chance. *If* I do get one, and it is not enough for me to live on, I will take it anyhow and supplement it with that money Cousin Katie gave me, as Tate thinks after the novel is completed, I won't have to worry too much about teaching full time.

 Regards to kin.
 Love,
 MF

* * *

Monday [28 Apr. 1947]

Dear R.

That is certainly too bad about the nurse and your help troubles. I wouldn't want her back.

Lytle said today he didn't think the Vanderbilt Fellowship was but $500; however, I will take it anyhow if I am so fortunate as to get it. He is writing Davidson today. Tate left this morning. He was impressed with my work, and I feel I have a most valuable connection in knowing him.

We are finishing the title page and dedication to my thesis today. It is dedicated to Paul Engle. I still don't know if Ruth is going to finish her thesis or not.

I won't have time to write the Davidsons for a couple of weeks. I wish if you have a chance you'd do it.

Very warm here. Regards to kin.

> Love,
> MF

* * *

### Tuesday [29 Apr. 1947]

Dear R.

Got your Friday letter and happy you were pleased over the possibility of Vanderbilt. I certainly hope to hear from them something this week. Even if it is only $500, it will be fine if I can get it. About the novel—there is no use talking about any novel until it is finished. I have been working on this one since before Christmas, but I don't believe in mentioning things you don't know will pan out or not. I don't care to find myself in Mary Sallee's predicament. I have gone far enough along in it now and received sufficient encouragement, however, to make me believe that the thing to do is finish it—which will take at least a year and a half. To do this you have to be somewhere there are other people in your field, people who can criticize technically etc. I couldn't finish the novel at home and that is why I am so anxious over the Vanderbilt business. The place there is full of people who can help me. I don't have to worry about getting the novel published. I have to worry about getting it written and believe me it is a most tremendous amount of work to think about.

Are you going to buy any more chickens this summer? I would like to raise some like last year only more. As long as you got to fool with 25 you might as well fool with 100. I mean in the back yard not at the farm.

> Regards to kin.
> Love,
> MF

* * *

### Wednesday [30 Apr. 1947]

Dear R.

Got a letter from Davidson today, saying that the fellowship there had been discontinued. So that is that. When it is given, it is only given to Vanderbilt students. However, continue to pray that the Lord will provide something else.

I settled the fur coat question today by sending it down to Strubes like I did last year. They will send it to me wherever I am next year without extra charge. Also, I don't have to pay postage sending it to them. It will cost $12.50 to have it stored, cleaned, glazed, repaired, and insured. So that is also that.

Trust you have your nurse back. I reckon you had to dispense with Mrs. Bruce since Miss Mary is back.

Regards to kin.

  Love,
  MF

    \* \* \*

   Thursday [1 May 1947]

Dear R.

Talked to Engle today, and he is trying to get something for me around here, but I doubt he will be able to do it. Anyway, he is trying.

Ruth was highly pleased with your letter, and I thought it very fine myself.

You have to stay for the degree or you don't get it, unless somebody in your family dies or gives birth to quintuplets. I already enquired, because I thought I'd be off a couple of weeks in advance. Since that can't be, I will leave here on the 8th via train, I presume. The trunk will get to Atlanta the day after I do, and then how will it get to Milledgeville?

Glad you have got somebody for the farm. What do these people do?

By the way, I got 4 graduation invitations. Who do you want them sent to? Four is all I'm going to get, so write me what you want done with them. I figured you would want one and Cousin Katie one, and I got 2 extra in case you wanted one sent to Frank and Josie, since they sent me all those cakes. I think I will give the other one to Ruth to send to her folks if she graduates, because she hasn't ordered any because she hasn't known if she'd graduate.

I see I have more money in the bank than I thought. It costs me $12.00 some weeks here now, but I think I will have plenty left over at the end of the month. Things go up and up around here.

Regards to kin.

  Love,
  MF

* * *

Friday [2 May 1947]

Dear R.

Enclosing a picture of Martha Bell, which kindly put with the ones of Sarah and Barbara. Cousin Katie sent me a leaflet of the Sacred Heart today. Weather very poor here, having entered upon the rainy season. What are you going to do with all these colts? Did you rent the house to the people from Kentucky? I thought you said Sister was going to give her car to Herbert and buy the Cadillac. What did she do?

Nothing doing around here but work.

Regards to kin.

Love,

MF

* * *

Saturday [3 May 1947]

Dear R.

Got one letter from you today. Ate lunch with Dr. Beiswanger today and enjoyed that. Sarah has gone home for the weekend, which leaves the house quieter. What color are you all painting the hall? What was that on Agnes's card about Louise coming? Is she going to spend the summer again? I reckon that would please Miss Mary mightily.

Nothing doing here but work.

Regards to kin.

Love,

MF

* * *

Sunday [4 May 1947]

Dear R.

Weather most decent—wearing that purple dress with the white on it, so must not have gained much over the winter.

Ruth still struggling over the thesis. It has to be in typed by Thursday, and she isn't finished writing it, so I don't know whether she'll get it done or not.

What did Miss Mary say when she found out Duchess had had Communion?

Nothing doing here but work.
>  Love,
>  MF

* * *

Monday [5 May 1947]

Dear R.

I am sending you two wire baskets for your desk and two other items for it—wrapped in some of my winter pajamas. Think you will find the baskets handy—you put your papers in them, letters etc. The other two things are self-explanatory.

What do you mean, "since Ruth is getting married, she figures she won't bother." Bother about what? I don't know what wrong idea I have given you, but kindly don't be passing judgment on her.

Will be delighted to see Dr. Beiswanger if he calls.

The "we" finishing the title page is Barbara.

Nothing doing here but work.

Regards to kin. Did you rent the house to the Kentucky people?
>  Love,
>  MF

* * *

Tuesday [6 May 1947]

Dear R.

Got two of your letters today, so presume I won't get any tomorrow. We have just learned that we will have 3 more exams than Engle told us originally, so I don't know if we'll pass them or not. Ruth's thesis has been accepted. I am mighty glad.

Glad you are getting rid of so many of your horses. How long is Cousin Katie going to stay?

I will leave here on Sunday and get to Atlanta on Monday so far as I can now determine.

Nothing doing here but work. Don't send any of my light clothes, as I won't be here but a month longer, and it wouldn't be worth it.

Regards to kin.
>  Love,
>  MF

* * *

Wednesday [7 May 1947]

Dear R.

Went and ordered my ticket today. The man said [I] could send the trunk the day before, which will do. Can't be sure when it will get to Atlanta but probably before I do.

They have changed the mail delivery schedule around here to 2 o'clock instead of 10, so I won't get your letter off until the 6 o'clock mail now. No letter from you today anyhow.

When are you expecting Miss Bancroft to arrive?

My regards to Cousin Katie if she is there. Regards to other kin.

Love,

MF

* * *

Thursday [8 May 1947]

Dear R.

My watch stopped this morning, and I have taken it to the jewelers to see what ails it. Will find out tomorrow. If something is bad wrong with it and it will take them a long time to fix it, I will just wait until I get home, and maybe you can send me one of those dollar watches hanging around your desk. Anyway, I hope nothing much is wrong with it and they can give it to me in a hurry.

I have an hour and a half in Chicago. Perhaps I will see Dr. Beiswanger tomorrow. It has turned [awful] cold here—this year is much different from last as regards weather.

Nothing here but work. How long is Cousin Katie going to stay?

Regards to kin.

Love,

MF

* * *

Friday [9 May 1947]

Dear R.

Got the watch back this morning. It needs cleaning and the balance is broken, and they can't give it to me here short of 6 weeks anywhere, so I will send it to you, and you can take it to Grants, and maybe will have it ready shortly after I get home. Don't you have some of those bureau models of Louis's that you could send me? I can get along without one here, but not for the trip home. I can't get anything here.

Didn't get any letter from you today. But a pamphlet from Cousin Katie. Will you tell her that I appreciate it and am enjoying it.

Ruth has gone to South Bend for to see Mr. Finnegan, having got her thesis in. Paul was very nice to let her use some of the stories she did for it. Haven't seen Dr. Beiswanger.

Regards to kin.

> Love,
> MF

* * *

### Saturday [10 May 1947]

Dear R.

Nothing doing around here but work. Thesis cost $21.00—20¢ a page, but I was glad to pay it. Martha Bell has gone home for the weekend. I wrote Mag Steinbridge today, so consider that off my neck. Is Mrs. Logan back for good?

We graduate on a Saturday, so I reckon I will go to early church Sunday, take the 9 o'clock Rocket, have an hour and a half in Chicago, and get home Monday. Don't like to contemplate the trip.

Regards to kin.

> Love,
> MF

Wrote Mrs. Semmes yesterday.

* * *

### Sunday [11 May 1947]

Dear R.

Sending this airmail, because my watch has started running again of its own volition—of course, I don't know for how long, but it seems to be all right, so you needn't send the bureau model.

Went to Communion for you this morning. Regards to kin.

> Love,
> MF

* * *

Monday [12 May 1947]

Dear R.

Glad you liked the desk businesses. My watch is still going, which I find admirable. About Ruth—she was working as hard as she could to finish the thesis and finished it. She gets back from South Bend today. That is funny about the Bonds going back together. How do you like this new man? Does Joan graduate in June or will she be around this summer?

Bessie is mighty gushy. How long will Catherine Garner be in Shreveport? Regards to kin.

    Love,

    MF

* * *

Monday [12 May 1947]

Dear R.

Got two of your letters today and the paper. That is too bad about Joan. Did the horse do all this to her?

Who will look after the farm with you in Savannah? Does Uncle ever go out there? Do I gather that the dispute about the fence is over?

It is right warm here, and I took a trip to the A&P, but they didn't have much down there. No, I don't want any sugar, but I could do with some of them bouillon cubes and them puddings. They appeal to my palate considerable. I don't know what kind of apples those are I get, except they are pie apples and cost 25¢.

Hope you got the dress.

Regards to kin.

    Love,

    MF

Have to remember to buy me some envelopes.

* * *

Tuesday [13 May 1947]

Dear R.

Martha Bell's mama and papa are coming to see her this afternoon, because she was supposed to have a wisdom tooth taken out this morning. She went to get it out and the doctor cauterized it instead.

Ruth not back yet. She was supposed to come back last night, but I presume the attractions of Mr. Finnegan proved too much.

Weather very poor here. I have had to stop writing for the last week and the coming one to try to prepare for my comprehensive. Engle hasn't set a date for them yet.

Regards to kin.

Love,
MF

\* \* \*

Wednesday [14 May 1947]

Dear R.

Got two of your letters today and Cousin Katie's and the numerous enclosures, all of which I enjoyed. Tell Cousin Katie she is free to move any of the irreligious objects in my room which interfere with her prayers.

Write me if I get any manuscripts back, as I am having them sent to Milledgeville.

Ruth got back yesterday. Mr. Finnegan is going to come up here when he gets through his examinations on the 27th and wait over to ride back East with her on the 7th.

I inquired for Mr. Stembridge, not Mr. "Willy"!

Nothing doing here but a great deal of work. Regards to kin.

Love,
MF

\* \* \*

Thursday [15 May 47]

[*On "Miss Mary Flannery O'Connor" notecard*]
Dear R.

Am having my comprehensives tomorrow and Saturday, so won't expend myself on this. No letter from you today. Regards to kin.

Love,
MF

* * *

Friday [16 May 1947]

[*On "Miss Mary Flannery O'Connor" notecard*]

Dear R.

One 5-hour comprehensive exam this afternoon and one tomorrow morning, and that will be the last. Got Sister's letter and appreciated and will write when this is over. Regards to kin.

      Love,
      MF

* * *

Saturday [17 May 1947]

Dear R.

Got your Tuesday letter today. We finished our last exam this morning. They were hard. Now I plan to get back to work on the writing, which I will be most happy to do.

Martha Bell had a tooth pulled yesterday, but it didn't cause her any discomfit. [*sic*]

My watch is still going, keeping better time than it did before.

Am writing Miss Mary today to thank her for her check. Nothing doing here but work.

Regards to kin.

      Love,
      MF

* * *

Monday [19 May 1947]

Dear R.

Think the writing paper handsome, but the envelopes too thin. People with such classy paper should only write on one side of it.

Appreciate the silver, but you certainly don't need to be giving me any graduation present, since you make the coming out here possible.

Went to a May procession at St. Mary's last night. It was very tacky—just like the sisters, you know, but very devotional and well intended.

That is fine that Miss Mary is taking over the house books.

Nothing doing here but work. Regards to kin.

      Love,
      MF

* * *

Tuesday [20 May 1947]

Dear R.

Had an airmail letter today from Robert Penn Warren, saying that if I applied immediately, it would be "likely" that I could get a part-time instructorship at the University of Minnesota next year. I had written him a couple of weeks ago inquiring about fellowships. Of course, I shall apply immediately and hope something comes of it. I would then get to write under Robert Penn, and that would be a great advantage.

Bought my ticket today and it cost $43.00—three dollars cheaper than before. Presume Cousin Katie left today. Regards to kin.

  Love,

  MF

* * *

Wednesday [21 May 1947]

Dear R.

Sent my application to Minnesota yesterday. Of course, I wouldn't like to be in Minneapolis, but if I get the chance to work with Robert Penn Warren, that won't make any difference what I like. I hope something comes of it.

Glad you got a woman for Duchess. You seem to be having much company for Cousin Katie. Presume she had left. Regards to kin.

  Love,

  MF

* * *

Thursday [22 May 1947]

Dear R.

I packed two boxes of books last night and will send them off shortly. I am going to express them collect as they are too heavy for me to carry to the post office, and if I send them collect, I won't have to sit around here waiting for the people to pick them up. I figured up I had bought $35.00 worth of books since September. However, if I smoked I would have spent more than that.

I presumed Mary Virginia wouldn't get out of these United States on an education score. It is too bad she isn't making her own money, and then she could go if she wanted to.

Enjoyed Nancy's letter. Why don't you and Gussie go to Atlanta on the 9th. I am thinking that would be a lovely trip for you in her car.

Regards to kin.

    Love,

    MF

* * *

Friday [23 May 1947]

Dear R.

Sister sent me a check for $15.00—ten of it she said was for my birthday, and the extra five for my graduation. Anyway, today I bought myself a dress with it. We are going to Engle's farm Sunday, and I thought I needed one anyhow. It is blue, buttons down the front, nothing fancy, and cost $14.95. Kindly tell her I got it. I wrote her that's what I thought I'd get. I think Ruth will come on the 15th of June. I don't know. She is now busy catching up on the work she didn't get done when she was writing her thesis.

Martha Bell has another tooth pulled this afternoon. This one is impacted.

Regards to kin.

    Love,

    MF

* * *

Saturday [24 May 1947]

Dear R.

Well, I am attended to for next year. Paul got me something on his writing program. I will teach one or two classes for which I get about 65 or 70 dollars a month. Not much money, of course, and I will have to supplement it with my own, but I won't have anything much to do but write the novel, and he thinks that by the end of next year, we will be able to get an advance on it from a publisher. Anyway, the thing to do is get it written now, and it will be fine to do that here. We are both pleased.

I am trying to get a room for next year from an old lady across the street. I don't know if she'll let me have it, but it is a single and costs $18 a month. This double I'm in now costs $15. I am going to see her this afternoon if it quits raining. Very pleased and grateful to the Lord about this whole business.

Regards to kin.

    Love,

    MF

\* \* \*

Sunday [25 May 1947]

Dear R.

Last night I looked down at my ring, and one of the diamonds was gone from it. Don't know when or where—none of the prongs were broken. I don't know how long it had been gone, but not more than a day, I reckon. Maybe I can find another to put in it sometime.

We are going to Engle's farm at two this afternoon. The affair doesn't begin until four, but it is 40 miles out there.

Regards to kin.

    Love

    MF

\* \* \*

Monday [26 May 1947]

Dear R.

Of course read the manuscript if you want to. Please send me the rejection slip out of it, and don't get the manuscript dirty, as I may be able to send it out again. That is one of the ones Allen Tate read and liked very much.

Now don't go telling people about my staying here another year or that I have an assistantship. These things have to get set in writing first. Also don't say Professorship—a professorship is something you get only after you have worked years—even Engle doesn't have a professorship.

We had a fine time at his place yesterday.

Dining with Miss Nutter tonight.

Regards to kin.

    Love,

    MF

Don't know whether I can get the room from the old lady.

\* \* \*

Tuesday [27 May 1947]

Dear R.

Well, one of the ladies in the next room found the stone to my ring. It was just on the floor in the bathroom, and she happened to see it. Mighty unusual to find something that small.

Haven't found a room yet. This house is not going to be open next year. I have applied for a room in the one that is, but I would rather not stay there if I can do better. The old lady across the street is going to tell me this week sometime if she can take me.

Sorry your nurse didn't work out. Mr. Finnegan expected tonight.

Regards to kin.

  Love,

  MF

* * *

Wednesday [28 May 1947]

[*Via airmail*]

Dear R.

I presume this will take some explaining. I wrote you Engle said he had me some money and I could teach a course. That was hogwash, I presume, to keep me from negotiating too fast for a job somewhere else. The thing is this: I have won a fiction fellowship given by the Rinehart Publishing Company for the first part of my novel. This is the first one they have given, although they offered one in February, but got no novels they thought good enough. The award is $750. As an outright gift; then when (*and if*) the novel progresses to the extent where they see it will be publishable shortly, they will give me an advance on royalties of $500 to $750 and a contract to publish the novel when it is completed. I have been working toward this ever since February but didn't tell anybody, because I didn't want to be commiserated with if I didn't get it. Engle got a telegram last Thursday saying that I had got it, but that it was not to be told until the following Wednesday, as they wanted all their publicity releases put out at one time. He announced then that it had been won and by somebody in the workshop, but he wasn't allowed to say to whom. He was mighty pleased. Saturday he told me that story about having $650 for me. I don't know why he did that, unless he was just excited and wanted to say something. I thought when he told me that, that somebody else had got the Rinehart money, but since I had some money—the $650—it was not so much of a disappointment to find I didn't get the other. Yesterday he told me I had won it, but I was not to tell anybody until the Rinehart release. I don't know if they have released it or not, but they were supposed to today. He thinks that he can get the graduate college to waive my tuition for next year as a consideration. So I will just come here and take a few courses and work on the novel. I am highly pleased and he is delighted. This throws a lot of credit on him. This is the first one that has hit the Workshop. I presume Rinehart will see that this gets in the Atlanta papers, but for Pete's sake, don't go telling people about it so that it gets in the paper through anything but Rinehart channels. They are very particular, and as Engle says—you don't upset people who give you money. By no means tell Mrs. Hines—just the family and Gussie if you want to.

It is 37° here and wet. If it is not raining here tomorrow, Sarah is going to drive us to Cedar Rapids.

We all passed our exams, although we don't know what grades we made yet.

Mr. Finnegan arrived and seems admirable. Regards to kin.

>Love,
>MF

\* \* \*

Friday [30 May 1947]

Dear R.

Had a decent time in Cedar Rapids, but didn't buy anything—ate, went to the picture show—*The Egg and I*; it was punk—and came back.

Of course Ruth's people are not coming to the graduation—people don't come to these kinds of graduations. I don't want any clothes; am much obliged for the silver, but as I said, you don't need to be giving me anything.

They had an anemic parade here this morning, and no mail and no stores open. It is still cold but not wet.

My train is supposed to get to Atlanta around 9 or 10 something. Don't know which, probably won't be on time anyway.

I mean to get those books off tomorrow, but so much has been going on, worrying about this Rinehart business that I haven't had time. I hate the idea of packing it all up and then unpacking it—such as the lamp. However, will be glad to get home and to work. Hope to work early in the morning and after supper when it is cool.

Regards to kin and Miss Bancroft.

>Love,
>MF

\* \* \*

Saturday [31 May 1947]

Dear R.

Two letters from you today and a card from Miss Bancroft, which I appreciated. Ruth lives in Lancaster, N.H.

We didn't do anything at the farm but sit around. Those that brought their own liquor drank it. Engle furnished the food but wouldn't be responsible for the other out in the country. The ones that got drunk all came home together. They were in an open car and it was storming, so they must have had a fine time. Ruth went, but not with the people I went with. It was very nice, and I had a fine time.

I am going to Des Moines with Sarah Tuesday to spend the day. I don't want to go, but she gets her feelings hurt easy, so I reckon I will.

Sent three boxes off today railway express.

Regards to kin.

> Love,
> MF

\* \* \*

Monday [2 June 1947]

Dear R.

Got your Wednesday and Thursday letters today, also a letter and check and a light gold choker from Cousin Katie, all of which I appreciated. Didn't write you yesterday, as there was too much going on. Barbara's mother spent the night here and they went home this morning. Barbara is mighty nice, and I like her mother very much; also her father. Barbara gave me a sweatshirt for graduation, and Sarah and Connie gave me Robert Penn Warren's *All the King's Men*.

Apparently, we are still going to Des Moines tomorrow—it is about like going to Atlanta from Milledgeville. I ain't looking forward to it.

Regards to kin and Miss Bancroft.

> Love,
> MF

\* \* \*

Tuesday [3 June 1947]

Dear R.

Didn't go to Des Moines as I was sick last night, and so stayed home to a dose of Sal Hepatica today. Staying home was worth getting sick for. I sho didn't want to go anyhow.

Got your Friday night letter, and I am happy you are pleased over the Rinehart business, but be pleased to remember this: the novel is not finished, and until it gets finished, this means nothing to me except $750, and a possible $500 advance later. Finishing it will be mighty hard work.

Ate supper with Ruth and Cyril last night and think he is very fine. Ruth just told her mother she was coming to visit me, and on top of the information about the marriage—which her mother had just got—it didn't sit so well, so I don't know if she will come or not. Anyway, I told her not to worry about it—come if she could, and if she couldn't, all right.

Graduate students don't stay at Currier. They are all to be in Eastlawn next year—a place near St. Mary's. I hope I can get a room there, but I don't know yet.

The trunk leaves here Friday on the afternoon train, so it should get to Atlanta Sunday. Couldn't you get Louis to express it? Or get it to the bus station or something?

Martha Bell has another wisdom tooth out this afternoon.

Regards to kin.

Love,

MF

Enclose some pictures.

* * *

Wednesday [4 June 1947]

Dear R.

Sent off another box today. Gussie sent me a note, which I appreciated. The river here is above flood stage, but they don't expect it to mess up anything.

I sho do have a lot of junk to take off. Next year, I'm not going to bring but half the clothes and half the everything else I've got here now.

Weather very poor.

Regards to kin.

Love,

MF

# Fall Semester 1947

Although Flannery earned her master's degree from the University of Iowa in the spring of 1947, she did return that fall for a postdoctoral fellowship. While the archive does not contain as complete a collection of letters from this period, it does contain several from that fall. While the September letters are similar to her letters from the previous two Septembers, with details about her new landlady, Mrs. Guzeman, and the heating situation in her new boardinghouse, these letters are notable for the new sense of independence that Flannery openly asserts in them.

For example, in the beginning of February, she directly asks Regina to start using her chosen name: "Would consider it very generous of you just to call me *Flannery*. That is who I am, that is who I am always going to be, and the people whom I will associate with and do associate with know nothing else. Very generous of you" (4 Nov. 1947). While she had previously explained to Regina that she was using the name "Flannery O'Connor" in her writing and that "They call me Flannery here" (26 Oct. 1945), Flannery's direct request and explanation here is a striking declaration of an autonomous identity. Once again, not having Regina's side of the correspondence is frustrating, as Regina's response seems to have been a complicated but ultimately supportive one, as Flannery notes in a later letter: "Consider your effort to call me Flannery admirable. May I ask what brought your consideration of it? What does Miss Mary think of your doing it?" (24 Nov. 1947).

In the archive, Flannery's signatures on these letters reflect an unstable but determined assertion of her chosen name. For most of their correspondence, Flannery signed her letters "Love, MF," or sometimes "Love, MFO'C." Over the course of November 1947, when she makes this request of her mother, it takes her some time to settle on a new signature. When she first makes the request, she still signs her letter "Love, MF." The next few letters seem to experiment with various new signatures—sometimes they are still "MF," perhaps out of habit, but with the "F" becoming more prominent. On her letter from 24 November 1947, for example, the letters "M" and "F" are scribbled nearly on top of each other, nearly illegible. In some letters, she signs "Flann," and others "Fl," finally settling on a simple "Love, F," mirroring the "Dear R" with which she addressed most letters to Regina. Flannery's assertion of her changing identity in these letters is one of the more intriguing aspects of the *Dear Regina* letters, one that deserves further attention by scholars. How does Flannery's claiming of a new name reflect changes in her self-identity? Certainly, it must reflect a self-awareness at some level of the other changes in her worldview that her experiences in Iowa brought about.

* * *

Thursday night [18 Sept. 1947]

Dear R.

A nice trip all the way up. Louis and your sister Tarleton were at the bus to meet us. Ate lunch, then got Agnes off, then went to look for a plow line, then got the trunk. It was still locked but put the plowline on it anyhow. Called Mary Boyd up and then went with Louis around and then ate and then caught the train, which was on time. This morning in the diner, met the girl who wrote me last year about getting an apartment up here. She and another girl from GSCW were coming up here to study physiotherapy. So we came on to Iowa City together. They were mighty glad to see somebody going there that they knew. Got here at 6pm and taxied to Mrs. Guzeman's. The same met me at the door and conducted me to the room. The room is fine, contains gold bed, rocker, padded straight chair, plain straight chair, big solid table, bookcase, bureau, lamp, bedside table, trash basket, suitcase stand, rug, curtains, and a closet almost as big as the room. She had already lined the drawers with paper and put blotters on the desk and a bureau scarf on the dresser. Also contains two large mirrors. I put my spread on and Mrs. Guzeman was mightily taken with it. She thought it was about the prettiest spread she had seen. I certainly like her. She is funny and very friendly. The business about the overflow room is settled—it is rented. So she has three of us. The other two seem very nice; however, you never know until you see more of them. There is an ironing board in one of their rooms, which I think belongs to Mrs. Guzeman, so it seems it is all right to use it.

It is very very hot here.

I hope your dairyman is on his way. I forgot the Unicaps, but if you will send them, I'll take them.

Sho like this place.

Love,

MF

Regards to Miss Mary and Gussie.

\* \* \*

Friday [19 Sept. 1947]

Dear Regina,

Am still extremely pleased with the set-up here. Have been introduced to where the ironing board is kept and understand from one of the other girls that the laundress does sheets for ten cents a sheet—she can do mine for that. One of the people here is a music teacher in the high school and the other a physical education teacher in the university. They are both working on their master's, and I would set them both in their late twenties.

Went to see Paul and was greeted with great cordiality etc. etc. etc. When he leaves for his lecture tour, Lytle will come up and stay until he gets back. He was much pleased over the *Mademoiselle* deal.

The trunk came and a bottle of powder that I didn't know I had put in had broken in the hang-up section and got over everything most. However, the spirits had only leaked slightly, for which I am grateful. It is very hot here, too hot to have any, yet.

The yellow bed sleeps mighty fine.

When you send the Unicaps, please send these two books: James Joyce's *Dubliners*, one of those small books on the bookkeeping desk toward the fireplace; and the book *Understanding Fiction*, which I think I left on the floor.

I am taking two things—the Workshop and a seminar of Warren's and will have to pay about twenty or thirty dollars tuition, but Engle said it couldn't be helped.

When we were in Atlanta, Cleo told me that she wasn't going to tell Sister when she was operated on, because she didn't want her to worry, but the idea was she wished Sister would come on up there and get her [to] visit so she could go on and have the operation.

Reckon the dairyman is expected soon.

Regards to kin.

    Love,
    MF

\* \* \*

Saturday [20 Sept. 1947]

Dear R.

Have about got myself settled here and expect to get back to work sho nuf Monday. Got your Wednesday letter today and enjoyed. I am glad Mrs. Guzeman has rented her overflow room, as it relieves me of the responsibility of visitors from any quarter. Also, the girl she rented it to is very nice, although a physical education teacher from New Jersey. The other one is all right, too, although a singing teacher from Omaha.

I don't find the cost of food up too considerably. Today for dinner I had spare ribs and sauerkraut, applesauce, cottage cheese on lettuce, big muffin, and ice cream for 56¢. That ain't bad. Wrote Louis and thanked him for his attentions in Atlanta.

I am certainly enjoying that black pocketbook. It is easy to hang on to.

My regards to kin.

> Love,
> MF

* * *

Sunday [21 Sept. 1947]

Dear R.

Come to find out the music teacher from Omaha—named Deloris—is a Catholic. Nice to have another one around.

It rained last night and is turning much colder. I hope you got your hay and stuff in. Did you all get much of the storm? What about the Rogers? Did they come in on top of the rat?

This is certainly a nice place to be in, and Deloris, who was here last year, says it is very warm in the winter. Mrs. Guzeman dusts around and empties the trash baskets once a week. She puts on a dusting hat to do this and is very funny.

I presume the little girl is still talking. Regards to kin.

> Love,
> MF

* * *

Monday [22 Sept. 1947]

Dear R.

Today I saw Fay Hancock that Janet Fowler told me was going to be up here. She is a Mrs. Somebodyorother and her husband is in the Workshop. They are going to move into one of the University trailers—have to draw all their own water.

It is right cold, and I am sleeping under a blanket, but the heat is on and the house is very comfortable in the daytime. I keep milk and rusk in the room here, also apples and such. It doesn't seem to disturb Mrs. Guzeman.

The gloves we bought in Macon have already split, and I have worn them maybe one time.

Have you heard from Agnes? Have you told Gussie the overflow room is rented? If you see Mary Sallee, tell her, too. That was stupid what you said was in the little paper. Better to keep your business to yourself and not let them know.

Regards to kin. Hope the wind didn't knock down any of your fences etc.

Love,

MF

\* \* \*

Tuesday [23 Sept. 1947]

Dear R.

Have got myself fully settled and to work. Thought that clipping impossible. Received a letter from Ruth reissuing the Thanksgiving invitation, so I reckon I will go down there then.

Found out today I will have to pay $48.33 worth of tuition. They have raised the price for out-of-state students. So it is a good thing I got the story from Mademoiselle.[2]

Eberhart's pictures came today. I don't think I will send one on to Mademoiselle until I hear from them. Paul says they are quick about paying.

Tomorrow I will go to one of the two classes I have—7:30 P.M. I know you are glad to be shut of the Woods. Regards to kin.

Love,

MF

\* \* \*

Wednesday [24 Sept. 1947]

Dear R.

Got your Sunday letter today. Don't tell Gussie I will try to put Mary Virginia up elsewhere; tell her that if she lets me know soon enough, I may be able to re-serve her a room at the hotel. It will be impossible to get her a room either out in town or in the dormitories, and if she doesn't tell me when she is coming soon enough, I won't be able to reserve a room. People come here for football games and to see their offspring, and you can't get a room a day ahead.

2. "The Turkey," one of the stories included in O'Connor's master's thesis, was published as "The Capture" in *Mademoiselle* in Nov. 1948 and reprinted in her *Collected Stories* in 1971.

Did the man Mr. Guin used to work for ever send you his recommendation? If not why not? (Uncle)

When Lytle comes, I will tell him Ed Dawson asked about him.

I have been eating every night with Anne, the physical education teacher. She is a very nice person indeed, in spite of teaching what she does. The other one is gone most of the time.

Enclose a letter I had from Frances Lewis for the Duchess's amusement.

Regards to kin.

> Love,
> MF

* * *

Thursday [25 Sept. 1947]

Dear R.

Am glad Mr. Guin has arrived and well-recommended. What does his wife look like?

Doesn't sound very good about Agnes. I hope she gets along better, but it would be nice for you to go up. If you're going, go before it gets icy, because there's no use to break your leg.

The books and Unicaps haven't come, but I dare say they will by tomorrow.

Has Sister ever heard from Frank?

My health is doing very nicely. No hives. Regards to kin.

If you see Mrs. Hines, tell her I haven't been able to give Paul the book yet because he has been away and will shortly go on his lecture tour, so I may not have a chance for a while.

> Love,
> MF

* * *

Friday [26 Sept. 1947]

Dear R.

Am invited to Fay Hancock Messnick's tomorrow night. They have just moved into a trailer. I have never been inside a trailer, so this will be an experience. Her husband is in the Workshop and from North Carolina.

The vitamins and books came and I am highly obliged, and will commence taking the Unicaps.

Glad you and Miss Mary are preserving the peace. When does Uncle get back?

None of the girls I knew last year are back; however, most of the men are. If a manuscript or a letter comes for me from the *Sewanee Review*, send it right on.

Regards to kin.

Love,

MF

P.S. Greatly relieved that Mary Virginia is routed away from Iowa. Would now like to route Mary Sallee away from same.

\* \* \*

### Saturday [27 Sept. 1947]

Dear R.

Your letter and the check from *Mademoiselle* came today. The check looks mighty good. I have just got back from visiting the Messnicks in their trailer, and it was all right if you like trailers. They are very pleased, as it is better than nothing. They have to go out to the bathroom and draw their water from elsewhere.

Does the man have any geese? He sounds like a nice man. You ought to have turkeys, geese, and guineas out there.

Haven't written Agnes but will do so. Also Sister, but there is a lot to do here, and I don't get around to such right off.

Regards to kin.

Love,

MF

\* \* \*

### Sunday [28 Sept. 1947]

Dear R.

Nothing ever doing much on Sunday. We went to see the picture "Dear Ruth" and it was pretty sorry, but had some good lines in it here and there.

I have written Agnes and Cousin Katie, so those are discharged.

I wore the new suit today and discovered as I was about to emerge from the house that the lining was falling out of the coat on one side. I will have to secure it. Weather very fine here.

I trust by now the Napier tea is a beautiful memory. Regards to kin.

Love,

MF

\* \* \*

Monday [29 Sept. 1947]

Dear R.

Got your Thursday letter and postcard, some Sacred Heart leaflets from Cousin Katie, and an answer to my letter to the Georgia Review from John Wade, asking me to send some of the chapters of the novel. I can't send anything until I get that manuscript back from the Sewanee Review. Of course, I would rather the Sewanee Review publish it, but I doubt if they will. It is long overdue, so send it on immediately it comes.

I trust the Hartys have bowed and scraped off the stage by now.

Naturally, I sewed the gloves up.

I paid my tuition today and felt poorly about giving them that $48.33; however, since I had just deposited the $300, I didn't feel too poorly.

The new man sounds mighty good.

The girl who is a Catholic here is not such a shouting one—the other girl is really much nicer. Her parents came over from Russia before the first world war. She speaks Russian well and doesn't act like the usual physical education person.

Regards to kin.

    Love,

    MF

\* \* \*

Tuesday [30 Sept. 1947]

Dear R.

No letter from you today, but an airmail from Mary Virginia saying she was planning to come here on the 24th (Friday) and stay over the weekend. (Bully x@*!!) I phoned the Jefferson, and they said they could reserve a room for the 25th, 26th, and 27th, so I reserved it. Deloris said she would swap beds (rooms) with me on the 24th. She has a double bed. I don't relish it in the least, but I wrote Mary Virginia to come on. It is very nice of Deloris to do it for that night. I am hoping maybe there will be a cancellation at the hotel or that Edna knows of a room I could get out in town. I'll call her and ask. Mary Virginia said of course all the plans were subject to change—if she's going to subject them to change, I hope she does it before the 23rd.

Be on the lookout for that manuscript. Sometimes they are careless about the mail around there.

I haven't got any Union Recorder since I've been here. Also haven't got the *Time* I ordered.

Regards to kin.

Love,

MF

\* \* \*

Wednesday [1 Oct. 1947]

Dear R.

Got your letter with the clipping from Miss Bancroft, also a letter from her containing a fragment of a Milledgeville paper of 1940 which was sent to me apparently to relish its antiquity. Very nice of her, but I confined it to the trash can right away. Her sister had picked it up off some package she got from a colored woman when she and Helen were in Milledgeville.

You never said if the Rodgers had moved in or not or how they liked it. I trust the rat was gone.

How did the clinic doctor know to tell Agnes that it was pre-cancer? Has Miss Mary ever heard from Frank?

I have run up on a good many weddings at St. Mary's in the morning. Today I ran up on a 50th wedding anniversary, where the old lady and gentleman were celebrating it at a high mass. Before the mass, they went up to the altar and the Monsignor read a service. Never had seen one of those before.

Regards to kin.

Love,

MF

\* \* \*

Thursday [2 Oct. 1947]

Dear R.

Got your letter on the back of Agnes's today and was glad to hear that the dairy-man is doing so hot. Glad she is feeling better and that they aren't charging her too much for the shots.

Met the girl from North Carolina today just for a few minutes but will call her tomorrow and eat with her sometime soon.

Went to dinner tonight with a novelist who is here, thence to drink beer, and thence to another guy's house to listen to records.

What about your sister Tarleton, when does her operation take place? She told me she was not going to tell you all when it was going to be, as she didn't want to worry you. Has Miss Mary ever been to Atlanta to visit her? When does the Uncle return?

Regards to kin.

Love,

MF

\* \* \*

Friday [3 Oct. 1947]

Dear R.

Got your letter on the back of Mrs. Curtis's. If people keep writing you, you won't have to waste any paper on me.

Paul—not Paul Engle, but another Paul who is here, a novelist, says it takes Mademoiselle about 4 months to get anything in after they've accepted it. So possess your soul in patience. He thinks I should write them to let me see the proofs, as they sometimes cut parts of stories. He's had some in there.

How do Mrs. Logan and Caroline like the new place? Have they ever got the refrigerator back?

You never said how the Napier tea was after the great build-up you gave it.

I saw one of the GSCW girls that I came up with on the train today. They had lost my address and I theirs. They don't like their work so hot. Think we will eat supper together Sunday night.

The Messnicks asked me to supper in their trailer after workshop yesterday, but as I was going elsewhere, I couldn't go. She said they would invite me again. She is working in the library.

Regards to kin.

Love,

MF

\* \* \*

Saturday [4 Oct. 1947]

Dear R.

Got my Rinehart check today and two copies of the *Georgia Review*. I took a year's subscription. I am glad I saw it before I sent them anything—the quality of the stories is so poor I would be ashamed to have parts of my novel appear in it, couldn't do me anything but harm. I will send them a good story I haven't been able to get rid of and they can take it or leave it. I imagine they are trying hard to bring the quality up, but until it comes up I ain't going to sacrifice my novel.

The gentleman Anne goes with sent her 4 reserved seat tickets to the football game today. He was away and couldn't come, and I got inveigled into going with her. It was dull, uncomfortable, and crowded, and I will know better than to go again.

Got the bill from Eberhart's. $9.50 which I will send them on an Exchange Bank check.

One of Engle's assistants was on the panel of the Arts Forum at N.C. He has told me a lot about it.

Haven't got a chance to look at the clipping but will do so.

Too bad Miss Mary is only going to be in Atlanta for the day.

Regards to kin.

> Love,
> MF

* * *

Sunday [5 Oct. 1947]

Dear R.

Ate tonight with the 2 GSCW girls. They say they have to work pretty hard. They invited me to supper next Saturday night. They cook where they live a couple of nights a week.

Spent my day typing an old story over for the Georgia Review and writing Wade a letter telling him what I thought about the quality of fiction printed in the Review.[3] I am anxious to see how the letter will be received.

Mrs. Guzeman says the washwoman will be around Tuesday, so I guess I will meet her.

Robert Lowell, the Catholic convert, this year's Pulitzer Prize poet, is coming this week. Paul (Griffith) is going to have a party, but I don't know if it will be while Lowell is here or not, as he is not going to stay all week.

Trust you got the room done over.

Regards to kin.

> Love,
> MF

---

3. O'Connor is referring to her story "The Crop," which was published posthumously in 1971. See letter of 28 Oct. 1947.

* * *

Monday [6 Oct. 1947]

Dear R.

Got the manuscript today. It was not a rejection but a return with a few suggestions about certain points. He said he was seriously considering it. As they were all minor points, I am going to do what he suggested and send it back. I certainly hope he takes it. A story in the *Sewanee Review* means twice as much to me as one in *Mademoiselle*. It means you can write work published on the highest level published today.

Paul (Engle) called about 2 o'clock this afternoon and asked if I wanted to go to Stone City and eat supper with Robert Lowell and a few others. Went and had a very fine time, although I was the only one of my sex present besides Mrs. Tiempo, the Philippino's wife. About 15 in all. Paul is going to spend the winter in Florida, Lytle will take his place. But there are also three young novelists here who are very fine, so the criticism will remain good, if not be better. Paul will be back in the spring.

I had a letter today from Barbara, saying they were coming next weekend. Sarah has a place to stay, and Barbara wanted to stay with me. I will write and tell her she can if she don't mind sleeping with me in the gold bed—it's three-quarter, sort of. Deloris would let me use hers, but she thinks her sister is coming. We will go out to the Amanas to eat Sunday.

Regards to kin.

    Love,
    MF

P.S. I will drop Mrs. Tarleton a hearty greeting by way of being kind to the sick and family-like.

* * *

Tuesday [7 Oct. 1947]

Dear R.

Got your letter and two Recorders today, so, so much for the Recorder. If Louis wants to pay Mary Virginia's hotel bill, it is OK with me, but I sho can't pay it myself. I wish she would decide to come on the 25th instead of the 24th. I haven't heard from her.

Went to hear Robert Lowell read his poetry tonight. He is very fine.

I have a lousy cold part as a result of riding to Stone City, I dare say, and also the change of temperature here—extremely hot all of a sudden.

Got my manuscript off to the Sewanee. I certainly hope [John E.] Palmer takes it, but he may not.

Regards to kin.

    Love,

    MF

* * *

Wednesday [8 Oct. 1947]

Dear R.

Got a letter from Mary Virginia today saying she would be here on the 24th and leave on the 27th. OK.

Glad the Rogers like the place. How does all that grey furniture look now that they've moved in? Is Selina still making strange with you?

My cold is better after some aspirins and oranges and a dip or two into my bottle of rotgut.

Am very anxious to hear from the *Sewanee Review* but I guess it will take some time again.

Wrote Cousin Katie and a note to Mrs. Tarleton in her illness.

Hope Louis gets the Caracker house if it's not a bum steer—if so, hope Miller Bell gets it.

Regards to kin.

    Love,

    MF

* * *

Thursday [9 Oct. 1947]

Dear R.

Anne is going to Omaha over the weekend, so if Barbara comes, she won't have to sleep with me, which will be agreeable to both of us. I hope there will be a cancellation on the 24th so Mary Virginia will not have to stay here.

Mrs. Guzeman was just in, and I was showing her my pictures and Mrs. Hines's book. She was highly took by it all and particularly your picture. Says she and the household here will come down and visit next winter. She is very funny. I keep my rotgut on the bookcase, and she saw the bottle and said, "What you got in that bottle, booze?"

My cold is better.

The girl from NC is not a friend of Blanche's, but knows the girl who visited Blanche.

Will you get Louis to send me a couple of typewriter ribbons?

Regards to kin.

    Love,

    MF

* * *

Friday [10 Oct. 1947]

Dear R.

Anne got off for Omaha this afternoon, and I am expecting Barbara tomorrow. Sarah is going to come, too, but she fortunately has somebody else to stay with. Sunday they plan to drive to the Amanas for dinner.

I bought myself a hot plate today and plan to heat water on it for my instant Sanka. Mrs. G doesn't seem to object. Her water is not hot enough, and I am accustomed to drinking hot water during the day, as I can work better that way.

Naturally, I can't and won't ask the GSCW girls to the Union to meet Mary Virginia. Those people work 24 hours a day and have their own friends. I will do the best I can for Mary Virginia, but she should know better than to expect too much. No advice along the entertainment line, please. She won't find this collegiate, and I am afraid the parties I go to would shock her, as she is extremely naive. She won't need the sweatshirt. That was meant to be a joke.

Regards to kin.

    Love,

    MF

* * *

Saturday [11 Oct. 1947]

Dear R.

Got your Wednesday letter replete with advice. I am very fortunate to have a chance to get a part of my novel in the *Sewanee* and every part I can get published before it is published as a book is so much to the good. If Rinehart doesn't want the novel, I will have no trouble having it published by another house. I would much prefer Holt, in fact. As for wanting the story in the Georgia Review, I do not want the story in the Georgia Review. I am only sending them this because of Lytle. I was not tactless in my letter. You should not pass judgments on these things you know nothing about.

Barbara and Sarah came today, and I have certainly enjoyed Barbara. We went for a bird walk this afternoon out in the country while Sarah attended the football game. We went to the city park and looked at the pheasants, geese, ducks, and bantams they have there—very beautiful birds. I see where I am going to spend a lot of time out there. Barbara wants me to spend a weekend soon in Des Moines, so I am going the next football weekend here. Then I'll avoid the stew.

Clyde McLeod, the girl from NC, and I are going out to the Amanas for dinner tomorrow with Robie McCauley and Anthony Hecht. They are teachers here and writers. Robie is the one who was at the Arts Forum. They have a car, which makes it possible to take in greater territory.

Paul Griffith is a novelist and assists in the Workshop.

Got the enclosed card from the Union Recorder. Regards to kin.

> Love,
> MF

* * *

Sunday [12 Oct. 1947]

Dear R.

The visitors from Des Moines departed this morning at 11. They seemed to have enjoyed themselves.

Robie, Tony, Clyde, and I had a very nice day. Went to a Mennonite place called "Homestead." Ate in a big room at one end of a long table. Came back to Iowa City and went to see the pheasants, and then went home with them (not the pheasants) and sat around all afternoon. Went to supper with Clyde and find her a very nice girl. She lives in the dormitory.

Just realized today that Mary Virginia will be here weekend after next, which seems a very short time

Anne not yet back from Omaha but expected tonight. The character she is with drives his car 90 miles an hour, so I hope she gets back.

Mrs. Guzeman had all her windows cleaned and storm windows put up today, because Sunday is the only day she can get the colored man.

Regards to kin.

> Love,
> MF

* * *

Monday [13 Oct. 1947]

Dear R.

Got 3 of your letters today—one of which addressed to 32 S. Bloomington had gone all over the country apparently. Enclose Mrs. Hines's clipping back, which I think is awful. I don't see how they ever manage to contort so much.

Mary Virginia cannot stay here except for the one night. I haven't given Paul Mrs. Hines's book, and I don't think I will.

Both Mr. and Mrs. Tiempo are in the workshop. Mrs. Tiempo looks like Louise Larkin and is lovely. I like her very much too, Mrs. Tiempo, that is.

Enclose my laundry list, and you can see the prices she charged for the things— blouses are .20. Do you think that high?

Also enclose letter I had today from [John E.] Palmer. Send it back please by *return mail* and *do not* show it to Mrs. Hines.

I hope they don't get Paul at GSCW.

Anne got back but very tired. When you send me something again, please enclose that Audubon bird book, as I have found another bird enthusiast.

Regards to kin.

Love,
MF

* * *

Tuesday [14 Oct. 1947]

Dear R.

Mrs. Guzeman has just been in to show me her new pocketbook—looks like something Aunt Gertie would have trotted out. She has put a little table in here for my hot plate so that I don't have to use it on the floor.

All the restaurants have stopped having meat on Tuesdays here. I went to the A&P yesterday looking for bouillon cubes, but they didn't have any. I would like some of those beef-liver ones at your leisure.

No coat or sweater have been needed here for the last four days. The storm windows make it too hot in the room at present, but that will be admirable when it gets cold.

Letter from Ruth saying they were still expecting me Thanksgiving. Would much rather stay at home, but feel obligated. No need of your sending me a check for it, however.

Trust Aunt Tarleton is better. Regards to other kin.

    Love,

    MF

* * *

Wednesday [15 Oct. 1947]

Dear R.

Got your Sunday letter today and would be obliged if you wouldn't write again on that requiem paper. The outside looks like it might be a request from the Purgatorial Society.

I haven't got any invitation to Anne Sallee's chrysanthemum show. Do you ever see Mary? What are they going to do with the house in Milledgeville when they move to Atlanta?

I hope you have sent that letter back. If not please send it right away. The letter from Palmer [editor of *Sewanee Review*].

I hope Mary Virginia burns her pleasure urge out before she gets here. I am not looking forward to her stay with any wild anticipation.

I have just come back from my Wednesday night seminar and have to hang all my clothes out on the porch to get the smoke out of them. I always manage to get in between two pipes.

Have the Garners moved into their new mansion yet?

Regards to kin.

    Love,

    MF

* * *

Thursday [16 Oct. 1947]

Dear R.

Got your Monday letter today. I don't drink the Sanka from choice. It is vile. But coffee keeps me awake.

The headlines this morning said Savannah had been "ripped" by a hurricane. How did it go? What do you hear from Cousin Katie?

Am I supposed to pay for Mary Virginia's meals when she is here? The Friday night she comes, there is to be a poetry symposium which I can take her to, and Saturday I think we will go to Cedar Rapids—mainly because I want to go buy a pair of shoes.

My watch—mainspring—broke this morning and is now at Herteens. Supposedly can get it back Saturday. I don't know to the tune of what price.

Told Paul (Engle) today about Palmer taking the story, and he was much pleased.

Regards to kin.

> Love,
> MF

* * *

Friday [17 Oct. 1947]

Dear R.

Got your Tuesday letter today. What is George Haslam doing in Milledgeville? Do you mean the Whites' house, and if so, where are they?

Can't you buy a teaspoon and send to Anne Sallee for me? I thought you would put my name on whatever you sent. However, don't buy any bowl and send it to her from me—buy a piece of silver—preferably the cheapest piece possible.

It is just like summer here and has been for the last ten days. I don't reckon it will last much longer.

Surprised by the card to see that Mary Virginia had been through here. I thought she was supposed to be routed a different way.

Regards to kin.

> Love,
> MF

* * *

Saturday [18 Oct. 1947]

Dear R.

Got your Wednesday letter today and a very nice letter from Wade of the *Georgia Review* thanking me for my comments on the fiction in the *Review*, which naturally he agreed with.

I have probably destroyed the card from the Union Recorder by now.

I gather this is the day for the Sallee show. Who all are you keeping of the guests?

I don't know what Mrs. Guzeman paid the colored man and wouldn't presume to ask her. However, he didn't do such a hot job on the windows, and it was a sorry time to put up storm windows, as it has been so hot.

Des Moines is 2 hours away on the train. I don't care about going, but there's not much way to get out of it. I may go the weekend after Mary Virginia's visit if nothing is going on around here.

Regards to kin.

Love,

MF

\* \* \*

Sunday [19 Oct. 1947]

Dear R.

Got my watch back yesterday and didn't have to pay but two dollars, for which I was grateful, as I had thought it would be in the neighborhood of five.

Enclose a clipping about Paul culled from one of the university publications. Kindly save it.

My shoes are falling apart, and we went downtown yesterday to try to get some and couldn't find a thing; therefore I am certain I will take Mary Virginia to Cedar Rapids.

I plan to write Mrs. Semmes this evening and ask her how she weathered the hurricane.

Regards to kin.

Love,

MF

\* \* \*

Monday [20 Oct. 1947]

Dear R.

Got your Thursday and Friday letters today. Naturally I do and have been doing my own shirts. As you could see by the list, I only sent her towels and sheets and such. The Audubon book and bouillon cubes haven't come, but I will be expecting them and am much obliged.

Reckon Miss Mary is happy her brother John is returning. What about your sister Tarleton? You never said whether Sister went to Atlanta to stay with her or not.

Got the Union Recorder today. Arnold Parker's thing was so awful I cut it out to save. If his wife writes like he does, she should *sell* a lot of books.

Still hot here. Regards to kin.

Love,

MF

\* \* \*

Tuesday [21 Oct. 1947]

Dear R.

The crackers and cubes came this morning and the book this afternoon, and I have been into both and am much obliged. The cubes are very fine for these meatless Tuesdays.

A change in the weather is expected, so it may be cold for Mary Virginia. I am looking forward with less and less passionate interest to her arrival as Friday approaches. I am hoping there will be a cancellation for that night so I don't have to upset everything around here.

We have a mission scheduled Sunday and Monday at St. Mary's. I never much like missions.

Have you and Gussie abandoned the idea of going to New York? If so, why?

The Sewanee Review does not pay—in money.

Regards to kin.

> Love,
> MF

\* \* \*

Wednesday [22 Oct. 1947]

Dear R.

Got your Sunday letter today and also an airmail from Wade saying he found the story I sent interesting and would hold onto it until he heard from me, but he would prefer one of the novel chapters, if I could send one immediately—which I can't do at present. He writes nice letters.

Are the lots to be laid out on the highway or in the place? How do you decide who gets what lot? I forget—does Uncle have a lot?

I hope Olivia has not quit you or entangled herself in nuptial relations. Is Donnie still around or has she gone to Philly?

Regards to kin.

> Love,
> MF

\* \* \*

Thursday [23 Oct. 1947]

Dear R.

Will write you early tonight, as I am going out to Paul's and will probably be too tired on returning. Stephen Spender (British poet) is here and this is a function for him. I was very happy to learn it was going to be tonight instead of tomorrow or over the weekend, as Mary Virginia's presence would have necessitated my staying at home.

We called the Jefferson tonight and they said we could probably get a room tomorrow if we tried around noon, as some professional convention lets out then. I certainly hope so.

That is handsome that Miller Bell is going to ditch the dump.

It has finally turned chilly, but I hope not for long.

Regards to kin.

Love,

MF

P.S. I ain't particular about sending Anne Sallee anything. Where is the other place Mary is considering going? When are they going to move?

\* \* \*

Friday [24 Oct. 1947]

Dear R.

Well, the buoyant one is here, happily overflowing in a room and bath on the 8th floor of the Jefferson. Oh brother. Is she loud! I took her to a symposium on poetry tonight and was right embarrassed at her comments and their audibility. Bless the Lord that it is only for the weekend. She is all joy and enthusiasm over the trip, and I have been fêted with all the highlights which would not interest anyone but her parent. She, Anne, and I are going to Cedar Rapids tomorrow if it's not pouring. It rained today. Sunday I am taking her to church and to see the Messnicks and probably to the cinema, and Monday with what felicity I will put her on the train!

Had a handsome time out at Paul's. Don't think much of Spender but met Frank Taylor, who is one of the editors at Random House. He is a big friend of John Selby's—albeit much younger—and was good to talk to. Robie and I left around 12, long before the breaking up time—and went to get something to eat. Robie taught at a place called Bard College, about 95 miles from New York. I am interested in the place as a possibility for next year. He is going to write some people. (He was one of the critics on the panel at the Arts Forum—representing Bard.) It is a small college, very literary and favorable to writers. Something may come of it for me.

Cleaned my room so as not to shock Mary Virginia.

Regards to kin.

> Love,
> MF

\* \* \*

### Saturday [25 Oct. 1947]

Dear R.

The trip to Cedar Rapids has been consummated, glory be. Now all I have to do is get rid of Sunday. Oh brother. She is so busy displaying herself until it is pitiful. I am sure all the waitresses at dinner tonight thought she was crazy. Tonight before dinner she met Paul Engle and Frank on the elevator, and told Paul that she enjoyed the symposium, that she was visiting me and etc., and he—generally pretty gay by 6 o'clock of an evening—invited her up to have a drink with them in Spender's room. She told them she couldn't because she had to meet me, and Paul said to tell me it was pretty good to be able to draw people away from Spender— or some such rot. She was quite set up by it.

I bought a pair of shoes and a hat in Cedar Rapids. Nothing much over there.

Weather here is pretty sorry. Regards to kin.

> Love,
> MF

\* \* \*

### Sunday [26 Oct. 1947]

Dear R.

For me the period of agony is almost at an end, but when you get this the happy child will be in Milledgeville, no doubt recounting it all to you. It rained all day and we have just sat around except for this afternoon, when I took her to the Messnicks. Her hotel bill was $11.25. I paid it tonight and my Uncle Louis may make checks payable to Flannery O'Connor.

I am not satisfied with the shoes I got yesterday and am going to take them back this week or next.

Deloris has a lousy cough and cold—went to bed for two hours and then got up and sat on the damp porch. She ain't long on brains.

Mrs. Guzeman was much took with Mary Virginia, who laid it on thick as usual. She gets off tomorrow at nine o'clock. I am very tired.

Regards to kin.

> Love,
> MF

* * *

### Monday [27 Oct. 1947]

Dear R.

At nine o'clock this A.M. the gracious traveller was on her gracious way and I was walking back singing songs of praise to the Almighty. I suppose I enjoyed her visit as much as would be possible for *me* to enjoy her for 3 long days. I think she enjoyed herself. She wanted to pay me back for the room, but I told her I couldn't take it, she'd have to force it on you in Milledgeville—and thus cleared my hands.

A letter from Mary Sallee today saying she wanted to come up here etc. etc. etc. I hate to be the cause of her coming and then have her not like it. As she probably will not. I don't know, she might.

A letter from Barbara inviting me to Des Moines on the 15th weekend.

What is wrong with Ben? The lupus?

Enclose the Bessie letter, which I couldn't make out anyway.

I see by the Recorder that Kitty Marie Smith is likely to contribute to the cause of human progress. I find this fascinating to speculate on.

Regards to kin.

> Love,
> MF

* * *

### Tuesday [28 Oct. 1947]

Dear R.

Went to the mission night services for the first time this evening and found it to be of the Barnum and Bailey variety and am most thankful I didn't take Mary Virginia Sunday night. You ought never to take a non-Catholic until you've heard what is going to come forth.

Bought myself some instant Maxwell House today, and I mean it is *fine*. It has it all over all the others and costs only 42¢.

A card from Mary Virginia from Chicago. I dare say by now you have heard all the extravaganza and nincompoopia and Iowacitia. You might write me some of the Iowacitia.

Two typewriter ribbons today from Louis, for which I have written the thank you letter.

I thought you understood that what I sent the Sewanee Review was the first chapter of the novel. That's all I have sent. Wade has a story called *The Crop*.

Why did Olivia quit?

It has finally cleared up around here. I hope for a while. I think I will go to Cedar Rapids Friday and take these shoes back. I would like to get me a wool jersey dress more dressy than the ones I have. I have in mind blue. Is Mrs. Lawrence having any sales these days?

Regards to kin.

> Love,
>
> MF

When does the drawing of lots take place?

* * *

Wednesday [29 Oct. 1947]

Dear R.

Got your Sunday letter and one from Ruth—they are really expecting me Thanksgiving apparently. I think I will go on Wednesday and come back Friday— that will be long enough for me.

I guess the Sunshine Kid is regaling the locality with her tales of travel. Have they mentioned the $11.25 yet?

Anne and Deloris have colds, but Mrs. Guzeman and I remain healthy.

Today it is cold. I will write Mrs. Hines when I get a chance.

Regards to kin.

> Love,
>
> MF

The Jackson victim sounds insipid.

\* \* \*

Thursday [30 Oct. 1947]

Dear R.

Talked to Paul Engle today. He said some woman in Athens sent him that article about me in the Journal and asked him if he would read her novel. Of course, he wrote her no, he couldn't read it. You see how careful I have to be and why I don't like all this publicity business. Believe me, there will be no more articles in the Journal. He thought the picture, incidentally, very seductive and bitchy.

Got the clippings. I never read those things. If you want to keep them, I'll return the bunch.

Anne was sick all last night, and this morning I called the doctor for her. She went over to the hospital and had sinus X-rays, but her sinuses were clear. She feels better now.

I don't think I will get to Cedar Rapids tomorrow.

Regards to kin.

Love,

MF

\* \* \*

Monday [4 Nov. 1947]

Dear R.

Have your Thursday and Friday letters in hand. Will try to remember to enclose the book ad this time.

Would consider it very generous of you just to call me *Flannery*. That is who I am, that is who I am always going to be, and the people whom I will associate with and do associate with know nothing else. Very generous of you.

I don't care about giving Ruth and the Messnicks fruit cakes. Not that friendly with the Messnicks and Ruth lives too far away.

Have only so far cooked eggs on the plate. I don't know how she would take to my cooking other stuff. I don't like to smell the house up.

Will enquire about the American Victorian.

Mrs. Guzeman sometimes has to be asked to turn the heat up; however, this place is better than most in town. I haven't had any colds since it has got cold.

Had a letter from a quarterly (*Furioso*) today asking me to submit something. Frank Taylor, the Random House editor who was here, had told them about me.

Paul Griffith had introduced me to him one night at Engle's. I don't have anything to send them. It is a good quarterly, though.

Regards to kin.

Love,

MF

\* \* \*

Tuesday [November 1947]

[*On "Miss Flannery O'Connor" notecard*]

Dear R.

The book just came, for which I am greatly obliged to you.

About the income tax: I don't see that it makes any difference to my end whether you claim me for a dependent or not. If you can justify it and save any money that way, file it that way. I gather that if I sell a story for another $300 and then get a teaching job here—which would amount to $261 between September 1948 and January 1949—you would then have to change your estimate, because I would have to file a return. It is doubtful if I will do either of these—although I think I am going to sell the story. If I don't get the teaching job, I will have to use some of that money of mine wherever it is—Exchange Bank or Atlanta or wherever. I don't want to use yours, because I would feel I had to hurry with the book. It is a good three years before I plan to be through with it, but I can worry along with what I've got. Poverty purifieth the spirit; I ain't got the Florencourt urge for great wealth, albeit I could do with a drop more.

Regards to kin.

Love,

F

\* \* \*

Saturday [November 1947]

Dear R.

The box arrived before I was up this morning, and I was delighted. Was then able to do more for Mrs. Messnick than stale soda crackers. She asked if you would give her the recipe for the cookies, and I said I would ask for it, so when you have time send it to me.

The jersey material sounds handsome.

Had a funny letter from Frances Lewis which I will enclose for the Duchess. Also one from Frank Taylor, which said in part—"I can only repeat what I said to you that pleasant evening at Paul's: that if for any reason Rinehart does not exercise their option on your novel, I will be most delighted to have the chance to consider it for Random House. Under the circumstances, I am afraid I can say or do nothing beyond this, except to tell you that it would be very nice to work with you." Nothing I didn't already know, but reassuring.

Regards to kin.

Love,

F

\* \* \*

Monday [November 1947]

Dear R.

Another letter from Mary Sallee today, and I gather she will be with me in February. It will be all right if she don't live too close. I am to keep my eye out for a room for her. Rooms are very hard to get.

That is certainly too bad about Ben. What does the new treatment consist of? Does he continue to work?

I will go to Barbara's on Friday and come back Sunday. I hope I will be able to get me some shoes there. I may get back to Cedar Rapids Friday.

One of my stories—the Accent story—was read on a radio program here today. They loused it up considerably. I wouldn't have let it be read except for Paul (G), who was trying to get them stories for it and who has been nice to me.

Regards to kin.

Love,

MF

\* \* \*

Saturday [November 1947]

Dear R.

The shirt and skirt and crackers came last night, and I am most certainly highly obliged to you. The skirt fits fine, including the length; also the shirt. I will adorn myself in the skirt tomorrow, it being the Sabbath. What I need now is a black underskirt long enough. I haven't got to mail this box of skirts yet because I haven't found the stuff to gum it up with, but I should get it off Monday.

$550.00 from Rinehart and $300 from *Mademoiselle* is right. Make it out *please* M. Flannery O'Connor, as that is on my social security card. I will be much obliged to you. Write me what the amount is and I will write a check for it out of the Exchange Bank money.

Cold again here. Regards to kin.

> Love,
>
> F

I plan to eat up a box of those crackers tomorrow. On Sunday I do a lot of eating.

* * *

Monday [November 1947]

Dear R.

Got your two letters today and also one from Mary Sallee saying the Iowa business was off. She is going to Florida for a while and then I gather will stay in Milledgeville. She don't weigh enough to stand the winter anyway. Today the whole place is loused up with snow—all over—very disagreeable.

I have a mental picture of you all in Bonner Park cooking wieners. Sounds like poor white trash. What ails your elegant sister?

Barbara's address is 1180 19th Street, Des Moines, but *don't* write me there. Her last name is Tunnicliff.

Glad you like the Guins. How do they like the place?

Does Ben realize the seriousness of what he's got? Don't sound like it.

Regards to kin.

> Love,
>
> MF

* * *

Monday [24 Nov. 1947]

Dear R.

Got your Thursday and Friday letters and the cubes today. Am highly obliged for the cubes and other contents. I haven't yet got around to all three kinds so I don't know which I like best, but I am much obliged.

Got my ticket to South Bend today—round trip coach ticket and it cost $15.90. Since this is more than I can afford, I will be happy to have you send in a little offering of $15.90. The Des Moines ticket was $5.60, but that is within my reach. A letter from Ruth today, saying they demanded I stay until Sunday. I still hope to avoid that, however. Her address is Mrs. Cyril Vincent Finnegan, Junior, 219 Baker Street, Mishawaka, Indiana (telephone: Mishawaka 5-5451). However, do *not* write me there unless it is some emergency. I don't want her having to forward my mail back to me. It might also be said in this connection that you are not always going to know where I am. I will be happy when the 7th of January comes and I can quit thinking about trains and go on with my work. You cannot work with your time chopped every two or three weeks.

Consider your effort to call me Flannery admirable. May I ask what brought you to the consideration of it? What does Miss Mary think of your doing it?

It is 18° above today, but it don't seem cold to me.

Regards to kin.

    Love,

    MF

* * *

Saturday [29 Nov. 1947]

Dear R.

Have somewhat recuperated from my fatigue. Cyril met me in South Bend, and thenceforward I was treated to a front pew view of their domesticity—which was somewhat terrifying. Ruth cooked a chicken for the first time. She had a letter from her parent saying exactly how it was to be done. My contribution was cleaning it. She was too squeamish, and Cyril's hand was too big to get in the back door—so I de-gutted it. The butcher had forgotten several things. I slept on a cot in the front room. They have a nice apartment, and boy was I glad to get out of it.

One of the GSCW girls I came up on the train with called me this afternoon and asked me to supper with them tonight. It seems Margo Flahive is visiting them. She was in my class and a member of the Newman Club. I go at six.

It was very nice of Paul to write Mrs. Hines, especially considering his condition. This is a secret, but Paul Griffith told me today when I had lunch with him that Engle is going away to be operated on. It ain't supposed to get out. His wife is also sick—she is under the direction of the head psychiatrist around here. They have their troubles.

Regards to kin.

    Love,

    F

* * *

Tuesday [December 1947]

Dear R.

Almost like summer here today. I have not felt the cold any this winter—however, the lowest it has been is 8 above.

Agnes's cards sounded very cheerful, but if she don't stop all that high pressure home-making to snare out the Harvard Business School for sons-in-law, she will be back on a slab. Do you know if Frank ever answered Sister's letter that I wrote for her this summer?

I ironed me two shirts tonight at the cost of great exertion, and I plan to make them last until I get ready to come home. I will try and write Louis.

Regards to kin.

 Love,

 Fl

* * *

Monday [December 1947]

Dear R.

Got your Wednesday and Thursday letters today and the Union Recorder. I hope you will have your shirts "laundried" before Christmas like Arnold Parker suggested. It ain't right to pile it up on him the holiday season.

You all seem to be playing a good deal of bridge lately?

Connie teaches at North Dakota University and don't like it.

The trip to New York, if made at that time, would not primarily be for the book, as I don't think it will be that advanced by then; but of course I would see the Rinehart people.

Very cold here now.

Regards to kin.

[*No closing signature*]

* * *

Thursday [December 1947]

Dear R.

Got your Sunday letter and was amused by the card from Mary Virginia. What festivities would I be planning? I hope you are not planning another of those herd parties like you had last Christmas—if so, be kind enough to have it before or after my visit.

Paul Engle left yesterday to have his operation. Lytle won't be here until January by the latest account. Paul Griffith and Robie officiate in the meantime.

Mrs. Guzeman made candy today and presented us all with a gob. It was fine. She gave me a fried egg and a piece of pie once, too.

Tomorrow I have to go to the railroad station and pick up my ticket. I have seen enough of that station this fall to last me some time.

Regards to kin.

> Love,
> Flann

*  *  *

### Monday [December 1947]

Dear R.

A pill box sounds like Mary Virginia. Your rosary beads will probably take on a few pounds.

Since when did you all get so friendly with the Nathan Morgans? or the Hamiltons? It sounds like you will spend the season attending nuptials.

Rather cold here.

Deloris still enjoying her flu—luxuriating in it.

Will not write again.

> Love,
> Fl

# CODA

Flannery would return to Iowa for one more semester during the spring of 1948, during which time she would continue working on the novel that would ultimately be published as *Wise Blood* in May 1952. Many of the stories she began writing at Iowa would be included in her first short-story collection, *A Good Man Is Hard to Find*, in 1955. That spring, she focused on writing and finding sources to fund her writing; she would be awarded a residency at Yaddo Artists' Colony in Saratoga Springs in upstate New York for two months in the summer of 1948. In the meantime, however, the lives of both Flannery and Regina would be completely and irrevocably changed by Flannery's diagnosis with lupus erythematosus, the chronic (and at that time fatal) disease that had claimed the life of Flannery's father in 1941. Diagnosed at the age of twenty-five, Flannery would spend the rest of her adult life living with Regina at the family farm in Milledgeville. Flannery O'Connor died August 3, 1964, at the age of thirty-nine.

As the letters in *Dear Regina* attest, her time at Iowa provided a rich apprenticeship for her productive—albeit tragically short—writing life and the success she would enjoy from it. The dynamic portrait of the artist in these letters provides invaluable insights into Flannery's development of her craft. Certainly, the künstlerromanic elements of these letters should allow scholars numerous new perspectives on Flannery's life and work. Just as importantly, however, it is my hope that these letters encourage a reconsideration of the role that Regina Cline O'Connor played in her daughter's life and work. Conveying a much more nuanced and complicated relationship than is typically understood between mother and daughter, *Dear Regina* also encourages new approaches to the mother-daughter relationships, both fictional and real-life, in the world of Flannery O'Connor.

# WORKS CITED

Als, Hilton. "This Lonesome Place: Flannery O'Connor on Race and Religion in the Unreconstructed South." *New Yorker,* 22 Jan. 2001, www.newyorker.com /magazine/2001/01/29/this-lonesome-place (accessed 10 Jan. 2021).

"Andalusia." Georgia College, Georgia College and State University, www.gcsu.edu /andalusia (accessed 9 Mar. 2020).

Bennett, Eric. *Workshops of Empire: Stegner, Engle, and American Creative Writing During the Cold War.* Iowa City: University of Iowa Press, 2015.

Cash, Jean. *Flannery O'Connor: A Life.* Knoxville: University of Tennessee Press, 2002.

Davis, David A. "A Good Mayonnaise Is Hard to Find: Flannery O'Connor and Codependency." *Southern Quarterly* 56, no. 1, Fall 2018, pp. 29–41.

Elie, Paul. *The Life You Save May Be Your Own: An American Pilgrimage.* New York: Farrar, Straus and Giroux, 2003.

Flanagan, Christine, ed. *The Letters of Flannery O'Connor and Caroline Gordon.* Athens: University of Georgia Press, 2018.

Gooch, Brad. *Flannery: A Life of Flannery O'Connor.* Boston: Little, Brown, 2009.

Justice, Elaine. "Flannery O'Connor Archive Comes to Emory University." Stuart A. Rose Manuscript, Archives, and Rare Book Library, 7 Oct. 2014, http://rose.library .emory.edu/about/news-events/news/archives/2014/flannery-oconnor-papers-emory .html (accessed 9 Mar. 2020).

Kahane, Claire. "Maternal Rage: Double Dipping in Language and Experience." *Women's Studies: An Interdisciplinary Journal,* Jan. 2021, pp. 1–17.

Kempf, Christopher. "The Play's the Thing: The 47 Workshop and the 'Crafting' of Creative Writing." *American Literary History,* Mar. 2020, pp. 1–20.

Leuchtenberg, William E. "New Faces of 1946." *Smithsonian Magazine,* Nov. 2006, www .smithsonianmag.com/history/new-faces-of-1946-135190660/ (accessed 25 Feb. 2015).

"Mary Flannery O'Connor Charitable Trust." CauseIQ. 2021. www.causeiq.com /organizations/mary-flannery-oconnor-charitable-trust,586309841 (accessed 31 Dec. 2020).

McCoy, Caroline. "Flannery O'Connor's Two Deepest Loves Were Mayonnaise and Her Mother." *LitHub,* 17 May 2019, https://lithub.com/flannery-oconnors-two-deepest -loves-were-mayonnaise-and-her-mother (accessed 9 Mar. 2020).

Miller, Monica Carol. "Flannery and Her Mother." Andalusia, Home of Flannery
   O'Connor, 14 Oct. 2014, https://andalusiafarm.blogspot.com/2014/10/flannery-and
   -her-mother.html (accessed 9 Mar. 2020).

————. "Country People: Depictions of Farm Women in Flannery O'Connor's Short
   Fiction." In *Reconsidering Flannery O'Connor*, edited by Alison Arant and Jordan
   Cofer, 112–26. Jackson: University Press of Mississippi, 2020.

O'Connor, Flannery. *The Cartoons of Flannery O'Connor at Georgia College*, edited by
   Marshall Bruce Gentry, Georgia College and State University, 2010.

————. Letter to A. 5 Aug. 1955. In *Collected Works*, p. 946. New York: Library of
   America, 1988.

O'Donnell, Angela Alaimo. *Radical Ambivalence: Race in Flannery O'Connor*. New York:
   Fordham University Press, 2020.

Powell, Padgett. "Breathing the Same Air as Genius." *Oxford American,* 27 May 2003,
   www.oxfordamerican.org/magazine/item/202-breathing-the-same-air-as-genius
   (accessed 15 Dec. 2020).

"Regina Lucille Cline O'Connor." *Find a Grave,* Jan. 2007, www.findagrave.com
   /memorial/17238816/regina-lucille-o'connor (accessed 20 Dec. 2020).

Westling, Louise. "Flannery O'Connor's Mothers and Daughters." *Twentieth Century
   Literature* 24, no. 4, Winter 1978, pp. 510–22.

# INDEX

*Numbers in italics represent illustrations.*